RENEGADE CHAMPION

RENEGADE CHAMPION

The Unlikely Rise of
FITZRADA

RICHARD R. RUST

TAYLOR TRADE PUBLISHING
Lanham • New York • Boulder • Toronto • Plymouth, UK

Published by Taylor Trade Publishing
An imprint of The Rowman & Littlefield Publishing Group, Inc.
4501 Forbes Boulevard, Suite 200, Lanham, Maryland 20706
www.rlpgtrade.com

Distributed by NATIONAL BOOK NETWORK

Library of Congress Cataloging-in-Publication Data

Rust, Richard R.
  Renegade champion : the unlikely rise of Fitzrada / Richard R. Rust.
     p. cm.
  Includes bibliographical references and index.
  ISBN-13: 978-1-58979-379-8 (cloth : alk. paper)
  ISBN-10: 1-58979-379-X (cloth : alk. paper)
  eISBN-13: 978-1-58979-411-5
  eISBN-10: 1-58979-411-7
  1. Fitzrada (Horse) 2. Pohl, Jane, d. 2001. 3. Show jumpers (Horses)—United
States—Biography. 4. Show jumpers (Persons)—United States—Biography.
I. Title.
  SF295.565.F52R87 2008
  798.2'50973092—dc22
  [B]   2008007156

♾™ The paper used in this publication meets the minimum requirements of
American National Standard for Information Sciences—Permanence of Paper for
Printed Library Materials, ANSI/NISO Z39.48-1992.
Manufactured in the United States of America.

To my former charges, starting lives of your own:
Henry, Jana, Ricky, Justin, and Ashley.
Having shared in your childhoods is my enduring delight.
Keep your disaster-to-adventure ratios under one point zero.
May the outdoors, horses, water, and wildlife always refresh your souls.
Remember from family experience:
horses and electricity don't mix;
never drink from a bottle showing a wild animal on the label;
and from your Grandma Jane,
work with the hand that's dealt, and draw another card.

CONTENTS

Foreword, *Rita Mae Brown*   ix

Preface   xiii

Acknowledgments   xviii

Introduction, *William Steinkraus*   xix

Part I

1   Jump-Off in the Big League   3

2   Independent to the End   15

3   A Good Horse Turns Outlaw   27

4   Learning from Cavalry Sergeants   41

5   A Death Sentence from Jane   63

6   Lost in Transit   81

7   Drowning in Quicksand   107

Part II

8   Honeysuckle to Skyscrapers: Fitz's Debut   121

9   Against All Odds: The 1946 National   139

10 The "Young Girls" Take on the Pros   155

11 Horse Sense Deserts Jane   167

12 In the Spotlight   175

13 Shotgun Wedding   187

14 The Way Out   201

15 From the Garden to the Pasture   209

Part III

16 Sowing Seeds   219

17 An Empty Stall   225

18 The Investigation   231

19 Last Class   241

20 The Next Great Adventure   259

Epilogue   269

Show Record   279

Glossary   283

Bibliography   285

Index   287

Note to the Reader   295

About the Author   299

FOREWORD

A life, like a novel, reads best when it has a clear beginning, middle, and end. Strange though it is, we perceive a person most clearly once they have died.

Jane Pohl lived from 1926 to 2001. The details of that amazing, instructive life rest between the covers of this book, as do the details of Fitzrada's life. Fitz was a horse and the truest partner she had in a life filled with victories, struggle, and disappointment. It's not my place to recapitulate that story but to put it in context.

We view Jane's life from the other side of a cultural Grand Canyon. Few of us would question a woman's ability to compete in the thrilling jumper classes. Perhaps a few more would question a woman's place in combat, but that too is fading as women acquit themselves with honor, willing to fight and die with their comrades.

Whether she wanted the job or not, she broke down the doors that led to women being included on the Olympic equestrian teams in 1964. Male or female, we owe her a debt of gratitude. Because the talent pool has widened, the United States is an equine powerhouse.

The daughter of a West Point army officer, Jane had little money. With a brother and sister in the brood, a dollar had to be stretched. Out on her own, Jane had to maintain her amateur status. Money was ever a problem.

Her discipline overcame that difficulty as well as Fitz's attitude. When you look at old film clips of Jane, even as a cute kid, her turnout is lovely. Whether wearing altered hand-me-downs or a borrowed coat, she was correct. Whatever horse she rode glistened. She paid attention to detail, and she respected the traditions of the hunt field as well as the show ring. If she had a motto in life, it might have been, "Do it right, or don't do it at all."

Her riding style was fluid, thrilling, and natural. The hunt seat is not superficially acquired. It took years to achieve that flowing style even with great heapings of talent. One rarely sees that style of riding anymore. Jane rode over all manner of surfaces. Many outdoor shows were on uneven ground. Through foxhunting, she learned balance regardless of footing, hills, and ravines. It shows. Her hands were lovely. She had just enough contact with the horse to give confidence, not enough to get in his way. If she had a fault, it was throwing the reins away on the landing, but better that, which she did occasionally, than keeping the poor animal on the bit and in a frame, which, apart from being ridiculous, looks stiff. At least to my eyes.

She took many of her fences at a hunting pace, not the measured, counting strides one sees today in the show ring. Show jumping has become so technical, so mathematical, that one needs No-Doz to watch an entire class. Jane took her fences with élan. Alas, that has vanished.

She was a complete horseman. She groomed her horses, picked their hooves, watched what went into their alpha, and cleaned up what came out of the omega. She cleaned her tack. She rubbed down her own horses. This intimacy makes good horsemen. She learned proper horse care as a child, thanks to the U.S. Army. Even had she become rich and able to hire a groom, the foundation she acquired would stand her in good stead. Today there are many brilliant riders, but there are few true horsemen. Jane Pohl had it all.

What she didn't have was a life partner. She was one of those women who if you put one hundred men in a room and ninety-nine were good guys, she'd pick the drinker, the abusive one. Once she surrendered her dreams of romance, life became emotionally stable if not emotionally full as she might have wished.

Buoyed by Fitz and her love of horses in general, she enjoyed vibrant, deep friendships. Not that she would blather on about it or make an emotional display. This was a creature of discipline, restraint, and incipient kindness.

Her physical courage and rock-solid sense of duty allowed her to face whatever life or people threw in her face. Jane was born when whining was not socially acceptable. No matter how hard her life could be, and at times it was painful, she shut up and got on with it.

In another respect she was a person of her time. She wanted to be judged on individual merit. She faced the prejudice against women just as she faced a six-foot fence—look on the other side of the fence if you can even see it, press on and over. Although she was denied an Olympic berth or accused of taking jobs from men who were professional and who had families to support, she kept her mouth shut, pressing on. And she did have a family to support—her son, Richard Rust.

As a single mother, although she had the benefit of marriage, she was one step above a fallen woman. She couldn't teach in public school. Divorceés were eyed with suspicion, the prevailing attitude being they were man hungry and would steal your husband. Many a divorcée would look at said husband and wonder why anyone would want him. Jane, wisely, never said this even though the albatross was hung around her neck.

The desire to be judged for one's self collides with reality. Athletic, hardworking women like Jane even today can't accept the concept of institutionalized oppression. They don't or won't identify with other women. Much of this is pride, and not a small part of it is an unwillingness to examine the stupidity that blights many lives and the pain it has caused in one's own. It fell to another generation to challenge that, even as it fell to Jane to show us all what one lanky, attractive, gifted woman could do on a horse.

Fitz died on September 11, 1952. He helped her through life just as she helped him. Knowing his time had come after a severe injury, he trusted the person he loved to walk him to the other side. One hopes that on June 21, 2001, when Jane's time had come, Fitz was waiting for her.

The other great love of Jane's life, her son, Colonel Richard Rust, sustained her. Without bragging, for she'd never do that, her pride in her handsome son was obvious. If she could read his biography of her, she would be deeply moved.

I think you will be, too.

Rita Mae Brown, MFH

PREFACE

Classes of a horse show were grouped into divisions: jumper division, hunter division, and so on. Points toward a division championship accumulated from order of finish in the division's classes. First place, a blue ribbon, might have earned five points; second place, a red ribbon, three points; third, a yellow, two points; and so on. So it was possible to win a championship without winning a single class, but the champion had to consistently finish in these classes among the top five places.

In Fitzrada's heyday (1946–1950), the few big shows lasted a week. Daily sports pages headlined rivalries in the unfolding points races and played up women threatening male domination in the jumping classes. Television was in its infancy, and the feature classes of the National Horse Show were broadcast live from Madison Square Garden.

America's royalty, the heirs to cosmetic, department store, and food fortunes, bred and touted their champion hunters at horse shows from Toronto to Virginia. The sport was an amulet of "old money," suggesting generational ties with foxhunting, private boarding schools, and summer mansions on the New England coast. Compared to flat racing, where healthy purses might provide repayment on investment, owning a show hunter stable could only be looked on as privileged recreation.

Hunters were bred and trained to be moving sculptures. Judged on conformation—the horse's physical proportions in pleasing the human eye—they were called strip horses because the saddles were pulled from their backs so the judges could better evaluate them. But they were also judged on manners, style, and safe way-of-going over natural fences likely to be encountered in foxhunting. Hunters were levelheaded, obedient, and steady enough for a rider to open and close a gate without having to dismount. Ideally, they remained calm when a car backfired or a deer ran into them. Lady jockeys were preferred for demonstrating the tractable qualities of these prize animals. Some hunter classes were for ladies only, and stables without lady jockeys forfeited these points.

The most coveted award at any show was the "Conformation Hunter" championship. Conformation hunters were too valuable to risk blemishing them by riding them regularly outside a ring in rough country. "Working hunter" classes were for horses regularly used for foxhunting, and points from these classes counted for the Working Hunter championship. Other championships within the hunter division were conducted, for example, Green Hunters, who were inexperienced and without a previous win.

In the jumper division, winning depended on clearing wooden rails by a sufficient margin to avoid an audible tick. Competitors were allowed to pause between obstacles if they desired. Ties were settled by jump-offs where the bars were raised successively. The heights could approach six feet, beyond belief compared to the four feet typical in the hunter classes. The top horses were typically razor fit and some were as hot as firecrackers. In the ring many of them jigged in place, collected by their rider into a tight ball, lathered in sweat, waiting impatiently to be released to attack the next fence in a rush. Neither conformation nor manners nor style mattered. Jumpers were an anomaly that many hunter purists considered perverse. Hunters had recreational utility, but there was nothing recreational about jumpers. Just as with racehorses, riding a jumper was at best a risky business, and at worst a trip to the hospital. It was highly unusual that a champion jumper, such as Fitz, could simultaneously be a working hunter.

In the days of Fitzrada, the jumping classes drew large crowds, even at local shows. The sport demanded the precision of figure skating and the courage of a lion. In pushing the limits of equine ability, falls were spectacular. Broken bones resulted more often to rider than to horse.

Fans debated who was the best rider of jumpers from among a handful of professional men. Most jumping classes were "open to all," whether amateur or professional, regardless of human or equine age, sex, size, or breed. However, few women entered. The sport was the equivalent of today's extreme sports. In a 2004 interview, Bobby Burke, Hall of Fame jumper from those days, said of the sport and Jane's entry, "You have to have to have a bit of courage. It's not the easiest sport in the world."

Today, Grand Prix jumping is the premier jumping event, time is often included in the scoring, and touches are not penalized. Women are plentiful. The horses are better controlled and go through the course in a more reasoned pace. Fitz was ideally suited to this timed competition, which in his lifetime existed only in the Olympics and outside the United States, and was closed to the weaker sex.

The Olympic equestrian events began in 1912 and were cavalry conventions. A dozen countries fielded teams that bred and trained exclusively for international competition. After the 1948 Olympic Games, the U.S. Cavalry gave up horses for tanks and helicopters and dissolved its team. Most other nations' cavalries did likewise.

The replacement of the army team with a civilian team brought controversy. Our best riders were professional men, but only amateurs could compete in the Olympics. A ray of hope emerged for the United States when our amateur women started beating the professional men in jumping. However, the Olympics were deemed too rough for women, and many riders from Latin countries could not accept the possibility of being demeaned should a woman beat them. Only five of eleven horses were able to complete the 1932 Olympic Stadium jumping course. Over half the horses in the 1936 Olympic Three-Day event fell at the water jump; three were injured so badly that they had to be destroyed.

The spectacular post–World War II jumping performances of Jane on Fitz, and a handful of her contemporaries, fueled public pressure to allow women to ride in the Olympics. These women considered themselves not protofeminists but amateur competitors, thrilled to be jumping against professional men. It was not until the 1964 Tokyo Olympic Games that a woman would represent the United States in Grand Prix jumping.

U

Simultaneously with writing this book, I was lucky to co-produce a documentary film about Fitz, titled *The Lady and the Outlaw Horse: Jane Pohl and the Renegade Champion Fitzrada*. The film revealed surprising differences and constants in jumping then and now.

Young horsemen and horsewomen seeing the film are astounded that a one-horse backyard barn successfully competed against the stables of America's wealthiest families. "Back then, it was about fun," Paul Fout wrote me after I sent him a picture of Jane riding his horse, Golden Chance, in the bareback class over the outside course of jumps at the Allentown horse show in 1948. Golden Chance wore a pajama costume Jane had sewn as a prank. In those days, Pappy and Ginny Moss arrived at shows without enough money for entry fees. For six dollars from a hastily assembled audience in the parking lot, Pappy would jump his horse over the hood of a car. Bobby Burke, Hall of Fame jumper, countered, "Now, it's about money." However, today's preoccupation with liability and technology obscures the importance of the individual, leaving the door open for the story of Jane and Fitz to repeat itself.

The fences in the film are very high, and few riders wear protective headgear. Female competition was sensational for challenging professional male dominance and morbid for allowing women to cripple themselves in front of paying spectators. Many viewers are appalled at Jane's riding, much less competing, when she was three months pregnant. But Jane was experienced with falls and accepted serious injury as remote.

While women are now less sheltered, horses are more protected. Some folks are offended that the army would want to destroy Fitz. Today, racehorse retirement charities exist. In the near future, the legal status of horses may change from agricultural animal to companion animal, creating other controversies. Intended to inhibit the slaughter of horses for commercial "by-products," it might end government agricultural supports for horse husbandry.

Attitudes have changed not only toward women's and animal rights but also toward breeds. In the days of Fitzrada, the Thoroughbred was a favored show horse. Today European breeds dominate Grand Prix jumping. In the 1940s the European horses were known as "cold-bloods," differentiating them from Thoroughbreds (hot-blooded and hotheaded). The jumper folks agreed with their racehorse brethren in exalting the Thoroughbred and doubting the athletics of the bulky breeds. Because of their lighter frames, athletic ability, and desire, Thoroughbreds are a joy to watch. The soaring feelings derived from watching the smooth spring, flight arc, and reach of a jumping horse are more vividly communicated. However, Thoroughbreds are often impatient and skittish.

Success of the European horses in Grand Prix jumping and the introduction of Thoroughbred blood into their studbooks led to their elevation from being termed coldbloods to warmbloods, distinguishing them as sporting horses from their origins as dray and harness horses. Major General Jack Burton (U.S. Army retired), member of the 1948 and 1956 U.S. Olympic Teams, had this observation in his 2004 interview for the film: "There are too many warmbloods now. I understand why—they're easier to train. Back then, you didn't bring a horse to a horse show until it could jump three foot six inches. Then too, you had to gallop—you had to be brilliant. Now it's all by the numbers, everything is striding. Today's hunter riders are like equitation riders. On the other hand, the jumper horses and riders are better than ever. Why? Because the riders copy the classic style."

Regardless of breed, desire in jumpers is more important than breeding. Walter Devereux, president of the National Horse Show Association, wrote in the November 1954 *National Geographic* magazine, "So much training is required to develop a jumper that he is apt not to be a standout until he is six or older. At that his training only serves to improve his inborn bounce. As any horseman knows, 'You can't put jump into a horse. It's either there or it isn't.' And if it is strong enough, it apparently can't help revealing itself. Steven Budd's Sir Gilbert, famed jumper of the 1930s was bought from a farmer who used the hackney as a plow horse. The farmer told Budd the horse was forever jumping over paddock fences, giving every sign of enjoying the experience."

Another aspect that has not changed over the years is the human role. "Any young horse bred for sport riding loves to jump. Jumping is just another outlet for his exuberance. A horseman who understands this and has sense enough to use training methods that take advantage of a colt's courage and natural instincts will need no spiked poles, whips, electric shocks, or murderous spurs. A horse will perform better for an understanding friend than for a bully who depends on fear and punishment" (Paul Holmelund).

Back in 1946, the Jumper Championship at the National Horse Show at Madison Square Garden was the most coveted jumping title in the country. The road there for Fitz and Jane Pohl was a five-year test of faith, patience, and understanding friendship.

ACKNOWLEDGMENTS

My thanks to Alexandra Shelly and Norm Fine for their patience, instruction, and love for this story.

The poem "Riding Lesson" in chapter 16 is from Henry Taylor, *An Afternoon of Pocket Billiards* (Salt Lake City: University of Utah Press, 1975).

INTRODUCTION

When I returned to jumper competition after World War II, one of the new (to me) riders I encountered was Jane Pohl, to use the maiden name by which I first knew her. Jane was not a great beauty, but she had a very open, natural, and unaffected personality, a good brain, and a good sense of humor and was a lot of fun to be around. With her jumper Fitzrada, she was a fierce competitor and a very good sport. She was also a sound rider whose style showed a marked Fort Riley influence. Fitzrada was a tough little horse who also had an army look about him, even aside from his cavalry neck brand, and showed enough wear and tear that you knew his life had not always been easy. However, he was very limber and athletic and could really jump. Jane had a lot of faith in him and, even better, had trained him to a point where she could ride him through the eye of a needle. The trickier the course, the more likely it was that Jane and Fitz would be in the thick of things, and they produced a lot of good performances, in both the jumper and the working hunter divisions, right up to the level of the National Horse Show in Madison Square Garden in the years following World War II.

After our military international team was disbanded in 1950, I became heavily involved in the newly created civilian U.S. Equestrian Team, and Jane got involved in raising a family and stopped coming up to the fall circuit competitions in the Northeast. I had entirely lost track of her until I read the very affecting memoir penned by her son, Richard, which filled in the missing decades for me. As a very personal account, it does not pretend to be wholly free of subjectivity and a free use of imagination, and having been based a lot on scrapbook clippings, it also passes on a certain quotient of journalistic hype. Even so, it does convey some sense of what the East Coast hunter/jumper world was like some fifty years ago. Those of us who come from older generations cannot but admire what the late Colonel Richard Rust achieved in producing, as a true labor of love, such a touching tribute to his mother and will also be grateful to him for having evoked so many fond old horse show memories.

William Steinkraus
Four-time Olympic medal winner

Part I

1

JUMP-OFF IN THE BIG LEAGUE

It was opening night of the 1946 National Horse Show. In the basement of Madison Square Garden, twenty-two-year-old Jane Pohl was nervously saddling her small chestnut gelding, Fitzrada. Those with an eye for horses would fault him for a thin neck and a plain head. Jane was a lanky five feet seven inches tall, weighed 130 pounds, and wore round tortoiseshell glasses. Tucked up under a hairnet, her brown hair was uncomfortably hot and damp. A genuine smile with prominent teeth usually identified her, but not now. The skinny horse stood quietly while she deftly adjusted his straps and buckles. She wanted a cigarette to soothe her nerves, but there was no time.

The National Horse Show had been founded by rich sportsmen in 1883. By 1915, it was one of the top jumping competitions in the world. Although civilians entered, jumping had been dominated from the beginning by military officers from Europe and Central America. *Harper's Weekly* featured the show with illustrations by famous sports artists that Jane had clipped and saved as a little girl in the 1930s. Members of the U.S. Army Equestrian Team had included future generals "Black Jack" Pershing, Billy Mitchell, and George Patton. The level of competition had not changed.

Jane heard the announcer's call for the open jumper class, the feature of the evening program. She led Fitz from his stall. As she stepped onto the ramp up to the show ring, she felt it springing up and down from the weight of other horses walking on it. She wondered if Fitz would notice its similarity to the ramp of a horse trailer and refuse to go up, one of his flukes.

Wouldn't that be great? she thought. *His first shot at the "Big Time," and he's disqualified for missing the class. I've got to lead him like he's been going up this ramp for years. Don't look back at him.*

He tentatively put a hoof on the ramp and braced. Jane felt the reins go tight behind her. She groaned.

"C'mon Fitz," she begged. She clucked to him and gave his reins an anxious tug. He rolled his shoulder to move forward, and Jane thanked God. She picked up the pace to maintain his momentum.

On the level with the arena, she tightened his girth, checked it one last time with a jerk, and swung up on Fitz. Of the fifty-five horses that entered the morning elimination for this class, only twelve had been selected for the evening. She felt lucky to be among them. Jane and Fitz moved to the "In" gate's aisle, where the eleven others waited. Butterflies rummaged through Jane's stomach. She and Fitz were just minutes away from fantastic achievement or highly visible public failure. She could not remember ever feeling so alone.

Some of the open jumpers in the aisle pranced in place, bumping other horses. They were fit and tight as piano wire. Some open jumpers were so high strung they could not be ridden outside a ring. Foxhunting on them would be suicide. In open jumping, the horse's style was not judged. Only clearing the jumps counted. Jane could sense the tension in their sweat and short breaths. Many of them had been "poled" in training, meaning that attendants standing on either side of the jump raised the top pole abruptly as the horse jumped, banging the lowest leg. The goal was to teach them to clear jumps with extra margin. Some poles were rimmed with tacks to heighten the sting. Jane believed the practice more probably taught them to be shy of jumps flanked by men.

The horses around her chomped loudly on their bits, fractious, waiting to release their pent-up tensions over fences. Standing still stretched their patience. Jane believed it took less effort for a Thoroughbred horse, like Fitz, to walk than to stand. Their riders were also edgy, lost in concentration, feigning nonchalance as they shifted in their saddles for a better fit or tugged at their breeches to move seams that chafed. The civilian men were riding bareheaded, their hair precisely combed and oiled to keep it in place. Their coats and breeches were of the finest British wool twill, custom tailored to hug the waist and flare at the hips. They were the most famous riders in the United States; almost all were professionals, training and selling show horses for huge prices.

A member of the U.S. Army Equestrian Team waited for his turn in the ring. He wore a service cap, brown boots, tan breeches, and a dark brown uniform coat, all hand tailored with the same flares to fit him perfectly. From her father's uniform, Jane recognized the ribbons on his chest and counted four gold hash marks on his sleeve, each indicating six months in combat.

Jane was the rare female in the assembly. Women usually rode in the hunter classes, where the fences were lower and horses were judged on safe style and manners. She was dressed in informal riding attire appropriate for ladies. Over the hairnet, she wore a black derby tethered by a thin cord to a big safety pin hidden inside the collar of her riding coat. On the dressmaker's dummy in her bedroom, she had taken the tweed coat's seams in for better fit three years ago, when it was new, and sewed suede to the inside of the breeches' knees for better grip in the saddle. She unconsciously plucked a horse hair from her coat and glanced at the gloss of her black riding boots. Jane had spit-shined them, as her father had taught her, just as she knew the officer's orderly had spit-shined his.

She briefly wondered if any of these horses might bite or kick Fitz. She imagined pandemonium breaking loose, horses rearing and bolting past each other, Fitz's legs shredded and bleeding from steel horseshoes trampling his pasterns.

"Get a grip," she muttered.

Jane forced herself to go through the course in her mind's eye. A wrong turn and a fence out of order would disqualify them. She listed the eight jumps to herself. Two worried her. The third jump, a four-foot-high single rail with no ground reference to help Fitz judge its location, would come right after the first turn, a sharp 180. *Fitz, we need to make that turn slow and deep so you can have at least two straight strides to decide where to take off,* she told her horse silently. And there was the last fence, the triple bar, four feet high with a six-foot spread. *Need some steam to clear it.*

After five years of work together, this was their first crack at the supreme test of show jumping's "Big League," the Jumper Championship of the National Horse Show at Madison Square Garden. Fitz was sixteen years old, perhaps past his prime. Tonight might be his only chance.

Throughout her life, Jane weighed the marvel of possibility in one hand and ran out of fingers totaling the impossibilities on the other. The old horse had never before jumped on a vibrating suspended steel floor. When the Budweiser Clydesdales had galloped out of the ring for their exhibition finale, the entire Garden shook as if in an earthquake. Even worse, tonight would be Fitz's initiation to a huge crowd completely surrounding him, above him, and hiding in the dark. Silence would be abruptly broken by the unseen crowd's gasps, applause, and echoes. The spotlights would cast conflicting multiple shadows from the jump rails, making it hard for Fitz to determine their location in space. He was used to the sun casting one shadow from each rail. Photographers' flashbulbs would burst from the void. The only things familiar from his past would be Jane and jumping. She'd have to be calm as a rock for him.

That morning in the hotel, she hadn't been able to find her glasses. The only other prescription glasses she had brought to New York were sunglasses. Wearing these now, she saw the horses near her in dim shades of gray. Above the solid gate ahead, the arena was bleached in electric floodlight—unnaturally white, stark, and cold. The gate was too high for her to see the jumps, but above the gate, flashbulbs popped randomly in the mezzanine and balcony. She felt for an earpiece and wished it had a better grip. Jane was so nearsighted that if her glasses fell off while riding the course, she would see the next fence only as a vague blur.

Owners from across the country had paid entry fees for fifty-five horses to compete in this class, but the National Horse Show schedule allowed time for only twelve in the evening class. Therefore, a morning elimination round had been used to select the best twelve. Each horse negotiated the course of eight jumps with judges scoring faults for touches, knockdowns, and refusals. In the elimination, Fitz had gone clean, without ticking a single fence, qualifying him for entry in the evening open jumper class.

Of the fifty-five horses, half were trained and ridden by professionals, and four were from the U.S. Army Equestrian Team. Pushing horses to jump beyond their ability was a man's world, the domain of professional horsemen and moneyed daredevil sportsmen. Injury to horse and rider was likely, and egos carried the day. The riding technique was rough, unorthodox, and individual, each rider having found what worked for him by experiment, gouging and snatching a horse through the course to instill in the animal a do-or-die sense of urgency. It was exactly the type of riding that had pushed Fitz over the edge six years ago, before Jane rescued him.

Just four women, all amateurs, were among the fifty-five that morning. They rode their own horses because no man would mount a woman on his horse for such a dangerous game. When the field was culled for the evening class, nine of the twelve surviving horses were professionally trained, and eight were professionally ridden. Of the twelve surviving riders, only two were women. The other woman was Caral Gimbel, who became the wife of baseball's Hank Greenberg, riding a professionally trained horse.

Very soon Fitz would be competing against the best jumpers in the country. Jane was a one-horse backyard outfit. She and her mother had shared the driving on the trip to New York from Leesburg, Virginia, pulling Fitz in a tarpaulin-covered wooden trailer behind the family's Ford sedan.

Among the twelve qualifying horses was Chamorro, ridden by Cappy Smith, perhaps the greatest professional trainer and rider ever. Cappy started breaking ponies for the Hippodrome when he was nine. Later, a South American cavalry officer competing at Madison Square Garden watched teenage Cappy ride and approached him.

"If you spend a year with me," the officer proposed, "I'll make you the best rider in the world."

"I already *am* the best rider in the world," Cappy replied instantly, and he proved it. Just before the war, instead of going to college, he turned professional and won the Jumper Championship at the National Horse Show at Madison Square Garden three out of four years.

In the morning paper, Jane had read about Cappy betting $1,000 with his rival, Alex Aitkins, riding Irish Lad, on the outcome of the impending Jumper Championship. It was a fantastic sum for 1946, the equivalent of a new car. Waiting in the aisle, Jane saw the two of them mounted nearby, conversing in hushed tones.

Another horse jostled Fitz. Jane watched to see if Fitz would pin his ears back and tense his neck as a warning to the other horse. Fitz was a skinny runt compared to those entered against him. She prepared to pull his head up to stifle him from retaliating with a kick or a bite and fervently hoped the other rider would do the same. Fitz stepped quickly to keep his balance in the confinement and offered no fight.

Beyond the gate, Jane heard the capacity crowd of 15,000 gasp and then groan. The current entry must have knocked down a bar. The gate attendant passed the word back that the horse in the ring had fallen. Jane wondered which fence caused the fall, but the attendant did not say more. She took deep, deliberate breaths and stroked Fitz's withers. She recalled a newspaper article from home speculating on the Virginia entrants heading north to this National Horse Show: "Jane Pohl, like all pilots of great open jumpers, is a fearless rider."

Hardly, Jane said to herself.

She found reassurance in fingering the nonslip rubber dots on Fitz's reins. Back home, the trashman, Jesse Randolph, had recommended them. Jesse, the pharmacist, mailman, plumber, barber, and a few farmer neighbors each kept a horse in training and raced on the lesser tracks in Maryland and West Virginia. All were one-horse barns like Jane's. Ingenuity was their long suit in competing against the big moneyed stables. Among the blue-collar underdogs, a victory for one was a victory for all.

"You show that fancy crowd what we're all about in Leesburg," she remembered Jesse telling her on the kitchen steps. The pharmacist caught her in the drugstore and gave her medicine of his own concoction to keep Fitz's legs from swelling on the trip to New York.

"Just bring us back a blue ribbon," he'd said when Jane had offered to pay him.

Fitz trained one ear ahead on the crowd beyond the gate and one on Jane, trying to sense any clue from her about what to expect. Then, he swiveled his ears back and forth uncertainly among competing sounds and stomped a foreleg. A few horses had cotton stuffed in their ears to mute sudden frightening noises from the audience, and another had to be blindfolded before he would pass through the gate into the arena.

Jane daydreamed, recollecting five and a half years ago when Fitz was an army mount in Hawaii. Jane was only seventeen but a promising rider. She'd been asked by a general who couldn't handle Fitz to reform the savage horse. She'd failed, and Fitz was scheduled to be destroyed. The next days were frantic in begging her father to buy Fitz from the army. "If you buy that horse," officers at the post stable warned Pop, "you're buying your daughter's death warrant." Fitz had sent more than a few people to the hospital, Jane included.

I'm two years out of college, her mind wandered. *Thought I'd be married to some lieutenant by now . . . pregnant at Fort Bliss, or Fort wherever. Instead, I've ridden this horse, rain or shine for the last five years.*

A burst of applause from the arena shook her. Under the hot wool riding coat, Jane's blouse was sopped with perspiration and stuck to her back. The hairnet was annoying on her ears and brow. She hoped a drip of perspiration wouldn't streak her lenses. It would be impossible not to smear them using her wool cuff. Technically, the course wasn't timed, and the rules allowed a pause between jumps. She wondered if they'd allow her enough time to clean her glasses. *Probably, not.* It just wasn't done.

The horse and rider ahead were announced by the loudspeakers and entered the ring. Jane and Fitz moved forward a length. Inches in front of Fitz's nose an attendant latched the gate closed. They were next. Jane felt small looking between Fitz's ears at the big entrance gate to Madison Square Garden's arena. Fifteen thousand people were on the other side. The longest minutes of Jane's life crept by while the rider ahead completed his round.

Jane saw the gate swing open as if in a dream. She pushed her dark glasses higher up on her nose and squeezed Fitz forward.

"Number twenty-two, Fitzrada, ridden by Jane Pohl," the loud-speakers boomed, and the gate closed behind them.

Although the National Horse Show in November marked the beginning of the New York Social Season, this 1946 opening night was particularly resonant. This was the first National after a five-year hiatus. The war was over and won. Joe Dimaggio had turned in his army boots for cleats and was back in the Yankee lineup. Mothers' stars (indicating a son in uniform), gasoline ration stamps, and somber wartime fashions were saved in trunks so that future grandchildren might share evidence of their family's sacrifice. Now, for eight action-packed days and nights, the National Horse Show's ritual and pageantry would capture the front pages, restoring a cherished past. In addition, it was a reunion for those horsemen scattered by the war.

Members of America's oldest families attended, wearing black silk top hats, white gloves, gowns, jewels, and furs. Their families had founded industrial empires: Vanderbilt, du Pont, Reynolds, Firestone, and others whose corporations were household names. Many of them had horses at the National, and some of the amateur riders were from these families. In the words of a society reporter, the audience was packed with people "who love horses, who know horses, who love to be seen, and who know where to be seen."

The National climaxed some 1,200 smaller horse shows across the nation. Seven divisions were shown: harness ponies, fine harness horses, saddle horses, hunters, jumpers, junior pony, junior equitation, and heavy harness horses. The most sensational division was jumping.

During the hour before the show, members of New York's high society filed leisurely to the "Golden Oval" of box seats surrounding the ring, waving and nodding to friends. The scene had not changed since the first National Horse Show in 1883. The automatic nodding once created a good laugh. Robert Bacon, a high-ranking member of President Theodore Roosevelt's administration, was unable to attend one evening. He invited his butler, maids, and footmen to occupy his box. Many passersby had bowed low to the Bacon box before they looked up to discover servants confused but respectfully nodding in return.

Boxes were rented for the entire eight days. Some boxes had been held by the same family for as many National Horse Shows as could be remembered, and there was a long waiting list. By joining the crowd in the seven-foot-wide promenade circling the show ring, people could get close to the horses on the inside or the debutantes and their families in the box seats on the outside. Sometimes the push was so great that overcoats and programs spilled over the rail into the ring, and the announcer asked people to move back.

On this Monday night, November 4, 1946, two uniformed army officers were among the crowd inching their way around the promenade. Major Delton Wilkins savored the elegant perfumes and orchid corsages. He had forgotten the genteel smells of "social life." During the war, Del served in the 1st Cavalry Division. But the division had left its horses in Texas and fought as infantry in the Pacific. In the jungle's steaming heat, fungal ulcers ate through men's flesh to expose bone. The memory of the ulcers' fetid stench suddenly pierced Del's thoughts. It was not the contrast in smells that shocked him but rather the realization that less than two years had passed.

The other officer, Major Rodney Yandle, nicknamed Rye, nervously walked his fingers on the railing and looked into the show ring as they shuffled along. He thought about "The" National Horse Show and their participation in it before the war. Both officers were members of the U.S. Army Equestrian Team. Prior to the war they had been stationed at Fort Riley, Kansas, where they trained to represent the United States in international equestrian competitions. In those days, only military teams competed in the Olympic equestrian events. On the chests of the officers' dark brown uniform coats, brass insignia and colorful campaign ribbons sparkled in the arena's lighting.

"Welcome home," gentlemen said tipping their top hats as the two officers passed. Tears welled in some of the older ladies' eyes. Rye dreaded the possibility of reminding someone of their lost son and having to converse and console. He dug in his pocket for a program and studied it to avoid eye contact. Delton, however, was beaming. "Thank you," Del nodded and replied to each.

Head still buried in his program, Rye suddenly grabbed Del's wrist. "Look at this!" he said. "Fitzrada is in tonight's open jumper class. Remember him?"

"Hell yes. My shoulder still hurts from when the son of a bitch threw me. I'll never forgive that sergeant who had me ride him in team qualifications. Should've destroyed Fitzrada. Sent two grooms to the hospital, didn't he?"

"Personally, I thought of him as a rite of passage to the team," Rye countered. "Great source of entertainment, too."

"*Purely* for the entertainment of spectators," Del snorted.

"Didn't they dump him to Hawaii as General Sultan's duty mount? Whoever did it must've ended his army career peeling potatoes in the mess hall. Program says, 'Owned by Colonel and Mrs. Herman Pohl and ridden by Miss Jane Pohl.'"

"That outlaw might've passed as bronc on the rodeo circuit, but not here," continued Del. "And ridden by a girl? A *girl*, damn it. Makes the army look like a bunch of fools."

"Worse if she wins," replied Rye.

Once in the ring, Jane saw in a daze the whitewashed fences, their potted shrubbery, the jump crewmen dressed in service caps and bow ties, each waiting near his assigned jumps. Through her dark glasses, she could barely discern the crowd beyond. She tried to find comfort in the familiar rhythm of Fitz's walk. She bit her lip and focused to cement the route through the course in her mind.

She pulled Fitz up facing the center of the arena and reached for a stirrup leather. Pretending to adjust it would give Fitz time to become accustomed to the light. If he became anxious, she would move him out immediately, but he seemed calm standing there, staring ahead with his ears pricked forward. When she felt she had milked the ruse beyond what was considerate, she sat up in the saddle, collected him, and walked him in a large circle to let him have a look around.

Then Jane squeezed him with her legs, and he broke into a canter. She focused on the first fence and immediately scolded herself to think beyond it. She squared her shoulders and set his pace but let him adjust stride to choose his takeoff spot. As he lifted to clear the first jump, the brush fence, she came off the saddle and bent forward to absorb his leap. The timing, flow, and connection were perfect. Then, at the top of their arc, she felt the seam in the seat of her breeches split open.

"Nuts," she said aloud and remembered to thank her grandmother.

"Throw away underwear with holes," Granny, who always wore dresses, used to advise. "Never know when you'll be in an accident, and they'll pull you out feet first."

Jane hoped the split was covered by her coattails and put it out of her mind. They cleared the next jump, a picket fence, and Jane turned her head to the right to find the single pole that worried her. She felt him follow her gaze, and certainty of destination filled him. She leaned into the turn with him, telling him with her legs where to adjust the radius so they would arrive straight into the jump. Her dark glasses made it impossible to see if there were shadows from the floodlights betraying the location of the single rail. She had to trust Fitz to sort it out. A shift in his shoulder told her what to expect. She stood slightly and crouched on his cue as he set to fly. Time slowed over the jump. At the peak, she felt him round his back and unfold his forelegs, reaching for the tanbark.

"Whew," she exhaled. The next fences—the high painted pole over a target panel, the Fairfield gate, and the log over oil drums— passed under them quietly.

With just two fences left, there had not been one single gasp or moan from the crowd. She imagined the audience holding its breath, riding with her, muscles clenched, hoping for a clean round.

"Almost home," she muttered. "Don't blow it now." The next-to-last jump, double crossed poles, went effortlessly. She caught herself focusing on the finish—the big triple bar with a six-foot spread—knew it wrong to lock onto the obstacle, and quickly shifted her focus to the ground beyond.

To Jane, the delay in flight seemed endless. They touched down, and the crowd burst into applause. She knew they had jumped the course clean, without a single fault.

"Oh Fitz," she gushed and leaned over to hug his neck. "We did it!"

He walked out of the ring on a loose rein, acting like it was just another day at work.

Three other horses finished the course without a fault: Cappy's Chamorro, Alex's Irish Lad, and a mare named Princess Peroxide. Jane was the sole woman and the only amateur. A jump-off would be required to decide the first four places.

In the ring, the jump crew raised the poles, and the judges measured them with tapes. Jane and Fitz waited again behind the gate with the other three. Cappy needled Alex about the their bet. Jane was silent. Her emotions were conflicted between joy over the previous round and anxiety about the next. The competition didn't get any tougher than

Cappy Smith, and the fences were going up six inches. Never had Fitz or Jane attempted a course where six out of eight fences were at least four feet six inches high.

Jane remembered Larry Lawrence's *Washington Star* articles published in the weeks leading up to the National, when Fitz won four Jumper Championships in five local shows. One article read, "Loudoun-Owned Horse Seen Strong Bidder for Top Garden Honor": "In a box stall on a farm out in Mount Gilead, near Leesburg, there is a little old 15:2 hands Thoroughbred, which this writer believes has an excellent chance of bringing to Loudoun the open jumping championship [at Madison Square Garden]. . . . Under the expert riding of his owner, the 16-year-old son of Fitzgibbon-Perada has rolled up a record season which surpasses any open jumper in the East. . . . As reserve we pick Chamorro, mostly because of 'Cappy' Smith's expert riding than the flashy gelding's ability." At stake was Jane's credibility as the rare female and an amateur, competing in the high-risk extreme sport of open jumping. But more important to Jane was Fitz's exoneration as a rogue. Five years had been a long time to wait.

2

INDEPENDENT TO THE END

In the spring of 2001, almost fifty years after Fitz died, Jane pointed up
at paintings of her horse on the wall of the Museum of Hounds and
Hunting in Leesburg, Virginia. She was seventy-seven years old, sitting
in a wheelchair. Cancer had eaten through her, and she knew she had
just weeks to live. Her glasses were now trifocals, but in this moment
her eyes gleamed with the same excitement of her youth. She was im-
maculately dressed in a navy blue skirt and stockings, tasseled flats, a
white blouse, and madras jacket. Under the sleeve, she wore a man's
Timex with hour and minute hands. A safety pin substituted for a missing spring bar in attaching the watch to its brown leather band.

The museum was holding an exhibit of work by Paul Brown,
a famous artist of polo, steeplechase, foxhunting, and carriage sports.
His pen-and-ink drawings had illustrated magazine advertisements for
Brook Brothers clothes in classic 1930s sophistication. Paul's media
ranged from watercolor to marquetry, but his favorite was pencil. Jane
had lent to the museum the watercolors and sketches of Fitz that Paul
had given her. The exhibit opening occurred when Jane was hospital-
ized in Loudoun Long-Term Care, taking radiation therapy and recovering painfully from a broken hip where cancer had weakened the bone.
She was determined to go, and her doctors consented.

That morning, the hospice nurse helped Jane take a shower and
noticed she didn't have any shampoo. The nurse asked her about it, and
Jane held out a bar of gray Redken soap.

"You wash your hair with bar soap?" The nurse was appalled.

"This cost eight bucks!" Jane waved the bar with a flourish.

Jane subscribed to magazines aimed at saving money. She had discovered that free plastic grocery bags could substitute for Saran wrap and was going to send in the tip.

The day before the opening, she had instructed me on which clothes to bring from home. "This is probably my last outing, and I want you to get the gold fox pin out of my top drawer," she added. "The fox is tipping his top hat and leaning on his cane like Fred Astaire."

"Yes Ma, I know him and his little ruby eyes well." It was hard to speak, realizing she was right about this being her last outing.

Even as a young woman, Jane wasn't glamorous. However, she was self-conscious of her appearance in public, where she wore clothes that never went out of style, many of which she made or tailored herself on a dressmaker's dummy that stood like a sentry by her bedroom door. At home, she wore patched jeans and my old shirts. During the workweek, she dressed up to teach elementary school, appearing to me as charlatan in costume.

Jane was good looking in a lean, athletic way. Except for special occasions, she wore no makeup or perfume. She smelled of horses, hay, saddle soap, and toil, and though she smoked a pack a day, nobody remembers her smelling like cigarettes. Supposedly, a horse never forgets the scent of the first human who rubbed it as a foal. To me, she smelled maternal, a uniquely personal and comforting scent that curiously did not change over the years, even when she was dying.

I helped her get dressed for the opening while she sat on the edge of her bed at the hospice. The pain in her hip made it impossible for her to bend over. After I helped her into her shoes and jacket with the fox pinned prominently on the lapel, she asked for her lipstick and compact mirror from her purse. The part of the compact that held face powder had been missing for years. Only the lid with its mirror and broken hinges remained. As was her custom, lipstick was the last touch. She was ready.

Awkwardly, I reached out to her, confused about how to get her from the bed to the wheelchair. She shooed me away, not willing to risk pain from her hip to my uncertainty. Carefully transferring her weight—a scant ninety pounds of it at the time—to her feet, she slowly pivoted and gently sat in the wheelchair, sucking air between her new teeth.

It was her disposition to deal with pain, control it, and find ways to work around it. Three-months pregnant with me, unmarried and keeping it a secret, she fell while jumping in the 1947 Pennsylvania National. As she lay dazed on her back, the horse she was riding deliberately rolled over and crushed her under his hindquarters. An ambulance rushed her from the show ring to the hospital, where X-rays revealed broken ribs. The doctor taped her up and told her not to ride for six weeks. The next day, rather than forfeit a class needed for championship points in that show, she rode with one arm, avoided taking painful deep breaths, and won. In the next week, she fell again at Madison Square Garden. Almost six months later, she broke her water carrying an anvil at our barn. I was born the next day.

When Jane was born in 1924, many women still rode sidesaddle. It was considered vulgar by many for a lady to spread her legs over a horse. Although that particular precept relaxed by the time Jane started to ride, a woman's place in horse shows had not changed. On the horse show circuit through the 1950s, the wealthy stables concentrated on expensive Thoroughbred foxhunters and hired professional horsemen to train and show them. But since hunters were judged on safe way-of-going, women riders were the best way to show off the animal's tractable qualities. All the hunter classes were open to women, and a few were closed to men: the ladies' hack class, ladies' hunter class over lower fences, and the Corinthian class, where, after the jumping, the judges checked appointments (i.e., tack and formal riding attire, including a silk top hat or hunt cap, hunt coat, vest, gloves, and hunting whip). On the saddle, an empty flask or barren sandwich box cost ribbons. The ladies' classes counted toward accumulation of points for the Hunter Championships, and without a woman in their arsenal of jockeys, owners would forfeit the points available to their horses.

Most professional horsemen were male. Women usually rode as amateurs. Nationwide, it was estimated that only 500 women rode in horse shows. These women rode hunters almost exclusively. Some were openly criticized for taking ribbons from men trying to make a living.

Unlike the hunters, in the jumper division only height counted, and the fences could go over six feet, too dangerous for women. However, the open jumping classes were, by definition, "open to all." The risks didn't stop Jane or the few rare women who began entering the open jumping classes in the 1940s.

Jeanne Hoffman's November 26, 1949, article in the *Sunday American,* "Girls Risk Limbs for Show Honors," chronicled the injuries these women sustained: "Orangeburg's Ethel Beck, who was sidelined for a full year following a nasty fall that resulted in a brain concussion, torn back muscles, and saw most of the skin torn off her face, explains it thusly: 'You expect spills in this business. We all get them sooner or later. If you go in with fear in your heart, you'd better park your saddle on a sofa.'" The article noted Jane's fall at the National in 1947 and named women who sustained broken pelvises and rode in shows with their arms in casts or with pneumonia.

Jumping was the only high-risk "athletic" sport where men and women competed as equals. "Three of us girls used to bum rides to see Jane and Fitz beat the men in the jumper classes at the bigger shows, like Upperville," Adele Hawthorne Miller told me after my mother died. "I guess you could say we were her fan club. We'd sprawl over the show ring rail and say to each other, 'Hey, if she can do it, we can do it!'" A few years later Adele had her first ride in the juniors' classes at Madison Square Garden. She was fourteen and petrified. Jane was there, saw Adele didn't have the right clothes for the class, lent her what she needed, and used safety pins to make them fit.

Fascination with challenge overpowered my mother's concerns about injury. Jane tended her own wounds. She considered Pap smears repulsive, refused check-ups, and was lucky to survive cervical cancer in her sixties, which could have been diagnosed earlier. Up until her aorta was about to rupture at age seventy, she had never been in a hospital overnight except to give birth to me. A year after the aorta replacement, she had open-heart surgery to receive an artificial valve. Her St. Jude valve was made of metal. Seated in the quiet of her kitchen, its clicking was audible.

"You sound just like the alligator who swallowed the alarm clock in Peter Pan," I told her.

"I looked up St. Jude in the dictionary when I was in the hospital," she said. "Did you know he's the patron saint of lost causes?"

She suspected the medical profession was motivated by profit as opposed to efficacy. The veterinarian's advice held more authority than the doctor's. At age twelve, I had a bicycle accident with muscle laid open to the bone. Spreading blue flesh, she described what she saw over the phone to our veterinarian for his opinion on ligament and tendon damage before hauling me to the doctor. She thought nothing of swallowing leftover antibiotics prescribed for her animals, breaking the big horse pills into smaller pieces appropriate for human dosage. She groaned at how much more expensive the same medicine was for humans.

As she grew older, horse liniment was conspicuous in her travel luggage for treating her sore muscles. She carried it in a heavy-duty quart plastic bottle. It was labeled in her printing, "Bigeloil," on a piece of white tape.

"Absorbine Junior is worthless," she'd state with conviction. "It's been watered down for humans."

On fishing or ski trips she could be counted on to produce a heating pad, ice bag, ace bandages, moleskin for blisters, and bootlegged veterinary antibiotics. These and her horse liniment were cheerfully forced on strangers who inadvertently mentioned their ailments. Many left her company with a discarded soda bottle half full of her horse liniment. Converts sent her Christmas cards.

Jane's friendships were mostly with men and based on shared passion for horses, the Washington Redskins, or fishing. She was leery of women, especially when the conversation drifted toward relationships, which she considered the "airing of dirty laundry." Having survived two painful marriages and excommunication from the Catholic Church because of divorce, she was paranoid about her past. Subjects of child rearing or cooking didn't hold her interest. She knew two positions on the kitchen stove: high and off.

"Your breakfast is on the stove," she would yell to me as she left the house for work when I was waking up to catch the bus to high school. That meant four pieces of raw, waxy bacon were sitting in a skillet the burner of which was on high. If I did not immediately jump out of bed and race to the kitchen, all would be lost in a haze of acrid smoke and the raucous screaming of the smoke alarm.

"I joined the army to find better food," I told her.

Jane was raised during the Great Depression. By then her father was a captain in the army and teaching math at West Point. He was careful not to wear his uniform in New York City for fear of being mobbed by unemployed men who blamed the government. Unable to justify the expense of paying faculty during the summer when the cadets were absent, the army put instructors on leave without pay. Jane's parents took summer jobs at Camp Redwing teaching swimming and riding to children of wealthy New Yorkers. The pay was meager, but food and rudimentary lodging were included, and Jane and her younger brother and sister attended camp for free. She never forgot the times when her family was hard up.

Jane refused to own a dishwasher or a clothes dryer, considering them unnecessary, and never threw anything away. When I came to her home on leave from the army, I took the initiative to haul off waist-high stacks of old magazines that clogged her house. Their titles included *Western Art, Skiing, American Heritage, Fly-Fishing, Scientific American, Wellness, Needlepoint, Money,* and *Household Cleaning Tips.* A window sash flew up, and she leaned out. "No, no, no! There are articles in there I want to read."

I returned the magazines to her house in a huff.

"After supper," I asked as she served two microwave dinners with side salads of plain lettuce, "would Madam care to view her twenty-year-old *National Geographic* magazines or her ten-year-old *Atlantic Monthlies?*"

"Aw, shut up," she muttered through a smile.

When Jane retired Fitz from the horse show circuit in 1950, he was twenty. By then, my parents were divorced, I was four, and we were living with my grandparents. My grandfather, Colonel Herman H. Pohl, was retired from the army and the nominal owner of three horses and a pony. They were Jane's responsibility, and she tended them by herself. All were for sale, except Fitz. As a business, it was barely a break-even proposition, but Pop considered it sufficient room and board for his daughter and grandson.

When my mother and grandparents looked at Fitz, the expression on their faces showed admiration afforded to no other animal, including humans, in our family. I wasn't so respectful. When nobody was looking, I rode my tricycle between his legs while he stood cross-tied in our old barn. From my perspective, he was huge. But he tolerated my foolishness, and I wasn't aware of his reputation as a killer.

When the din of the crickets rose in the late afternoon heat, she would open his stall door and clip a lead shank to his halter to lead him to pasture. I held my hands up in the air and wiggled my fingers for her to lift me. Although just in her late twenties and weighing a wiry 130 pounds, her knees popped from years of riding as she bent down to scoop me up. I reached high with my heel to get it over the horse's bony spine.

Fitz's hooves resounded in deep hollow clops on the rough oak floor planks as she led him outside. His iridescent chestnut coat was slippery, shifting under me in the rhythm of his walk. I worried about sliding off and placed one hand flat on each side of his withers. Veins stood out through Fitz's thin warm coat.

"Are earthworms under his skin from him eating dirt in the pasture?" I asked. She laughed. Iron-on patches covered the threadbare knees of her blue jeans. Her hair was light brown—mud blonde, she called the color. It was cut short below her ears, with a part and a clip holding the long side off her face. Perspiration ran down her neck and disappeared under the frayed collar of a linen dress shirt splotched with spilled gentian-violet and scarlet-oil horse medicines. The sleeves were rolled up above her elbows, showing lean tan forearms. On one wrist she wore a sturdy plain gold bracelet and on the other a boy's watch with big numerals and a plain leather band.

"How are you doing?" she asked, looking up to me. Squinting into the sun, she used her hand as visor over her tortoiseshell glasses. Anyone could see she never had the benefit of braces.

"Fine," I said, stretching the truth.

When we got to the pasture gate, I leaned over to put my arms around her neck. She cradled my waist in one arm and swung me to the ground.

Jane let Fitz go and paused to watch him hike uphill to thicker forage. The pasture slanted to the west from the ridge of Mt. Gilead. In the Valley of Virginia below, dairy silos were white dots scattered among green pastures and woods in full leaf. Beyond, the Blue Ridge Mountains rose in the haze that was their namesake. Smells of honeysuckle and sumac lingered in the humidity on Mt. Gilead. Fitz bowed his neck to rip a sheaf of orchard grass from its roots. He munched, switched his tail angrily at flies on his flank, and stomped a foreleg to discourage them further.

"Go hang this up in the barn." She handed me Fitz's lead shank. I ran back to the barn at full tilt, trailing the shank in the dust behind me, proud to have stayed on.

"Slow down! You know better than to run around horses," she yelled after me, "and *pick up* that lead shank. Tack's too expensive to drag in the dirt."

Jane's father, Pop, had filmed seven hours of silent 16 mm home movies from 1930 through 1955. In the late 1990s, Jane's grandchildren were in grade school and begged to watch this footage. They lay at her feet, chins in their hands. Searing heat from the old projector's bulb filled the room with the smell of hot oil and dust. In fading color against a backdrop of steep verdant mountains, a bucktoothed high school girl with curly brown hair cantered lithely on the army's outlaw horse toward a small jump. Jane watched from the edge of her rocking chair. Her face was wrinkled, much shorter gray hair was thinning, and she wore a brand-new set of perfect teeth.

"Gawd, that jump was awful," she said. "This is Schofield Barracks, Hawaii. A week later, he broke my nose and gave me a concussion."

"Why didn't you sell him after that?" one of the kids asked.

"I just knew he'd straighten out. Besides, nobody would've bought him. . . . Look! Here he is clearing six foot six at Meadowbrook." On-screen, Fitz and Jane arched in slow motion over an impossibly high fence of white poles, touched down, and cantered out of frame.

"Were you scared?" they asked.

"Terrified." Her voice was vibrant.

At a splice in the film, the scene changed, and Jane's grandmotherly narration stopped as if she'd been slapped. The screen had jumped backward in time to a younger Jane, maybe eight years old. The projector's whir was conspicuous in the pause.

In black and white, Pop knelt on all fours. Jane's younger sister, Jennet, ran at him from behind and jumped on his back like a movie star cowboy, kicking his ribs hard and laughing. He bucked her off. She righted herself, stuck her tongue out at him, swaggered with mischief, and started pummeling him with her little fists. Eight-year-old Jane stood excluded in withering humility, starkly out of place in the vaudeville scene, apparently ordered to pose there.

Then and now, Jane watched the playmates with longing. She felt her grandchildren searching the frame for importance. Just as when she was a child, she wished the movie of her life would return to a horse scene.

Pop was a strong figure in Jane's life. He was the son of a Catholic brick maker in Alexandria, Virginia, and the oldest of seven boys. His father, Gus Pohl, forbid his sons to attend college, insisting they work in the brickyard. Herman accepted a wrestling scholarship to Lehigh, and his father disowned him. With funds at Lehigh running short, he secured an appointment to West Point from Senator Carter Glass of Virginia. Determined that all his brothers should attend college, he prevailed on the senator to send two of his brothers to West Point and one to the Naval Academy. Twin brothers enlisted in the navy. The six brothers funded their remaining sibling through Georgia Tech. Each was disowned for leaving home.

Herman was captain of the wrestling team at West Point and graduated first in his class of August 1917, a curriculum abbreviated a year for the war. He distinguished himself in World War I as an engineer officer in France, was promoted early to captain, and was picked to be a White House aide. His duties there included military liaison and protocol.

Jane Andrews (later known as Jane Sr. to avoid confusion with her daughter, Jane Pohl) was an only child from a prominent family. Her parents divorced when she was five, and her mother took her to Europe to avoid the scandal in 1906. For the next eight years, they lived in grand hotel suites in Paris or Dresden with summers in the Hotel Moy, Interlaken, Switzerland. Governesses considered Jane Sr. dull and raised her to be invisible. Returning to the United States when World War I erupted, Jane Sr. graduated Phi Beta Kappa from Vassar in 1922. After graduation, she and her mother visited Washington as the guests of Senator Borah, father of Jane Sr.'s college roommate.

The senator arranged an invitation to a White House ball. The Protocol Office assigned Captain Pohl to escort Jane Sr. Over the succeeding months, he courted the reserved, cultured girl, believing she would make an ideal officer's wife. However, Jane Sr. was a Presbyterian and refused to convert to Catholicism. The Church agreed to marry them on the condition that she raise their children as Catholics. They wed on April 25, 1923, in Washington.

Jane Sr. had not known family life and was ill prepared for marriage, especially to a man with Catholic blue-collar expectations of his wife. Having never cooked a meal, she went to the markets in Washington, D.C., with a cookbook she had purchased on her honeymoon. A grocer helped her select a supper menu from its pages and stocked her with the produce and utensils necessary to prepare it. Lacking experience with measures or stoves, the recipes were indecipherable to her. Sullenly, Pop scraped her untouched suppers into the garbage. Jane was born eleven months later on March 11, 1924, followed by a son, Richard. Jane was her father's joy until the third child, Jennet, was born.

Pop's preferential affection for his youngest daughter was unabashed and lasted all his life. However, Pop respected athletic achievement above all other human endeavors. Much of his early film is West Point track meets, football, and baseball games. The vast majority of his family footage is of Jane riding and competing in horse shows from age six. His pride in her wins was keen motivation and a source of jealousy for Jennet, which further encouraged Jane's riding. Unfortunately, Pop's career disappointed him, and he turned to alcohol. Jane adored her father, forgave his cruelty, and conjunctively nurtured a grudge against Jennet.

I drove Jane to the rear of the Museum of Hounds and Hunting. The exhibit was upstairs in the ballroom. She didn't want to be carried up the front stairs in public view. Two kind, sturdy young men met us inside the back door. It was dingy in the servant's entrance to the old mansion.

"We'll carry you up the back stairs in your wheelchair."

"How?" she asked, dubiously looking up the stairwell.

They tipped her chair backwards and she winced, lurching forward at the waist to keep her balance.

"Wait!" she ordered, "I have to get used to this." Probing for a tolerable balance between pain and haste, she lowered her shoulders back into the chair. "How many old ladies have you guys dropped?"

"Uh, none."

"How many have you carried up these stairs?"

"Well, none."

"I thought so," she joked. "I'm not sure I want to be the first."

On the way up, she peered over the railing, somewhat enjoying the adventure. When the wheelchair was safely planted on the ballroom's floor, she thanked the men. I pushed her from painting to painting, admiring with her Paul Brown's economy of line and sense of horses—remarkable for a man who never owned or sat on a horse.

A few patrons lingered in front of Jane's watercolors. In the paintings, Fitz stands out from the spring landscape. He is moving in his element, alert, confident, gracefully powerful. Sky-blue streaks highlight the sheen in his chestnut coat and the glint in his eye. In the painting titled "High Lepper [Leaper]," Fitz bends his neck as his tightly tucked forelegs clear a white coop with five poles above it. His shadow darkens the poles. Straightened hocks, nearly vertical, suggest the incredible height of his jump. Jane is out of the saddle over his withers, wearing a derby, a white blouse, tan breeches, black boots, and glasses. The last painting is titled "An All 'round Good Ride, to Fitz and Jane, Sincerely Paul Brown '53." Fitz is suspended inches above the ground trotting at a comfortable clip with flared nostrils, head up, ears focused on what's ahead. Jane is out of the saddle, balanced, resting her hand on his shoulder.

These paintings were unique for their personal connection to the exhibitor. The patrons were curious, and Jane explained. When she was showing Fitzrada at Madison Square Garden, a man approached her in the basement stable. The stranger said he had enjoyed watching her horse so much that he wanted to do some sketches. She led Fitz out of his stall. Without any introduction, the man started drawing rapidly. Halfway through, he showed her his sketch.

"I gasped." Her eyes lit up in the telling, and she raised both withered fists suddenly from the armrests of her wheelchair. "You're Paul Brown! I've been a fan of your books since childhood."

"We talked for an hour after the sketch was finished. He had noticed the '9J' and 'US' brands on Fitz's neck and shoulder and wanted to know the horse's background. He took the preliminary sketch and said he'd be in touch. A month later, two sketches arrived."

"I sent him a thank-you note, and he wrote back asking for action photos of Fitz. A few weeks later the photos were returned, along with a note saying he'd let me know when he'd finished a painting. Several years later, these beautiful watercolors arrived."

"Paul caught the horse's attitude, personality, and way of going perfectly," she said. "Thanks to him, I have a priceless gift—memories of Fitzrada."

3

A GOOD HORSE TURNS OUTLAW

On April 15, 1930, a puny chestnut colt with a white star on his forehead was foaled. A deep bed of fresh straw received him in the foaling barn at Fort Robinson Army Remount Depot in Nebraska, one of three such depots in the United States supplying the army with thousands of horses. The colt's sire, Fitzgibbon, and his dam, Perada, were army Thoroughbred breeding stock. This foal was intended as an officer's mount, having been bred for lighter and faster duty than the sturdier mustangs purchased off the ranches for cavalry duty. The post quartermaster named him Fitzrada to identify his lineage, as was customary and useful. In this case, the name served as a warning label. Fitzgibbon's offspring had the reputation for being scatterbrained.

Fitz nursed from Perada into the summer. Soldiers came to their paddock regularly to handle the new crop of foals. Since horses defend themselves with their hooves, the troopers made a lavish show of handling Fitz's legs and feet to foster his trust. They slipped a halter on his head and led him around Perada in circles. He was shy, but the men were persistent, and Fitz came to know the routine.

In the late fall he was branded with a large "US" on his left shoulder, as were all army horses, and moved to a new barn with the other weanlings, leaving Perada behind in the broodmare paddocks. To identify him more specifically, "9J" was branded on his neck and recorded on his certificate of registration as a Thoroughbred foal with the Jockey Club in New York, the equivalent of a birth certificate for Thoroughbreds.

Missing their dams and sore from brand burns, the weanlings whinnied into the night. Out of loneliness grew a sense of cold vulnerability that could not be ignored. The feeling drove them to the ordeal of forming a herd. Just as with children, these young horses romped and chased each other, but the play could turn vicious from bullies climbing the pecking order. Although the soldiers fed liberally, fights broke out over who would control a section of the trough. Some weanlings ran away from confrontation. Some were oblivious, some nervous, some inquisitive, and some just stupid. Fitz was a runt and lost his fights with the bullies. But he was alert and tended toward a cautiously inquisitive personality. Too small for breeding, he was castrated the next year when his testicles dropped. Castration would make him more tractable as a service mount.

Since heavy work can damage bone development in younger horses, Fitz's first four years were spent at the remount depot in relative leisure. The soldiers put Fitz on a lunge line and worked him in a circle. His halter was replaced with one of tighter fit called a caveson, and a long lunge line was attached to its nose. A trainer, usually a corporal, stood in the center of the pen, holding the line's other end. An assisting soldier held Fitz.

"Wa-a-lk," the trainer commanded in a strong, lilting tone. The assistant led Fitz in a circle scribed by the end of the lunge line.

"Who-o-oah," called the trainer, and the assistant halted Fitz.

"Traw-o-t," and the assistant led the horse into a trot, jogging by his side.

After a few days Fitz was beginning to understand. The assistant let go of the caveson and hovered a few feet away with a buggy whip.

"Wa-lk," the trainer called. If Fitz didn't move out on his own, the assistant flicked his rump with the whip. The young horse flinched and moved forward. Fitz was quick to discover that words with inflection meant he was to act, and each word demanded a specific response. Soon, the assistant was no longer needed—or so the trainer thought. Fitz grew confident that he understood all the words, went splendidly for a week, and then became bored. Just like a kid who's too smart for his own good, it was inevitable that Fitz would test the trainer.

Most soldiers in charge of training the young horses had been cowboys before they enlisted in the army. Compared to the subsistence living they knew on the open range, wearing a uniform had its advantages: decent food, hot showers, clean clothes, and free dentistry. Icing on the cake was regular pay with bars and fast women close by. Cowboys thought that the lunge line was for sissies back East or officers who played polo and chased coyotes with foxhounds they bred and kept in the post kennel.

The army's ex-cowboy trainers believed the way to break a horse was to show him who's boss. You couldn't trust a horse until that was settled. But officers' backgrounds were with sporting horses, not working cow horses. Officers valued courage in their mounts and did not advocate breaking a horse's spirit.

"Charging into Sioux at Little Bighorn," the cowboy trainers could have cited history, "I wouldn't want my horse making any damned decisions for himself."

However, cavalry duty could be brutal. Colonel Paul Wimert, U.S. Army (retired), served as attaché to the Cavalry School of Venezuela in the 1960s. In a 2004 interview at his Virginia home, he recalled participating in a jungle patrol with the Venezuelan cavalry: "We got to the first river. The brigade commander told me to bring forward the two horses in poorest condition. He drove these two into the river and shot them. While the piranha were feeding on their bodies, the brigade [400 horses] crossed. That was the price to cross each river. Had the commander not done this, he would have lost dozens."

The winter wind whipped the amber stubble of Fort Robinson's plains. Exhaled breaths from Fitz's nostrils turned to white steam and were swept away. He was feeling frisky and paced sideways on the lead shank as the trainer walked him to the lunging ring. Skim ice crunched underfoot in mud puddles. The long hairs of his chestnut winter coat glowed in the morning sun.

"You gonna give me a hard time today?" the trainer asked Fitz, paying out the lunge line from the center of the ring.

Fitz stood alert with his head high staring across the paddocks and snorted. A gust of cold wind swept his tail.

"Walk," the trainer commanded.

Fitz stood still.

"Walk!" the trainer yelled. "Ain't got time for this shit. I got four more to go, just like you, before chow."

Fitz ignored the trainer.

The whip's lash sizzled through the air as it made its way to Fitz. The zipping noise startled him, and then, *S-s-snap.* It hit his rump with the pinpoint pain of a wasp sting. Fitz bucked and bolted to get away. Round and round he ran until the sting faded, and he slowed to a walk, still blowing hard.

"Walk," the trainer commanded, and then, "Whoa."

Fitz heard him, but the horse's mind was still rattling, unsure about what had just happened, and he kept walking.

"Common, halt!" the trainer spat. "You're puttin' me behind schedule."

Whizz, whap! Fitz felt another sting and bolted again.

With several more repetitions, Fitz was tiring. His flanks heaved. Steam shot from his nostrils, and his coat was drenched in sweat. He readily heeded the command to halt.

"Walk," said the trainer in a quieter tone. Fitz hesitated to move forward, and the trainer frowned.

"If that'n won't learn," a sergeant ordered from the next paddock over, "don't waste time on it, or we won't make quota for the month. Send it to the auction barn and start on a fresh 'un."

"Naw Sarge, he'll come round," the trainer replied. "He's a Fitzgibbon colt. I had three of his last year. They all think they know more than me, but I change their minds. Just takes a week longer."

"Alright, a week, and no more."

The trainer twitched the whip shaft. It rippled, but the lash never left the ground. Fitz saw the shaft spring and flinched into a walk.

In the next month, a bit and lunge reins were put on Fitz. These practice reins were hooked from the bit to a circingle wrapped around him where a girth would eventually go. The reins served to collect his head into the right position while he went through his workout on the lunge line. He learned the feel of the bit and its constriction in preventing him from extending his head when he wanted to move faster. Then, a few weeks later, the lunge reins were replaced with a trainer walking behind Fitz holding the ends of long reins. Days later came a saddle. When the girth was cinched up, it was tighter than he had known from the circingle. He lurched ahead and ran in circles on the lunge line until he settled into the strange feeling and calmed to a walk.

If Fitz quickly figured out what was asked, he was fine. But if he didn't get it, he got frustrated, and the whip didn't help. He reared, and the trainer whopped him hard, repeatedly. Fitz was put back on the lunge line to wear him down until he was too tired to resist. In Fitz's case, boredom and fatigue were mistakenly interpreted by the trainers as submission.

Broken to saddle, Fitz was shipped by rail with dozens of other green four- and five-year-old horses to the U.S. Army Cavalry School at Fort Riley, Kansas, where he was trained for duty as an officer's mount. He was taught to carry himself more elegantly and efficiently, practiced drill movements required to march in parade formations, and was introduced to jumping. At just over fifteen hands two inches, Fitz was a borderline runt, just six inches taller than a pony, but his trainers thought he might have potential as a sporting horse. Despite a coarse head, flopping lower lip, and thin neck, his structural conformation was excellent with a deep sloping shoulder, long pasterns, strong hindquarters, and straight hocks. These traits promised long, comfortable strides. Fitz was often ridden by officers who held Thoroughbreds in high regard and were gentler than the ex-cowboys at Fort Robinson. He did well at cavalry school, eagerly accomplishing all that was asked of him, including remaining calm while riders fired pistols from his back or wielded sabers to pierce straw dummies as he jumped small obstacles.

Fitz was admired for his smooth movement and clean jumping style. He was excellent at folding his legs tightly under himself when he jumped. This ability was cherished as an athletic gift. The word spread at Fort Riley, and officers were picking him for their mount in recreational horse shows. He was entered for the Officers Charger's Trophy, and many scoffed that he was too small to be seriously considered. The entrants were judged on ability to jump three-foot-six-inch fences, conformation, quality, substance, and manners particularly suitable for parade and show purposes. Quality was evident in the elegant perky way he carried himself. Substance was heart and honesty, as demonstrated by a willingness to confront obstacles and tolerate frightening commotion. Amazingly, he won the Officers Charger's Trophy two years in succession, quite an honor considering the hundreds of suitable officers' mounts available at Fort Riley. What Fitz lacked in height and strength he made up for in grace, and he clearly liked the attention that came with winning.

One day a lieutenant approached Fitz wearing a strange helmet and carrying a long mallet. The officer rubbed Fitz with the mallet, and the horse remained calm. Smallness is an advantage in polo, especially in stopping and turning quickly. Fitz's hocks were well developed from jumping, and he was quick in the short sprints that are key in polo. He learned to cant his body as a counterweight to support a rider leaning far out over the ball while maintaining a perfectly straight track. The rider then could precisely time his mallet's downward stroke to coincide with the fall of Fitz's shoulder in a galloping stride. When it all came together in perfect synchrony, the mallet head would sing through the air from the combined power of the horse's shoulder and rider's torso and arm. A ball hit this way had a distinct and satisfying report that told both horse and rider the ball was sailing.

On the polo field Fitz became deft at bumping bigger horses out of the way. He was quick enough to get his rider's knee ahead of the opponent's and instantly set his shoulder into the opposing horse. Because his shoulder was lower than those of taller horses, his bumps were unsettling, and other horses yielded to him.

One of the polo players was such a fan of the little horse that he decided to ride him in the Fort Riley steeplechase races. Although Fitz had little chance at winning against taller horses in three-mile races over timber, it was obvious he loved jumping at speed. Fitz learned to judge distances and adjust the length of his stride en route so as to have his feet just where he wanted them for the takeoff. He could tell from sight, while closing rapidly on the next obstacle, exactly how much effort would be required to clear the wide water jumps or the high brush fences with ditches and rails in front of them. He even mastered jumping banks at a gallop. Fitz couldn't see the landing spot on the other side, which could be dangerously lower than the takeoff, but in the thrill of a race he didn't care. His riders called it "courage" and spoke the word with reverence.

It was unusual for a horse to be good in such disparate events, but Fitz seemed to like the change. Being intelligent, variety kept his interest. So, even though he was a runt, Fitz became a local star. It was this stardom that led to his undoing.

The Army Equestrian Team, based at Fort Riley, represented the United States in international competition. Olympic equestrian events had been initiated in 1912 and were exclusively for military teams. Through the 1920s, the U.S. record was an embarrassment. The U.S. Army horses were a poor match for the European teams' horses, which had been deliberately bred for competition since the 1912 Olympics. So the Army Remount Service adopted methods to breed horses specifically for the team and combed the country for the best sporting mares to breed to army Thoroughbred stallions.

To improve riding technique, Captain Harry D. Chamberlin was sent to the Italian Cavalry School to study the new "forward seat" invented by Captain Federico Caprilli. The technique advocated coordinating the rider's center of gravity as closely as possible with the horse's. Rather than lie backward over a horse's rump when jumping a fence, Caprilli advocated rising forward in a crouch from the knees and extending the arms, the rider's spine holding the same arc as the horse's neck. This freed the horse to extend his head for a greater range of balance. The technique made it possible to safely and consistently jump heights of five feet or more. Chamberlin returned to Fort Riley to teach forward seat. The Cavalry School started a yearlong Advanced Course in Equitation, sending its graduates to initiate horsemanship programs at each of the army's fourteen cavalry regiments. After the 1928 Olympics, all team members were graduates of this course.

The concerted effort paid off in the 1932 Olympic Games, where the U.S. Army Team won five medals. However, the victory was hollow. With their economies in depression, not many countries sent their military teams to Los Angles. So the U.S. Army Team looked forward to proving itself at the 1936 Berlin games.

Meanwhile, forward seat riding spread to the U.S. civilian horse show circuit, considerably raising the bar for jumping competitions. Spectators flocked to see a sport with the raw power of professional football, the kinetic delicacy of figure skating, and the injury risks of prizefighting. Sports pages headlined Jumper Championships as they unfolded during the big shows, just as today's press follows changes on the leader board in golf tournaments. It was a man's world, however, as ladies still rode sidesaddle in long black skirts. For a woman to wear slacks in public was considered poor taste, for her to spread her legs over the back of a horse, vulgar.

The 1936 Olympics are best remembered for Hitler's refusal to present medals to Jesse Owens and the other black athletes. Among equestrians, these games became notorious for the water jump on the cross-country course. Out of forty-eight horses entered, twenty-eight fell there, and three were injured so badly they had to be destroyed. However, all the Germans jumped the left side, even though it looked like the hardest path, and none of them fell. Under protest from the other teams, the pond was drained, and the officials found no rules violation. For the first and only time in Olympic history, one country captured all six equestrian gold medals. World opinion hovered between suspicion and outrage.

Against this backdrop, the U.S. Army Team prepared at Fort Riley for the 1940 Olympics. Fitz's second successive capture of the Fort Riley Officers Charger's Trophy was noted. He seemed willing enough to work hard, so the team drafted him in 1939, with reservations about his small size being a handicap in jumping the large fences of international competition. He was a proven jumper and had the heart to go the distance on the racecourse and the polo field, but Fitz had never been asked to jump higher than four feet.

The team did not have time to waste on marginal prospects. If a horse didn't work out, they could always get another. When the limit of Fitz's jumping ability was found, he was schooled over solid fences. If he hit them, they would not give way, supposedly to encourage him to try harder. Jumping at this height required athletic ability and a compliant attitude. Inevitably, he banged his knees, and it ruined his confidence. Subsequently, the height was reduced, and Fitz was required to repeat, again and again, what he had already mastered. He was no longer being ridden for recreation, and the work went largely unappreciated. Multiple members of the team rode him, each placing different emphasis on what was asked, which confused the young gelding. Incessant jumping eroded his natural ambition.

Jack Burton, major general (retired) and member of the 1948 Army Olympic Equestrian Team, has been instrumental in coaching and officiating Three-Day events, including subsequent Olympics, for over fifty years in the United States and abroad. In a 2004 interview, he explained Fitz's behavior: "All the fluids and ideas that were making him go well suddenly turned sour and went the other way. . . . Some people are bright and cheerful and then they get depressed, and they don't want anything to do with anything. Well, the same thing with horses. . . . He just turned off."

When Fitz refused a fence, his rider whipped him and spurred him in place until he jumped it. Fitz was thin skinned, and spurs used too hard produced immediate and frantic results. He came to associate training with punishment and rebelled. Fitz took to cantering to a jump and refusing, ducking his shoulder and throwing his rider into the jump, then trotting away as far as he could get. When the men caught him, he was immediately mounted and punished.

Bobby Burke was interviewed in 2004 at a Virginia horse farm. Bobby enlisted to serve with the 1st Cavalry Division patrolling the

Mexican border shortly before World War II. After the war, he knew Jane and Fitz; had a long, brilliant career as a professional horseman; and was inducted into three show jumping halls of fame. At the interview, he wore a parka buttoned against the winter wind and a stained slouching cowboy hat. He rubbed his gimp leg, crushed in a fall and stiffening in the cold. In clipped sentences, he remembered Fitz: "He was just one of those kind that just wasn't gonna take it. . . . Horses that are really intelligent, they'll fight you . . . like a [rebellious] kid."

The army's solution was to bridle Fitz with increasingly more severe bits, hoping that the greater leverage on his jaw would contain him. But this had the opposite effect. Soon, slipping a bridle over his head could not be attempted without his rearing. The grooms used a twitch (a short loop of chain or closeline on the end of a stick; the horse's upper lip is placed in the loop, distracting the horse and allowing grooms to accomplish their tasks while the horse stands still) to subdue him. He now knew that whenever anyone approached him, pain would follow. Warning off man and horse alike, his eyes adopted a perpetual smoldering glint. He pinned back his ears and bit those who wandered within his range. One soldier was evacuated to the post hospital holding a piece of his ear in his hand. Another made the mistake of turning his back. Fitz bit him on the buttock, lifted him by his trousers, and threw him into the wall.

Fitz reared whenever he was handled, and once he got started, there was no holding him—something was going to break, tack or men. They gave up on trying to shoe him. The loathing in his eye was replaced by a numb and eerie patina. The men couldn't tell if his spirit was withering or, worse for them, hardening. They referred to him as "the outlaw."

The sergeants concluded he was a killer and suggested he should be destroyed. The team was reluctant. As the highest U.S. authority on horsemanship, destruction of a horse for behavior could have been considered contrary to the team's ethic. However, Olympic medals had higher priority than research and development on reforming the rare rogue.

Fitz stood listlessly in his stall, as far as he could get from the door, his coat dull and ears limp, serving a terminal sentence. He left his feed and water untouched until the middle of night so no one would witness his sole remaining dependence on humankind. When grooms came to muck his stall, he started attacking them with his front hooves. The team decided Fitz had to go, but *where?*

U

Meanwhile, in Hawaii, General Dan Sultan had been without a personal mount for some time. He requisitioned one from Fort Riley, writing directly to the Army Horse Show Team, asking them to recommend a horse. The Army Horse Show Team seized this opportunity to get rid of Fitz. They knew that Fitz was too small to carry Sultan's 200-plus pounds and that no one could ride a horse with such a disposition, but the team also recognized that if they sent him to Hawaii, so far away, Fitz would never come back to Fort Riley. They wired General Sultan about Fitz's winning the Officers Charger's Trophy two years in succession and promised to ship him immediately.

U

"Look at those goddamn fools," the master sergeant of the team's stable said near the loading chute on the day Fitz was to be shipped. "There must be two dozen of 'em . . . and more coming." He glared at the crowd of soldiers elbowing each other to get to the front for a better view. There was a small circle of bare ground in front of them with a loading chute in its center. The chute led up to the bed of an army van for hauling horses. The sergeant shook his head and approached the onlookers with menace in his step, campaign hat raked forward on his brow.

"Outta here, you goddamn slack-jawed morons," he yelled. The crowd reluctantly dissolved.

The sergeant went back into the stable scratching his head, and the crowd started congealing again. Once inside, he summoned a trooper who was cleaning tack.

"Call the veterinarian and tell him to meet us at the rail siding with tranquilizer," the sergeant ordered. "Then get the old draft mare,

Sweetie Pie, saddled up. You're gonna lead that bastard Fitzrada to the loading chutes at the rail siding."

"But Sarge, it's four miles to the rail siding. Can't we load him on the truck?"

"I don't give a damn if it's four *hundred* miles. We're only gonna get one shot at loading him, and I ain't wasting it getting him on a truck and then have to try again down at the rail yard. Sweetie Pie is as calm as we got. Hopefully, the bastard'll take her lead."

Sweetie Pie plodded calmly out of the stable with Fitz following on a lead shank dogged to the horn of her stock saddle. Fitz was stiff, limping a bit and blinking his eyes against the bright sun. Cheers had penetrated the stable a week prior, when Fitz's shipping orders arrived. Since then, he'd been locked up tight. The sergeant had nightmares about not being able to catch Fitz on the day he was to be shipped, so he kept the horse in and counted down the days on his wall calendar. Despite the sergeant's tirades, he didn't want to risk his men handling the rogue horse any more than necessary. On this morning, he had hesitated to mark off the last day.

"I don't wanna jinx this," he muttered, putting the red pencil timidly back in his desk drawer. "I'll save the pleasure of marking the last X 'til after the bastard's gone."

As Fitz walked behind Sweetie Pie, he seemed groggy, but soon he loosened and flared his nostrils to inhale the fresh air. The further he walked, the more interest he took in his surroundings. The crowd grew as it paralleled Fitz's route, staying one row of buildings away and out of sight of the sergeant, who drove a jeep slowly at a safe distance behind Fitz. The men ran from the corner of one building to the next hoping Fitz would explode where they could see it. Their disappointment mounted as Fitz went smoothly over the four miles right up to the entrance to the railcar loading chute.

This is going too easy, the sergeant thought.

Sweetie Pie walked into the chute and started up the ramp to the boxcar. Behind her, Fitz smelled a trap and stopped. The lead shank went tight. Sweetie set her shoulder into Fitz's load, and the trooper screamed in pain as the shank cut into his kidney. The shank broke and flew out of the chute, hitting Fitz in the face. Spectators stabbed the air to catch it, and when one of them did, the others piled on. Fitz was wild eyed and pinned his ears back for a fight. Grunts, whoops, sounds of boots sliding in the dirt, and painful human cries ensued.

"You," the sergeant barked at a bystander and pointed to a thick hawser coiled on the ground, "give me one end of that rope. We're gonna snug this rope up behind the bastard's rump and pull him forward into the chute."

The soldier looked confused.

"Move!" Spit flew from the sergeant's lips.

A corporal jumped in and popped Fitz's flank with a quirt. Fitz turned sideways and reared, striking for men with his front hooves. The veterinarian leaped forward from behind, stabbed a big hypodermic syringe to its hilt into Fitz's hindquarter, slammed the plunger home, and leaped away as Fitz twisted to get him. The syringe dangled by its needle from Fitz. As the drug took effect, Fitz sagged, and his eyes dulled. He was lathered in sweat from fear and struggle. Not a soul moved—all eyes were fixed on Fitz.

"Stop your dimwit lollygagging!" Sarge barked, breaking the silence. "Get that bastard into the boxcar before he collapses!" They scrambled to pull and push him forward. Fitz wobbled up the ramp like a drunk. The sergeant wiped sweat from his brow when the car door was shut and latched.

The railcar was filled with other horses destined to be distributed to army posts scattered across the Pacific Ocean. A rain barrel inside the car collected water from the car's gutters. Hay bales were stacked at the other end. A groom traveled with the horses and looked after them. After a three-day journey, Fitz and the other horses were transferred from the railroad car into an army transport ship in the port of San Francisco.

Just as at Fort Riley, Fitz rebelled at the bottom of the chute leading into the ship. Narrowly missing injury in sedating Fitz, the army veterinarian was flabbergasted when he read in the shipping orders that Fitz was destined to be a general's remount. He wondered if the general had been a bronc buster as a younger man.

4

LEARNING FROM
CAVALRY SERGEANTS

In 1938, three years before the attack on Pearl Harbor, Pop received orders transferring the family to Hawaii. He'd been in the army twenty-one years, and thanks to the lingering economic depression and shrinking military budgets, he was still only a major. Pop would oversee public works construction projects in the Pacific, mostly harbor improvements, administered by the Army Corps of Engineers and funded by the Works Progress Administration, which had been started by President Franklin D. Roosevelt to provide jobs for the Depression's unemployed. It was not the troop command Pop hoped for to get him back on the fast track for promotion, especially now that war with Germany looked possible. But he would meet congressmen and senators who might remember him when drawing the cutoff line on a future promotion list when it came to them for approval.

He was not alone in mixed emotions. At age fourteen, Jane had mixed feelings about leaving Fort Belvoir, Virginia, and moving yet again. Jane knew Hawaii was a romantic place with erupting volcanoes, exotic flowers, and black sand beaches, but the curse of growing up in the army was frequent changes of schools and friends. The Pohls had moved every two or three years.

Pop and Mother had enjoyed seeing the country, but the marriage was stale. Pop placed high priority on his career and was disappointed at being demoted one pay grade in a 1930 government cost-cutting measure. He was a domineering German husband, and his wife responded with resigned, sometimes sullen obedience. During the Depression, they had been stationed at West Point, where he taught math and re-gained the rank of captain.

On Saturdays he took Jane, then in elementary school, and his movie camera to West Point's intercollegiate athletic events: baseball, wrestling, hockey, track and field, and his favorite, football. Pop quoted General Douglas MacArthur to her: "On the fields of friendly strife are sown the seeds that upon other fields, on other days, will bear the fruits of victory." From the competitors' faces, Jane saw what it took to excel. Beyond the brink of exhaustion, soiled sweat dripped from their noses and chins, yet their eyes still held intense concentration. Jane was impressed with the nobility of their determination, especially when the effort was likely to be futile. She came to share her father's pride in acts of sportsmanship and reverence for gumption.

As for Jane's siblings, the middle child, Richard, was unusually caring and adored by his sisters. He was a solitary boy and placed no demands, preferring to make model airplanes in the privacy of his bedroom. His father was hard on him, wishing Richard had more masculine drive. Pop frolicked tirelessly with his mischievous youngest child, Jennet, and expected Jane to act like an adult. Jane's jealousy of her sister festered, and Jennet lorded it over her.

As a cadet, Pop had been instructed in equitation and mounted pistol marksmanship, skills expected of all officers regardless of whether they were destined for the cavalry. His interest in recreational riding did not extend beyond several excursions he had made while stationed at the White House. Pop would take a week's leave and sign for a horse from Fort Myer to visit a friend from World War I who had retired in Berryville, Virginia. The trip was sixty miles each way. He did thirty miles a day, invigorated to be away from Washington, D.C., and spent the night at the inn beside the stone bridge at Broad Run, east of Leesburg.

Mother's first opportunity to ride came at West Point as a military wife. In her early thirties, she immersed herself in riding, taking instruction from sergeants at the post stables, and introduced her children. Jennet, age four, could not be trusted to refrain from slapping a horse in glee and was not put on the back of a horse for a few years. Mother alternated her other two children on a horse she was riding, named

Ross, and led them around the stable. Richard was timid about being so far off the ground. Jane was six, her legs too short to reach the stirrups, but she picked up the reins, beaming, and pretended to be riding the huge beasts on her own. Over the next weeks, she learned all the horses' names and visited their stalls regularly.

At a West Point horse show, Mother rode Ross to win a jumping class that included the touring Army Equestrian Team. The team was insulted to be beaten by a woman, a first for them. Official dinner parties were awkward for the next few days with muted congratulations, and senior traditionalists avoided the subject altogether. Shortly afterward, Mother broke her ankle in a fall with Ross. When the ankle set, it remained the size of a grapefruit, and she was never able to ride again. With the other post wives, she turned to contract bridge and amateur theater. At home, Mother escaped into science-fiction and palmistry books to avoid her husband and raised her children passively.

Jane rode at all the army post stables where they were stationed. The one place that Jane could hold her father's attention was in the riding ring. By twelve, she was entering classes at post horse shows. He faithfully came with his movie camera to film her awkwardly bouncing around courses of small jumps. For the preceding five years, when her father had been assigned responsibility for flood control on the Illinois and Ohio rivers, they lived where there were no army posts. To fill the void, she clipped photos of famous horses from magazine articles, made paper saddles for them, and imagined herself riding them. Jane read Harry Chamberlin's books explaining forward seat riding. Having won the silver medal in jumping at the 1932 Olympics, his concepts were gaining acceptance in the civilian community.

Chamberlin stated women could more easily take the forward seat than men because they carried more of their weight in their pelvis, closer to the horse. The only disadvantage for women, he felt, was that they were too weak for hard riding. But Chamberlin promised that the new seat made riding much less strenuous for the rider as well as the horse.

Jane remembered a very young horse that carried its head unusually low. She consulted Chamberlin's books but was still puzzled. Mother suggested writing Colonel Chamberlin. Pop helped her compose the letter. She rejected the typewriter as disrespectful and labored with a fountain pen. Colonel Chamberlin graciously responded from his post in New Mexico. He cautioned about heavy work before age five, while bones were developing, and added, "The head *should be low and well extended*. This allows the loin to become strong and hollowed out." Jane preserved his letter in her scrapbook for sixty-five years.

    When Jane arrived on Oahu, she was tall and bucktoothed, wore glasses, and anticipated torment as a high school freshman. She longed for her hollow adolescent shell to be inhabited by a cheerful self-assured personality—perhaps a cross between Velvet Brown, the young heroine of *National Velvet*, and Katherine Hepburn. She missed the family dog and cats, who stayed behind because of quarantine restrictions. The one good thing about moving to Hawaii was the prospect of riding army horses.

    The family drove across the country to catch the troopship, USS *Chateau Thierry*, in San Francisco, bound for Hawaii. Pop hung canvas water bags from the front bumper of their Ford "woody" station wagon. In some stretches of desert, they drove seventy miles without seeing a gas station. Three hundred miles was a good day, and they stayed the nights with friends on army posts. The highlight of the trip was a week at Eaton's Dude Ranch in Wyoming. Jane witnessed cowboys breaking horses and saw terrified horses violently pitching cowboys into the ground. On the army posts, Jane's riding had been contained in a fenced ring under instruction or with her mother. At Eaton's she was allowed to ride alone. She rode up forested canyons and found vistas of prairie that reached to the horizon without a sign of human impact. The hours of solitude brought a previously unknown intimacy with her horse.

    During the first three days at sea, Jane was ill from the ship's rolling movement and the hot, stale air below. The passengers accumulated bruises from banging into railings and smacking their heads on low passageway coamings. Jane, Jennet, and two other girls were berthed in an officers' stateroom with one porthole with barely enough room to stand between the bunks. Since the ship was designed for soldiers, the women shared a men's head (toilette) and shower, reserved for females during certain hours of the day. When Jane first went to the head to relieve herself, she was shocked to see polished steel commodes in full view of each other and no shower curtains. Modesty forced her to bathe out of a cup while seated on her bunk with the door locked, careful to hold the cup level against the ship's roll in her free hand to keep it from spilling. She didn't feel clean when it was done.

Jane's first impression of Oahu was verdant spectacular geology. Schofield Barracks went into shade in the afternoon from Mt. Kaaia, rising 3,000 feet in just two miles to the west of post. Within a week of her arrival, Jane went to the stable to ask about riding. It was dark in the stable aisle. For the minutes it took her eyes to adjust, the forgotten smells of hay and horses lifted her spirits. A portable Zenith radio the size of a small suitcase played Artie Shaw's "Begin the Beguine." She walked the aisle, peering into the stalls, building her courage to ask the stable sergeant how she might get to ride. Black soldiers in work uniforms were brushing horses secured in cross ties and mucking out stalls with pitchforks, tossing the manure into wheelbarrows parked in the aisle.

She heard the faint ringing of horse shoes being hammered into shape and followed the sounds to the forge, buying time to muster confidence. She remembered forges were separated from stables because of the fire hazard.

A groom held a horse on a lead shank outside the forge's shed roof. A farrier leaned into the horse's shoulder to shift the horse's weight and growled at the horse when the hoof didn't come up in his hand. He wore thick leather chaps tied around his waist like an apron. He pared the horn tissue of the hoof and rasped the hoof flat. A stable dog sat nearby impatiently waiting for the hoof parings to fall, ears up, wagging his tail in the dirt.

A sweating soldier pumped the furnace's bellows. Air hissed in the coals, and Jane could sense the heat from where she stood. A blacksmith rotated a steel bar in the white coals and jerked it from the fire to his anvil, where he beat it into a U. The ringing of his blows sounded in steady rhythm. He dropped the hot shoe into a bucket of water for quenching. It hissed and bubbled.

"Miss, would you like a horseshoe nail ring?" the farrier asked Jane while bending over a hoof. Finger rings made from the soft-metal horseshoe nails were popular with kids.

"No thank you, corporal," she replied, proud to know his rank from the two chevrons on his sleeve but mortified. Three years ago she would have been delighted with the ring, but now she was embarrassed that he saw her as a child in need of a toy and not a young woman.

Jane thought it was time to stop delaying her trip to the stable sergeant and turned to walk back to the barn. Barn cats, there to control the rodents, sunned themselves beside the stable. Jane smiled to herself, remembering the story of the Hawaiian name for cats. Hawaiians were amazed to see missionary women arriving in the 1800s carrying small unknown animals in their arms like babies. The cats were often sick and gaunt from the long voyage. The missionary women kept saying, "Poor, poor, kitty." The Hawaiians deduced these strange animals were called "popokee."

A weathered cavalry sergeant approached the sunning cats with his hands on his hips. He stared at them and shook his head. The cats mewed at him. Some got up casually and rubbed themselves on his boots with dubious sincerity, hoping to be fed.

"You lazy fleabags," Jane heard him mutter. "It's a sad damned day when you have to feed barn cats."

When he discovered Jane watching him, he stood up straight and faced her, but even from the distance that separated them, she guessed him to be shorter than she was.

"Sergeant Mope," he introduced himself, louder than necessary. "Can I help you?" He had three chevrons on his sleeve.

A buck sergeant, Jane thought, *the first of the sergeant ranks. His face is so ruddy. He's mighty old to be just one step over a corporal. I bet he's been busted. Maybe more than once. Fighting, insubordination, drinking? Probably all of them.*

"I'm looking for the stable sergeant," she replied.

"I'm headed there now. Follow me." He did not offer a handshake.

He walked ahead of her at a brisk pace to a tiny bright-white clapboard building with planted flowers blooming by the steps. Sergeant Mope removed his broad-brimmed brown campaign hat, which reminded Jane of Smokey the Bear. He tucked it neatly under his arm, stiffened, and sharply knocked twice on the door.

"*Enter!*" a voice from inside rasped. Jane tensed.

Master Sergeant Smith stood in brown army riding boots and breeches. Although his back was turned to them, Jane could see his cheeks bulge as he chomped down hard on a plug of tobacco and searched through a sheaf of papers. He turned his head only enough to see Mope standing at attention and did not see Jane.

"What the *hell* do you want?"

"Master Sergeant Smith, we're out of cat food again. I suggest we have the veterinarian spay some of the cats." Mope stood rigidly at attention and spoke to the back of Smith's neck.

"*Hoddamnit* Mope," Smith bristled and looked up from his papers toward heaven for relief, "if I want your opinion, I'll ask for it! It's better to have too many cats than not enough."

Smith wheeled around angrily to give Mope more "advice" and saw Jane. He bit his tongue to stifle an epithet and quickly removed his campaign hat. Even though this was Smith's office, swearing in front of officers' daughters could bring reprimand. Mope tried to hide a smile at Smith's embarrassment.

"Try the mess hall," Smith growled at Mope. "They served fish yesterday."

As Mope pulled the door shut behind him, Smith looked at Jane. In the pause, a hot wave of regret spread through her. *Bad timing*, she thought.

"I'm having a typical day," he confessed. "What do you want, Miss?"

"My name is Jane Pohl," Jane stammered, "and I want to ride."

"Where did you come from?" Smith let out a long sigh.

"My father, Major Pohl, was stationed in Peoria, Illinois, and Fort Belvoir, and before that, West Point, where he taught mathematics," Jane replied tenuously, not knowing if there was a right answer.

"That's more than I need to know. What have you done with horses?"

"I rode at West Point and Fort Belvoir."

"What makes you think you can ride *my* horses?" Smith was not impressed.

Jane felt her cheeks and ears turning red. "I'll do anything for a chance to ride," she pleaded.

Squinting, he measured her to see what she was made of. Under his scrutiny, her face flushed again. She lowered her eyes and turned for the door.

"All right," he relented. "Come back tomorrow at fourteen hundred hours and see Sergeant Mope. Tell him to tack up Belle of the Valley. Don't be late."

"Thank you, thank you, Sergeant Smith," Jane burst out. "I'll tack up Belle for you. I don't want to be any bother . . ."

Smith held up his hand to stop her gushing.

"You are *not* to tack any of *my* horses, and don't thank me. Just be here at fourteen hundred tomorrow."

Jane contained herself until she was out the door and leaped off the top step to run home with the good news. She wondered what Belle would be like and prayed that she would do well on the mare. Jane spent the rest of the day searching packing boxes for her riding clothes and checking their fit. Weighing a little less than 120 pounds, she had grown to almost five feet six inches and started to develop hips. So she borrowed Mother's old jodhpur boots and breeches. They were too big in the waist and too short in the leg.

The next day on the bus to the stables, she fidgeted. By the time she had walked the short distance from the bus stop, perspiration had streaked the inside of her glasses. She searched her pockets for a tissue. Finding none, she pulled out a shirt tail to clean her wet lenses. Jane felt suddenly unprepared, like a kid in school for the first time. It made her angry with herself that she wasn't more confident. She was a half hour early.

In a fenced riding ring Jane saw children, a few officers, and several wives riding. Orderlies were sitting on the fence watching and talking. A cavalry sergeant stood in the ring dressed in tall brown boots, riding breeches, and campaign hat. He held a riding crop in one hand and nervously swatted the calf of his boot with it. The sergeant eyed the children, trotting their horses in a circle around him, and told a girl to halt. He walked to her horse, tapped her stirrup with his riding crop, grabbed the heel of her boot, and pulled it firmly down.

"Keep your heels down," he said loud enough for all to hear. "Relax your shoulders." He stepped back and looked at her posture.

"Good. Now trot."

As soon as her horse broke into a trot, she stiffened. The sergeant put his hands on his hips and shook his head.

"*Relax* your shoulders!" he barked. Jane told herself to remember these tips.

On the other side of the ring, an officer on a bay horse approached a jump in an easy canter. The horse's coat was shiny with sweat. The horse rocked in a steady rhythm, ears up, looking at the jump. He gathered himself to spring off his hind legs. In perfect timing, the officer leaned forward from his knees, and his hands went forward to give the horse use of his head as the animal extended his neck for the jump, clearing the rail by a wide margin.

At the next fence, the horse again gathered himself for the leap, but this time he bolted to the right around the fence. The officer was thrown to the side in his saddle but hung on and regained his seat. He kept the horse in a canter, spoke sternly, and then calmed him. The officer called two grooms to haze the horse into the same jump. They took positions on either side of the jump.

Jane watched intently as the horse approached again. The horse saw the men blocking its escape. The bay hesitated, and the officer squeezed him hard with his boots. The horse rocked back and sailed over the jump. The bay cleared his jumps with such excess height that Jane thought he must be green.

Jane saw Sergeant Mope among the spectators and approached him. Jane noticed one of his front teeth was broken. His face was deeply lined from years in the sun.

"Yes Miss Pohl, you're early. Groom doesn't have Belle ready yet," he stared at her from under the shade of his campaign hat.

"May I help with the grooming and tacking?" Jane asked eagerly.

"That's okay with me, but only if Master Sergeant Smith isn't around. I know some army post stables cater to you kids and your families. But, far as I'm concerned, you're here for the horses, not vicey versey." Mope paused to search Jane's face for signs of character. "There's no perfect horse. Each one can use training. I'm gonna say what to do, and you do it. Give any of my remounts bad habits, I'm gonna bark," his eyes narrowed, "and you'll respond, immediately."

"I want to learn," she said, trying not to look at his broken tooth and taking heart that he might bend Smith's rules for a kid with commitment. She guessed he lived in the barracks with his men and wondered if he was hard on them. Maybe he'd been a cowboy. It would be rude for her to ask. Officers did not fraternize with sergeants, nor did their kids.

In the stable Jane brushed the dust off Belle and struggled to fit the bridle to her head. She decided the cheek straps had to be let out. After several adjustments, she still wasn't sure the bit was correctly located in Belle's mouth. But the horse was patient, and Jane felt comforted that she wouldn't get bucked off.

Jane mounted and rode toward the ring. It felt so good to be riding again. The officer she had seen jumping the green horse was leading the horse back to the stable. He looked up at Jane on Belle and smiled.

"You must be Jane. I met your father this morning. He said you'd be here. Colonel Van Deusen." He held up his hand to shake hers. "I learned to ride from a bunch of crusty old cavalry sergeants. Their bark's worse than their bite. Let your stirrups out a hole or two. Belle's more of a saddle hack than a hunter. A good horse to teach you equitation before you learn how to jump." Jane later learned that Colonel Van Deusen had jumped at the National Horse Show in Madison Square Garden with George Patton before World War I. He was one of the first graduates of the Advanced Equitation Course at Fort Riley. He gave up his show jumping career at the request of his wife after she witnessed a bad fall. But Colonel Van Deusen was the most respected horseman on post.

Leilehua High School was not what Jane had expected. Close to 90 percent of the students were Filipino, Japanese, or Chinese. They were shy, polite, and gracious. Most had been born in Hawaii, and they spoke near-perfect English with accents. Their parents relied on them to translate everything from legal documents to comic strips. The quiet natures of these students meshed comfortably with Jane's adolescence. She was relieved that they would not taunt her for her awkward looks and strange German name.

Jane witnessed their poise in enduring racial slurs from the white students and began to see her own passive despair as too much like a dog cowering with its tail between its legs. With Hitler annexing pieces of Europe and the Japanese conquering China, Jane had more in common with the Japanese American students than her Caucasian classmates.

"Hey Pohl, you're a hun and a Catholic aren't you?" the school-yard logic unfolded as Hitler invaded Norway, Holland, Belgium, and was heading for Paris by the end of the 1940 school year. "My dad says Catholic churches keep guns in the basement." "Government ought to round up all you huns and put you somewhere you can't spy for your Nazi relatives."

Jane went to the stable after school and on weekends. The cavalry sergeants took turns standing in the center of a well-worn circle of dozen children and wives trotting around the ring's long perimeter. Colonel Van Deusen's daughter was among them. For Jane's instruction, it was back to the basics in coordinating her hands, spine, and legs to anticipate Belle's movement. The objective was to make Belle's job easier. Jane's posture had to be balanced, supple, and confident with her shoulders back, chin in, carrying a little hollow in her lower back. Pulling on the reins with her arms was not allowed. Instead, she was told to close her fingers to a fist, and when Belle obeyed, she was to relax them. Focusing on all the pieces was too much to keep track of at once. She was embarrassed at being singled out but thankful that no one would snicker. Any sergeant would bite a kid's head off for such a breach of training etiquette.

When it was Mope's turn to instruct, he insisted his students ride with no stirrups. He peppered his instruction with tips and lore from his cavalry career, and she recorded them in a spiral notebook when she got home, illustrating the margins with doodles of horses.

"Now, trot! Sitting trot," Mope ordered the line of novices.

"Oh no," Jane groaned. It was much easier to ride without stirrups at a walk, and next easiest was at a canter, but the trot was the worst. The tops of her thighs burned from having to hold her calves forward to fit securely in the hollows behind Belle's shoulder blades. The backs of her thighs cramped from trying to grip the mare's belly with her heels.

"It hurts, dudn't it?" Mope asked them.

"Yes, sergeant," the bouncing chorus responded.

"You can't ride 'til you develop a seat with grip," Mope continued. "If I had enough lunge lines, I'd have you riding with no stirrups *and* no reins. When I was a young private at Cavalry School, we did what you're doing for *weeks*. That's why us cavalry troopers are bowlegged."

Jane hobbled at school, and classmates kidded her about being a gimp. But when the soreness went away, she could feel what Mope was talking about. Using only her thighs, she felt glued to Belle in a way she never thought possible. She could relax her knees and ankles.

"When you can sit-trot for ten minutes with no stirrups, I'll let you put 'em back on your saddles. Now you know why stirrup irons revolutionized warfare. Be pretty tough to wield a saber without 'em, wouldn't it?"

"Yes, sergeant," from the chorus.

"Anybody, know who invented the stirrup?" Without waiting for a reply, he answered, "The Chiney-men."

When Mope told Jane to put stirrups back on her saddle, she was delighted to be promoted one step closer to jumping.

"When you first get on," Colonel Van Deusen advised her at the stable the next day, "stand up with the stirrup irons under the balls of your feet and push your heels down as far as you can. That'll stretch the calf muscles to be as hard as Hitler's heart." He tapped the back of her boot with his crop for emphasis. "Then slowly sit in the saddle, holding your heels down and your calves stretched."

"Why?" she asked.

"Communication," he replied. "Say you're driving a cab in New York City, and the passenger's feeding you directions in traffic. He could tell you, 'Turn left at the next light,' or he could say, 'Maybe, uh, somewhere up here, uh, you might turn left.' What would you rather he say? Takes a little time for your horse to react, and you must allow for it. It's different for each horse. The army tries to train them identically so any trooper can pick up the reins on any horse and both of them will know what to expect. But hey, it wouldn't be any fun if all horses were the same. If they were, they'd be called motorcycles."

She checked out copies of the army cavalry manuals on horsemanship from the post library, and her questions became more technical. Jane volunteered to help around the stables, even where she wasn't entirely welcome. She held horses while the farrier shod them and learned how faults in the way a horse moves could be corrected with weighted shoes and rasping their hooves at angles. The veterinary officer showed her how to give horses shots and apply poultices. He taught her to run her hand down a horse's legs and feel for ailments—like splints, ringbone, and bowed tendons—and told her how each was caused and treated. From the orderlies and troopers she learned tricks about distracting horses so they'd hold still or load onto a truck. Master Sergeant Smith gave up on trying to keep her out of daily stable operations.

Within a few weeks Jane was able to make Belle walk out in a brisk pace and change gaits smoothly, but she looked longingly across the ring at others who were schooling their horses over fences.

"You gotta learn to maneuver a horse before you can jump," Mope answered her unasked question.

The sergeants had their students trot in a big figure eight, threading the needle at the center. It was terrifying at first, but the horses knew the drill. Jane and the others became comfortable in judging distances to pass between horses without collision. Then came parade drill movements. They were formed into a column of three abreast and ordered to trot.

"I don't want to see any accordions out there," the instructor warned.

Each rank of three had to wheel together, changing direction simultaneously, just as the cavalry troopers were expected to do it. After several months Jane could get Belle to change leads at a canter (called the flying change) in preparation for turns in each direction. Soon after, the sergeants put her on more difficult horses and taught her the faults of each and how to correct them through schooling.

"When you show a horse," Colonel Van Deusen told her, "the trick is to show off what it does well and avoid what it does poorly."

Jane thought about that for a long time. She had heard about "morning glories," racehorses that ran well only in the morning training and were slugs in the afternoon races. Morning glories were sold as hunter or jumper prospects, as nobody knew how to correct the problem. Jane discovered horses were right handed or left handed, just like people, in that they felt stiffer at the canter turning in one direction as opposed to the other.

Gymkhana competitions were regular events at post horse shows. The sergeants gave each kid a glass test tube full of water to carry in each hand along with the reins and ordered the class to walk, trot, and canter. The winner was the rider with the most water remaining. They played broomstick polo, trying to score goals by hitting a basketball. A favorite game was to pin a balloon on each kid's back with the objective of breaking each other's balloon by back slapping. There were relay races where the riders had to exchange coats while mounted. Horses took off for the barn with their riders' arms pinned behind their backs in the sleeves. The smart kids put the reins in their teeth during the change. These exercises developed quiet hands, a secure seat, and good balance in riders and prepared horses for the mayhem of battle.

"Go get Belle and meet me over by the jumps," Sergeant Mope ordered Jane one afternoon, more than two months after she started to ride here.

At long last she was going to jump. Jane was silently elated but scared. She didn't want to make a fool of herself, especially in front of spectators.

"Horses know when you're afraid," Sergeant Mope said, pointing at her heart with his crop. "Your fear can spill into them, and they'll refuse. Some horses are timid and need to feel your confidence. Some're hotheads and need to feel your calm."

Jane chewed her lip.

"This old yellow-leg cavalry sergeant thinks you can do it. Now," he squinted, "you too gotta think it about yourself."

"How?" Jane asked weakly.

"Pull your chin in. In fact, I want you to work on your posture from the time you walk up to a horse to catch it in the paddock. Horses can tell what you're made of just by looking at you. Now, trot Belle around the ring until both of you are relaxed. Then jump the two-foot rail, come right back to a trot, and settle her."

Jane got Belle moving in a brisk trot on a loose rein.

"Pick your head up and look where you wanna go, *not* down at where you are. Keep the same pace. Collect Belle; it'll warn her she's gonna have to do something different."

Jane turned in and lined Belle up straight to the low rail. She was gripping Belle hard in anticipation of the jump. When Belle took off, Jane was rigid so that when Belle reached out with her head to clear the rail, the mare slammed into the bit. Jane had a death grip on the reins and felt the jolt right through her shoulders.

"*Ouch!*" Sergeant Mope screamed. "Don't hit my horse in the mouth! Get loose. Bend at the waist to follow the horse's head with your hands."

The next time around she came out of the saddle way too early. Belle propped on her front legs right to bounce Jane's weight up, then jumped. The saddle rose and punched Jane in the seat, shooting her over Belle's shoulder. Jane did a somersault in midair and landed on her back. The breath was knocked out of her in a rush. Belle had stopped and stood quietly beside her. Jane still held the reins in her hands. She gasped, but no air came into her. Her eyes grew big from the terror of suffocation.

Sergeant Mope hovered over her. "Good girl for not letting go of the reins."

Jane tried to smile but couldn't. Her eyes watered from the cramp in her chest, and she was mad at herself that Mope might think she was crying. Breathing returned to her in shallow gulps. Her stomach cramped. Mope held out his hand, and she grabbed it. He jerked her upright.

"Horse has got to have her front end free so she can push it up and over the jump," Mope ignored her discomfort. "You gotta help your horse by keeping your weight centered. Got it?"

Jane nodded weakly, unable to speak. Mope swatted the dust off Jane's back with both hands.

"Get your breath and back on Belle. Trot 'til both of you are settled and try again."

On the next attempt, Jane concentrated on sitting deep in the saddle right up to the jump. But she got left behind on the jump and hit Belle in the mouth again.

"*Ouch, Ouch!* That's enough. You keep hitting my horse in the mouth, and she's gonna be as scared of jumping as you are. Go on a walk, away from here. Get Belle loose, gentle on her mouth so she'll forget. Try again tomorrow."

Over the next week, she did get it. It was like riding a bicycle. Once she jumped correctly, she had a reference. At night in bed, while foliage rustled outside her screened window and the Plumeria blossoms sweetened the ocean breeze with a vanilla scent, she closed her eyes and practiced the movement in her mind, slowing it down to savor its delicacy and study it from all sides. Her hands and knees wiggled under the sheets as she summoned memories of the thrilling power surge of the takeoff, the arc of flight, the horse's hooves receiving the ground and resuming their rhythm to the next fence. Jumping was an ecstasy she never tired of conjuring. In school she drew pictures of horses over fences when she should have been taking notes. The sergeants worked her steadily up to three feet on Belle and then put her on Pat, a horse who could jump higher.

For Jane the toughest test of her riding was to jump a wooden sawhorse that was barely wider than it was tall. It was impossible to prevent a determined horse from running out on this obstacle. The necessary discipline came from schooling. After the horse grew accustomed to jumping the wide sawhorse, narrower ones were substituted. Jane learned there could be no ambivalence in the path to and through the jump. She had to let Pat know precisely and continuously where he must go.

When Jane felt Pat waver, she applied leg to push the horse back onto the line. The trick was to stay ahead of Pat in her mind, envision their path through the jump immediately ahead, the turn to the next jump beyond, and so on. With concentration, Jane could imagine the two of them several jumps ahead and rely on it to happen just as she envisioned it. If Jane felt Pat falling to the inside of a prescribed imaginary arc, she applied inside leg to push him out. When Pat wandered to the outside, she held the horse with her outside leg and rein. Over time, she learned to expect what Pat would do or forget to do. Then she had merely to remind Pat just before the anticipated problem, and he would straighten, as if saying, "Oh yeah, I remember."

Jane's gift as a rider became her ability to maintain her legs exactly where they needed to be, allowing her to crouch forward from the knees and reach with her hands to follow the horse's head in extending for balance over a jump. Her weaknesses were looking down at the fence as she passed over it and *throwing the horse away* by reaching too far forward, losing contact with the horse's mouth. Both were an interruption in telling the horse where to go on landing.

Jennet also came to ride at the stables. Considering the priority that Pop placed on filming Jane's progress, giving her older sister a run for her money may have appealed. At thirteen, Jennet was a tomboy, quick and strong as a cat, but impatient. In the weekend shows, Jane and Jennet competed in the same equitation classes and rode as a team in the pairs hack classes. With their tight braids bobby-pinned like laurel crowns and matching white hacking jackets, they looked like Swiss milkmaids. Jennet had an active group of kid buddies and enjoyed mischief better than having sergeants bark at her, so she didn't put in the hours that Jane did. That was fine with Jane.

As Jane's riding improved over the next year, she entered progressively more advanced classes in the post horse shows, riding as many as three horses in the same class. Her more challenging classes had been in the hunter division, where horses were judged on manners, form, and safe way-of-going, and the jumps did not exceed three feet six inches. With a week's notice as to which horses would be available to her, she worked to polish herself with each. One afternoon she was in the ring trying to maintain a perfectly even pace through a course of schooling jumps. She had been riding in Hawaii for two years, recently turned sixteen, and was a lithe five feet seven inches tall. Mope perched on a rail by the schooling jumps.

"Put him away," Mope called. "He's had enough."

"But Sarge," Jane pleaded, "he's almost got it. Just a couple more?"

"Nope, he ain't getting any better," Mope said sliding down off the rail. Then, walking away, he said over his shoulder as if it was an afterthought, "Go get Pat ready. You're riding him in Saturday's open jumping class."

Jane froze. She had never entered a class in the jumper division before.

Only the best enter that class, she thought. *The fences are the highest of any in the show. For sure, I'll be the only female. Oh my . . . I could be competing against Colonel Van Deusen.*

On the day of the show, a crowd of several hundred sat in the covered grandstand. Navy and army officers wore white uniforms. Their wives wore dresses and hats. Pop and Mother were among them. The commanding general, his wife, staff, and guests socialized in their box seats. All stood as the Hawaii Division Band marched into the ring, playing the National Anthem. Sixty horses waited under tents erected to shade them. Almost forty riders from ages ten through fifty were entered in the dozen classes of the show. The riders were officers, their wives and children, some sergeants, and an occasional civilian with his own horses. The classes were sorted by ability. In this show's open jumping class there were a handful of officers, two sergeants, and Jane. Like most army kids, she wore riding clothes out-grown by previous owners. She'd learned to sew and tailored them to fit as best she could. For this feature event, three photographers from the Honolulu and the post newspapers stood inside the ring with the jump crew. Enlisted men in khaki crowded the rail to get closer to the action.

Jane wrote of the experience two years later in a composition for her college freshman English class: "The green ring in front of me glistened in the sunshine. The low white grandstand to my right was filled with laughing officers in white and their families. The trees rustled in the cool breeze. Far to my left the Koolau Mountains rose against the sky, their summits hidden by clouds of rain.

"The white jumps were being set up in the ring in front of me and as I turned to put my foot in the stirrup, my stomach felt empty, tight and it hurt, my mouth was dry and my knees shook against the saddle.

"As I jogged back to the open field behind the ring, I heard the familiar cries wishing me luck, and I tried to swallow my fear caused by the excitement. I gathered my horse beneath me and put him into a canter to warm up.

"Around and around until sweat showed on his neck above his shoulders. Then walk, drop your reins and stirrups, relax.

"Suddenly Mope came tearing out.

'Bring him over here.'

"What would I do without that wrinkled old sergeant who always gave me last minute advice and helped me with my horses.

'Put him over that jump and them bring him back here.'

"As I turned away and steadied Pat into the jump, I unconsciously tightened up on the reins and hit him badly in the mouth as he landed.

"Mope gave me hell, told me to relax and everything would be fine.

"The other horses had taken their turns around the course and so far the lowest score was three faults.

'Pat—in the hole.'

"I had dreaded that call.

"I gathered my reins, fixed my toes in the irons, stood in my stirrups to get my weight down in my legs and tried to get my nervous horse safely into the ring. As I circled him for that first jump, I tried desperately to relax. It was a nasty jump, a brush with bars on each side and no wings. Pat rushed in and refused, ducking out to the side. Two faults! I felt my anger melt my fears and relaxed. It was the first time Pat had ever refused with me, and it was my fault completely. Mope made sure I heard that [it was my fault] as I circled back into the jump. I pulled my crop out of my boot and hit him with all my strength—every stride. Whack, whack—up and over—clean.

"I gasped for breath, gathered the reins which had slipped through my fingers, and gripped his moving body with my legs—hard. He tried to run out again on the next jump, but I pulled him back into it and legged him over.

"The rest was easy, jumps he knew: a brush, a single rail, a triple bar—more leg, squeeze, squeeze every stride, work him up into the bit and then let your hands follow his mouth over the jump.

"Then here it was: a triple in and out, three single posts and rails, about twenty-two feet apart, and each one higher than the last. Guide him into the jump, hold him and leg, leg, let him find his own stride. [I was] left behind on the first—he almost hit it. Get forward, leg, hands, up and over, leg, leg, up and over.

"I gulped for air for my tortured lungs and let Pat pull the reins through my fingers as we galloped out of the ring. His orderly [groom] grabbed him by the bridle and pulled him around by the bit. I jumped to the ground and patted his sticky, sweating neck with my cramped hands. The applause and the orderly's grinning face told me that we had the lowest score so far. Then walking around and around with Pat rubbing his itching head on my shoulder, blowing through distended nostrils and the swish and splat of his tail against his soaking, heaving flanks, and the plop, plop of his weary hooves on the hard ground.

"Once again that tight empty feeling returned and I crossed my fingers. Grinning soldiers turned away from the fence and said that I 'had it in the bag.' I smiled wanly back and said to keep them crossed for me, please! Deep inside I kept saying, *It isn't possible, you can't win a class as big as this, you never have before. But maybe I can.*

"It was all over. The team of black percherons trotted into the ring, with their empty wagon rumbling behind them, to collect the jumps and clear the ring. A knot of judges conferring in the middle, oblivious of the percherons, the tense silence over the stands. That feeling deep down inside—then the ring master calling four numbers and mine among them!"

It can't be true. Pat hold still! I can't get my foot in the stirrup iron. What's the matter with me? I can't bend my knee to mount.

"Two soldiers held Pat and helped me to mount. I trotted up to the ring gate and was told that I had won first place and to lead in."

It's true—oh Pat, you angel—thank you God! I'm going to cry. Stop it, stop it. Gather your reins and try to look as if you deserve it, at least.

"A tiny woman entered the ring, fear of horses written on her face, determined to do the duty expected of her, and a lieutenant in attendance carrying ribbons and a huge silver plate. She came up and tried to slip the blue ribbon in Pat's bridle, who immediately tried to push her over by rubbing his head against her."

Oh Pat, she's a general's wife—stop it!

"Something heavy and cold was placed in my hands with an accompanying handshake and congratulations.

"Thank you ever so much. Isn't Pat wonderful?"

Oh you dope, what a dumb thing to say to the commanding officer's wife.

"A canter around the ring, the reins slipping through my fingers and Pat bucking like a three-year-old.

"Numerous hands grabbed the bridle, an army photographer, congratulations, and I was so overcome by it all I just stood.

"Mope came running up with another horse.

'Sergeant Mope, I . . .'

'Get up on this horse—you're in the next class and you're late.'

'Mope, isn't it wonderful—I can't ever thank you enough.'

'Fix your stirrups—here's your number. Wait, the curb chain's twisted. Remember what I told you about showing this horse.'

"Then a pat on the knee, a silent laugh and a quick wink, and I was sent into the next class."

5

A DEATH SENTENCE FROM JANE

General Dan Sultan had been stationed at Schofield Barracks, Hawaii, for many months without a horse assigned to him. He had been a football player for West Point. Because of his size, Sultan had not been an avid horseman, but this could all change with the right horse. He had corresponded with the Army Horse Show Team asking them to select a mount for him. He might have conjured visions of himself on a classic Thoroughbred foxhunter type, towering high above his infantrymen as he marched them down potholed roads on their maneuvers. The big horse would be covering two of their strides with every one of his. Sultan rested one hand on the saddle's pommel, his attention turned to the rear, discussing something urgent with his mounted staff. The horse would make sure-footed decisions completely unaided.

When Fitz arrived in Hawaii by army horse transport ship in early 1941, he was examined by the veterinary officer and certified "free of disease and fit for service." More than a few sergeants waited at Schofield Barracks' stable to see what the Army Horse Show Team considered worthy for General Sultan.

"Aw shit," Master Sergeant Smith groaned seeing the small skinny gelding, "Surely this is a Transportation Corps screw-up, or someone at Fort Riley wants to get busted down to private."

"Riding this runt, General's gonna look like a monk on a burro," Sergeant Mope commented.

"Just for that crack," Smith roared, "you're the lucky bastard that's gonna tell him his 'special ordered' Thoroughbred remount is here."

"I take it back, Sarge. General's gonna look like Black Jack Pershing himself on this gorgeous chestnut charger."

"You might practice that speech on the way to headquarters. Take these papers and get the general to sign for his horse," Smith slapped open-mouthed Mope on the chest with a fat manila envelope of Fitz's records since foaling almost eleven years ago.

Mope swallowed hard and turned to find a lift to headquarters.

"He's nicely proportioned, sir." Mope offered, standing at attention in front of the general's desk while the gray-haired man finished his signature with a flourish.

"Lieutenant," General Sultan called toward an open door in the paneled wall of his office, "have my *new* horse saddled tomorrow for thirteen hundred hours."

"Yes sir," the reply came from the general's aide, who then summoned Sultan's orderly and called the stable.

The orderly was responsible for keeping the general's gear. He polished Sultan's boots, cleaned his saddle and breeches, and that night laid the riding uniform out for the general in the old man's dressing room. The next morning, Fitz stood patiently as the general's groom brushed him and picked his hooves clean. Fitz accepted the bit and the saddle without complaint. But there was something eerie about the horse. He acted like he was in a coma, but he was acutely aware, like a poker player waiting out a bluff. The orderly didn't like being left alone in a dark stall holding the horse's reins, waiting for General Sultan to arrive. Fitz made no move toward the manger for a bite of hay, as most horses would out of boredom if not habit or hunger.

Finally, they were summoned outside to the mounting block in the ring. The aide waited attentively beside General Sultan. Smith and a few of his sergeants observed silently from the rail. The general concealed his shock at the horse's size and skinny rib cage.

"Well," he said in mitigation, "the horse came from the Army Horse Show Team, so he must have something going for him." The orderly held Fitz by the bit. Sultan stepped up on the mounting block, put his foot in the stirrup, gathered the reins on the horse's withers, and swung his leg over Fitz's back.

Fitz grunted and shifted his legs quickly when Sultan got on. It came as a shock, as Fitz had never carried such weight. The horse braced while the general adjusted his seat and reins. General Sultan sat up straight and nodded to his orderly to release Fitz. Sultan squeezed slightly, and they walked off with chopped steps. Fitz's uncertainty with his feet did not inspire the general's confidence. Sultan tightened up, and so did Fitz. In a few seconds, everyone there, including the general, knew this was going to end badly. In fact, it escalated so quickly that there was nothing they could do to stop it. Fitz lunged to get his head free, jerking the reins from Sultan's grip, and shot into a racing sprint. The general had been pulled forward by the reins and stayed with him through the acceleration. Fitz arched, lifting Sultan, and then hit him hard in the seat. The sergeants were over the rail as the general was launched to land in a crumpled heap. The sound was sickening. They lifted the old man carefully to his feet. Fitz ran crazed in the ring, stepping on his reins and snapping them.

Shrugging the men off, the general swatted dust from his uniform and glared at Fitz as more men tried to corner the horse in the ring. Sultan hoped this was an aberration and told his aide that Fitz needed more time to settle after the trip and landing in a new stable. News of the accident spread through the military community and to Jane. She had heard a handpicked Thoroughbred mount was coming from Fort Riley for the general but did not know the horse had arrived.

Days later, Sultan rode Fitz again, with a more severe bit. Memory of the fall was on his mind as he mounted Fitz. Again, Fitz stood patiently while the orderly had his head. The general nodded and tensed. The horse moved forward and trouble started almost immediately. Fitz bowed and sidetracked, unresponsive to the general's strong attempts to pull him back on line. Sultan kicked him to move forward onto the bit for some control, and Fitz started to wheel on his hind legs. Expecting a fall, the orderly ran toward them, and Fitz shied. The general managed a hasty dismount and let go of the reins as the horse spun from under him to race around the ring dodging jumps.

"I've got to have a horse I can use," Sultan told his aide.

Master Sergeant Smith assigned a strong young ex-cowboy corporal to Fitz.

"Break this horse so's your mother could ride him in Macy's parade and never have to look up from her knitting," Smith instructed the corporal.

From the moment the corporal approached him, Fitz recognized the threatening posture and smelled resolve on the man. Old memories of Fort Riley returned, and Fitz's behavior deteriorated. Two months passed with five different riders, including a captain who wanted Fitz for polo. A few had success—until they pushed him.

A few weeks after Jane's seventeenth birthday, Pop came home from work, rested his briefcase on the front-hall table, and paused. He stared into the polished silver bowl for receiving officers' calling cards. The bowl had been a required fixture just inside their front door in every set of quarters they had inhabited, a total of seven so far, spanning half the globe.

He looked up the stairs, where Jane was studying, and focused on a small crucifix that also followed them around the world. The opportunity he was about to offer his daughter weighed on him. She was likely to be injured, but she'd earned the right to choose for herself. Nearly thirty years ago, his father had forbid him to chase a dream, and it had been wrong.

The problem was, she wouldn't choose, she'd leap. He couldn't entirely argue with that either. Pop was an officer in Hawaii, a long way from a stoking a kiln in his father's brickyard. Attempting the improbable was a virtue Pop admired. Risk made it more virtuous.

Besides, Jane was the most levelheaded of his children. When Jane was ten, she became infatuated with driving. Pop let her sit on his lap and steer the car in the driveway at a crawl. She'd made him promise he'd let her get her driver's license as soon as she was legally old enough. He'd agreed, knowing the age was fifteen everywhere they had lived. They moved next to Ohio, and Pop was horrified when she informed him the age was twelve. The summer after her twelfth birthday he taught her how to shift gears, made her change tires, and had her drive him everywhere. She proved herself behind the wheel and had never been in trouble at school, so he honored his promise, and she didn't let him down.

"Jane, come here," he called up the stairwell.

From his tone, she sensed she was in trouble. Although she descended the stairs reluctantly, she couldn't hide her athletic grace. Inadvertently adding to her anxiety, he waited until she stood in front of him and finished pushing a lock of hair from her glasses.

"General Sultan asked me if you'd like to work with his new Thoroughbred remount, Fitzrada. The horse is unfit for duty, bucks everybody off."

"*Would* I?" Jane's eye's widened, picturing a refined officer's charger in the mold of a gorgeous conformation hunter.

"General Sultan doesn't want the horse destroyed, but that's the only alternative if he can't be used. Said he knew your show record and bet you wouldn't give up. He wonders if a girl's demeanor might be a way to reach this horse."

She was overwhelmed that General Sultan had heard of her, let alone that he thought enough of her to request her help.

"Go over to his office after school tomorrow. There'll be a letter from the general authorizing you to ride the horse, which you'll need at the stable."

Jane filled with blind excitement. She had never ridden a Thoroughbred before. Every army horse she rode was part Thoroughbred. She visualized herself flying over fences, accepting compliments on the horse as she turned over the reins of this "made" hunter to a grateful General Sultan. She imagined Pop grinning at her with pride.

What Jane did not yet grasp was that she was Fitz's *last* chance.

"Holy cow," Jane said, examining the folder of records she'd been given in Sultan's office. *Served as mount in the Advanced Equitation Course?* She unconsciously bit off a fingernail. *That means he was in the U.S. Army Equestrian Team's stable! He's only eleven. In his prime. What could possibly be wrong with him?*

She hurriedly knocked twice on Master Sergeant Smith's door, forgot to wait for his reply, and marched into the office brandishing the general's letter at him. Smith frowned at her from behind his desk until she composed herself. He skeptically lifted the wiggling page from her grip.

"Who-eeee," he sighed, running a hand through the thinning gray hairs on his scalp while he read. "You may have bitten off more than you can chew on this one."

"But Master Sergeant Smith, he was on the Army Horse Show Team."

"Something's not right in the fuse box between his ears," Smith cautioned. "This horse's smarter than a West Point lieutenant, sneaky as a supply sergeant, and spoiling for a fight." Smith's eyes narrowed to slits. "You can't tell what's gonna happen or when. Flip his switch, and you could get killed."

A stiff silence settled between them.

"Look, I'm not in the business of disobeying generals' orders." Smith tried another tactic, "I know how hard you work around here and the good you've done with my horses. But you're a kid, got your whole future ahead: marriage and raising a fine crop of young 'uns. You sure you want to risk that for a life in a wheelchair? Or worse?"

"Sergeant Smith, all I've got is horses," Jane's voice was cracking at the possibility of losing this chance, "and it's likely that's all I'll ever have."

"Yup, you've got a gift, it's true, but there's no shortage of horses out there. Why don't you let this one go? I've got a corporal working on him. The horse ain't getting any better. Probably won't ever come around."

"I told General Sultan I'd try," she said, mustering as much resolve as she could, "and that's what I'm gonna do."

He shook his head slowly. He was frustrated with the general allowing such a risk, but a smile crept over the old master sergeant's face. Although he hated to admit it, he admired her gumption.

Jane opened Fitz's stall door. Fitz didn't turn to see who was approaching, as horses usually did. Not even his ears moved. When she patted his neck, he ignored her. She remembered lumps of sugar she kept in her pocket as a treat for horses when they'd done well. She fished one out and offered it to Fitz. He didn't move. She held it to his nose so he could smell the sweet, sticky odor and then lowered it to his lips. Nothing.

Never seen a horse refuse a lump of sugar, she thought.

"I was somewhat disappointed, to say the least, when I saw a small, thin chestnut with a long neck and ugly head awaiting me," she wrote in a composition for a college English course two years later. "He was a strange horse, showing no response to affection, disdainful of man and all the delicacies he offered."

Fitz was indifferent to Jane's grooming and saddling him. Speaking to him as if he were an old friend, she thought her words sounded forced and wished she was better at camouflaging her nervousness. She ran a body brush in each hand down his chestnut coat, over his muscles and joints, appraising his proportions. She liked the refined slippery thin-skin feel of a Thoroughbred, much different from the horses she knew. His legs were cool to her touch as she checked for signs of past injuries. They were true and unblemished, also unusual among the horses she rode. An appreciation filled her, but it was tempered by his history with the general and the corporal. Her intention was to work him at a walk and, if things were went well, at a trot. If he went nuts, she'd put her arms around his neck and slide off to mitigate her fall.

Holding her breath, she settled lightly into the saddle and didn't sense any animosity. It was more like sitting on a block of modeling clay. She wondered if he was plotting. At her signal, he moved off in an easy walking stride that felt honest, and Jane relaxed.

"The next hour we tried to find out as much as possible about each other, and I was amazed to find that, despite my first impression, I was riding a truly wonderful animal, obedient and responsive to my aid. It must have amazed him to have a woman riding him after all these years of knowing only men."

From his reserve, Jane wondered if he was waiting for her other shoe to drop. There was, however, something he couldn't hide.

"The following days brought us closer. . . . Nothing can surpass the thrill of having him completely balanced between my hands and knees, executing the school [dressage] movements handed down from the Spanish Riding School in Vienna. . . . The first time I jumped him, I knew at last what it was to be on a horse that loved to jump. It was written all over him. I could feel it running through the reins as he took hold of the bit coming into a jump. I could feel it in the muscles of his back; in the free, wide leap he made over any obstacle; and in the way he collected himself when he touched the ground looking for something else to be cleared. He went out of his way to jump; ditches or holes that could be walked through or stepped over were jumped over as if there were a six-foot barrier built over all."

But a week later, Jane was riding him, and for no apparent reason, Fitz froze, pinned his ears back, tucked his tail up between his legs, and stood rooted to the ground.

I've had it with all of you! his body language shouted to Jane. *I'm not doing another damned thing!*

"You are such a strange horse," she whispered to him. "Are you mad at yourself for showing me you like to jump?" Jane shortened the reins and gripped with her knees. She touched his stiff flank with her heel, and his ears pinned back further.

She tried to turn his head and touched the other flank. He tightened and took a short breath, and she had a twinge of premonition. The next instant, he exploded underneath her and arched into a plunge. She grabbed for his mane and braced. Enraged beyond caring about injuring himself, he locked his knees and slammed both forefeet to the ground to create the biggest jolt he could. She lost her grip on his mane and flew forward out of the saddle, falling onto his neck hard enough to knock her breath out. Fitz crouched for the next explosion, and she smashed back into the saddle finding both stirrups. Another leap, and he charged off with his ears laid back. Jane hung on. Divots flew from his hooves as he headed straight for a paddock fence. Fear seized her. She didn't know if he would jump it or crash through it.

A stride shy of the fence, he propped on his front legs and ducked a shoulder. Jane flew by his head and hit a wooden panel in the fence with her shoulder. The impact cracked the board. He shied away from her and trotted to the other side of the ring with his head high. She sat up, shocked by what had happened, unaware of her injury. It had come out of nowhere, as if he'd been hit by lightning. Jane knew she must win these contests. Otherwise, he would remember his victories, and she would have little chance with him. Hours later, searing pain developed in her shoulder, and she went to bed with an ice bag on it. Calcification in that shoulder would require surgery fifteen years later.

Grooms told Jane the corporal was having no better luck. She knew she'd never be strong enough to ride Fitz into exhaustion to gain his obedience first and then his trust. Obedience would have to be by-passed. As Jane later put it, "I had to pay my dues and suffer through his episodes." She could sense his willpower and intelligence but felt he expected the worst and was waiting for confirmation. Despite the times when Fitz was moving briskly, obviously enjoying being a horse, Jane felt tension festering just below his surface.

As a younger girl, Jane had come to consider her own anger at childhood injustices in the school yard and at home as inappropriate. So there was a part of her that admired Fitz's spirit. There was another part that felt sorry for him that his moods were so fragile.

For a change in routine, Jane decided to ride Fitz away from the stable, initially only at a walk with a girlfriend mounted on a steady horse. Hibiscus flowers and Bougainvillea bushes with tiny white blossoms lined their trails, and the air was scented with ginger. The girls rode to the beach in bathing suits and stripped the saddles off, hoping to swim their horses, but the animals would turn for shore when the water lapped their bellies. In a composition for her English class, Jane wrote of Fitz's progress, "I loved riding him over the mountain trails or through the pineapple fields. He enjoyed life, and nothing passed us unnoticed. When feeling particularly good, he would dance along on stiff legs, the muscles in his neck bulging under his satiny skin, his small ears pointed at some distant object, while he noisily blew through his nostrils pretending he was a wild stallion." The pineapple plantations were guarded to prevent theft of the fruit, but riding was allowed. On one excursion, the girls decided to smuggle pineapples under their sweaters. They stuffed two pineapples each to their chests. Not even movie stars known for their voluptuous figures had such enormous breasts. The guards were flabbergasted and quickly looked away. In 1941, any confrontation with a girl over her bosoms was unacceptable. Even staring at a woman's chest could get a man fired.

Fitz's progress was halting. "But at the same time, I had to combat the effects of the corporal, who rode him often and whose heavy hands on his sensitive mouth drove him crazy. . . . [One] hot day when the sun drove him out of his head, he stood on his hind legs, pawing and whinnying. I led him four miles trying to calm his frayed nerves while his anguished whinnies rang out over the barren sands of Lualualei.

"The captain at the stables wanted him for polo because he was fast and handy. . . . He talked to General Sultan, who in turn asked me what I thought about the horse. I told him how beautifully trained he was, how he loved jumping, and how completely crazy polo would drive him. The result was that I was still allowed to ride him."

Jane rode Fitz several days a week over the month. Half these rides ended with her being thrown or having to dismount as a precaution. But there were other times when he went splendidly. She entered him in the more elementary classes of the monthly post horse show. "The pride and joy I knew when he won a red [second place] in the hunter's class for performance and way of going, and a yellow [third place] in the road hack class for manners, I shall never forget."

In a month, Pop received orders promoting him to lieutenant colonel and transferring the family to Fort Bragg, North Carolina. He was to assume command of the 96th Engineer Battalion, a segregated black unit. They would be leaving Hawaii at the end of May 1941.

Jane graduated from high school, and the packers came to put their household goods in crates and barrels for shipment. Jane felt growing remorse about leaving Fitz, her friends, and Hawaii's idyllic way of life and verdant volcanic beauty. She continued to ride Fitz while waiting for the family's departure. She would miss him, but he was the army's horse, and saying good-bye was part of army life.

Jane decided to ride Fitz on the Hale Kula Parade Ground as a change from the confinement of the ring. The sun was bright, and Jane wanted to soak Hawaii into her memory before she left. She rode bareheaded, lingered on the panorama of verdant, jagged ridges rising sharply in the near distance, and inhaled the faint smell of ginger. The parade ground was three miles long and almost a mile wide. At the far end was a double set of railroad tracks and a highway.

Jane urged Fitz to a canter and smiled at how good he felt in steady pace. Suddenly and for no apparent reason, he seized the bit and lunged. In the first stride, she felt his carriage drop out from under her as he reached for full extension. Jane was startled but grabbed a sheaf of mane to avoid being unseated by his acceleration. Fitz ran in a panic, straight as an arrow. Her view of the grass below smeared, but she didn't recoil from the speed. She'd ridden horses at a flat-out gallop before but never for more than a brief sprint. Usually, runaways made for the stable, but Fitz was locked on the opposite direction. It should have been a clue to Jane that something was drastically wrong.

"Whoa, Fitz!" she tried to calm him in confident tones. And then to herself, *Parade field's three miles long. Got plenty of time. He'll run out of gas.* She crouched for a more secure seat and let him run. Her eyes watered from the wind.

Halfway down the parade ground, he wasn't tiring, and her confidence in her tactic eroded. Jane leaned far back in the saddle, stirrups out front with "both feet on the dashboard," and then pulled and held the grip. Her calf, thigh, and back muscles burned as she kept all her weight on the reins. Fitz galloped on, unfazed. Individual hoofbeats were indistinguishable in her ears.

Next, she tried to turn him. She'd been taught that tighter and tighter circles could spiral runaway horses down to a trot. Jane let one rein go to pull on the other with both hands, but his strength was incredible. He set his jaw to her rein, and she couldn't flex his chin off-line. He roared on, determined as a freight train.

Jane remembered one more trick. If she could get a rein wrapped across the front of his nose, it might be enough additional leverage to turn him. The bit twisting his mouth in the same direction might also help. She leaned forward and extended tenuously out on his neck, careful not to lose her stirrups. Hugging his neck with her left arm, she let the wind take a foot of slack in the right rein. His shoulders pounded on like pistons. As she leaned off his shoulder, the bright green plain came closer, increasing her impression of speed. She had a flash of a western painting by C. M. Russell with an Indian brave firing a pistol from under his galloping pony's neck. The warrior clung to the pony with one heel hooked over the pony's withers and an arm over the pony's neck. If Jane lost her stirrups, it was over. There would be no way to pull on the rein with any force. She extended her toes to keep them. The inside of her knees began to chafe raw in trying to maintain her purchase. Desperately focused on the rein's target, his lurching nose, she did not feel her skin abrading.

With the rein's slack flapping on her elbow, she managed a side-arm pitch to throw the loop under Fitz's chin, hoping in the retrieve to have the loop over his nose. But the wind swept the loop right back past her before she finished her cast. It was hopeless. Then she saw another way.

Going over the top of his ears would achieve the same result. She took advantage of the lifts from each of his racking strides to inch herself back on top of his neck. Steadying herself with one hand on his pulsing mane, she groped with the other hand to push the loop over his ears where it thankfully worked down to the bridle's nose band.

Jane put her feet forward and hauled back on the looped rein with both hands. But Fitz only leaned into the bit, twisting his jaw, and galloped on. She felt the grip in her fingers and knees fading. The sound of rapid thudding from his hooves and the roaring whistle of the wind filled her mind. A numbness of fatigue and fear crept through her.

The railroad tracks approached, and Fitz had not lost any steam. Jane knew what was going to happen. At this speed, he would trip in the railroad tracks, fall, and break multiple legs. And she knew if her skull hit a rail at over thirty miles an hour, she'd likely die.

With less than five seconds to the railroad tracks, she accepted that she would have to abandon Fitz. Both of them would have a better chance without her on his back. She had to bail out, *right now*.

Jane prayed for Fitz, took her feet out of the stirrups, leaned forward to steady herself with a light grip around his neck, and rolled her right leg over his back. Her toes hit the ground first, then her head. She saw stars and then black.

Fitz somehow cleared the first set of tracks, found firm ground between, and cleared the remaining set handily. Still at full gallop, he landed on the highway, tried to turn on the concrete, and slipped. Steel horseshoes have no grip on hard pavement. He went down hard, landing on his back with enough force to break the wooden tree in the saddle, and slid into traffic. Car tires screeched and horns blared as drivers frantically swerved to avoid him. Still sliding, he lifted his head and wallowed with his neck to get up on a foreleg. Sparks flew from his front shoes trying to find a hold on the pavement. Hair and hide ground into the concrete and was ripped free. Fitz crashed into the far curb, taking the impact in his legs, gained his footing, and galloped off, wild eyed, stirrups flailing in the air, and broken reins trailing from his bit. Blood dripped from his raw shoulder and hip.

Jane sat up and looked dimly for Fitz through the fog of near consciousness. She was having trouble breathing and put her hand to her mouth. It came away wet with blood. Jane looked down and saw a steady thin stream of blood pouring into her lap. Cautiously she probed the bridge of her nose. Puffy numbness spread to include both cheeks. A dull headache was forming.

"Damn, my nose is broken." Then horror flashed inside her as she remembered the railroad tracks, the highway.

"Fitz?" she asked. He was nowhere to be seen.

Jane got up and stumbled to the road, dizzy and holding her head, dreading what she would find. Raw pieces of hide and bloody mats of chestnut hairs marked where he had fallen.

Jane picked up Fitz's blood trail at the far curb and staggered in a weak trot from one red spatter to the next. Her head pounded from the concussion and swelling sinuses of her broken nose.

Two sergeants in a jeep saw the bloody girl padding down the road and stopped. Putting her in the jeep, they offered to take her to the hospital, but she would have none of it. The sergeants gave her a rag to hold under her nose and followed the trail of blood and broken bridle pieces. They found Fitz quivering by a maintenance shed. His eyes were bulging in terror, nostrils distended, still blowing hard. The bridle was gone, and her new saddle, a Christmas present, was broken at a sick angle. Blood oozed from his flank, soaked his hind legs, and dripped slowly from his belly. He resisted attempts to be caught by the three of them, wheeling and trotting away.

"Thank 'ou," Jane offered, "bud, I bedder do dis. He dudn't like men."

The sergeants gave her a length of rope from the jeep, and she baby-stepped toward Fitz.

"Easy," she said to Fitz in soothing tones. "Nobody's going to hurt you." At length he succumbed, and she tied the rope around his neck. One of his hocks was swelling badly, and flesh on the point of that hip was ground away to white, which Jane assumed to be bone.

Jane wrote, "I led him back to the stables trying to calm my anger caused by fear I had never known before. What a beautiful sight we must have been, a bloody, dirty girl leading a sweaty, equally dirty and bloody horse who was dancing nervously on the end of a rope. His nervous prancing made me angrier and angrier, and I knew that if I lost my temper, everything would be completely ruined, so for fifteen agonizing minutes I clenched my jaws and counted up to thousands."

Jane was over the tack room sink, halfheartedly cleaning dried blood from her chin when Pop arrived. He was relived that she was functioning, and he winced at the swelling in her face. He told her he was taking her to the hospital and left her for news on Fitz.

"Sir," Master Sergeant Smith stood at attention, "I thought General Sultan was crazy to suggest your daughter, good a rider as she is, might make a decent horse of that rogue. God knows . . ."

"Not your fault," Pop cut him off. "How's the horse?"

"He's gone bad lame in the stall, sir. Could be tendons, ligaments, bone chips. At least one leg, maybe three. Won't know till we get him cleaned up, and he won't let anybody near."

On the way to the hospital, Jane burst into tears when she heard the news and realized Fitz might never be able to jump again. She couldn't stand the idea that she had been responsible. If she had bailed out earlier, he might have turned for home on the parade ground and arrived back at the stable with no more than a pair of broken reins. The doctor told Pop she had a concussion and to bring her back if she didn't keep improving.

Over the next week, a black-eyed Jane held Fitz for the vet while he dressed the horse's wounds. Most of the damage was superficial. The major worry was the suspensory and sesamoid ligaments in the right foreleg. The ligaments had been strained and were hot and swollen. Jane knew this injury was common to racehorses, polo ponies, and jumpers. It could produce permanent lameness. The strain could also start the bones to ossify and fuse in the forelegs. If this interfered with a tendon, he might not be able to fold his knees sufficiently to jump. Jane slathered an iodine salve on the swelling each day to promote circulation and wrapped it in sheet cotton.

Amazingly, he was sound after the swelling subsided. Jane decided to start over by getting on him bareback, with just a halter and shank. Fitz had complete control of where to go. He did spook on occasion, and she had to dismount quickly, hanging onto the shank. But mostly he was content to munch on the lush grass with her on his back. Jane reasoned all she could do was ask, and she had to respect his "No" for an answer.

The week before the family was scheduled to ship to the states, Pop came home from work, again paused in the front hall, sighed, and called for his oldest daughter. She limped down the stairs, favoring an ankle twisted in a fall. The remnants of her black eyes had faded to light yellow.

"Jane, I don't know how to say this, so I'll just say it," Pop uneasily shifted his weight. "General Sultan gave his permission to have Fitz destroyed."

The metallic taste of consequence shot through her. She went weak in the knees and felt sick to her stomach. She regretted that she had not understood the responsibility that came with General Sultan's flattering offer. Then she felt desperate outrage that the army would shoot him. When he went right, he was a wonderful horse. He just needed to find his way.

"I know," Pop said softly. "You gave the horse your best, but time has run out."

Jane ran up the stairs to lock herself in her room. She wailed face down on her bed. Jane didn't know how to fix Fitz's problem, but she knew he was worthy of many more tries. Fitz's plight wasn't his fault. Buried deep under his abuses, she sensed a willingness. His two wins of the Officers Charger's Trophy at Fort Riley were tangible evidence.

However, the army had its mission. As Jack Burton, retired major general and member of the 1948 Army Olympic Equestrian Team, put it in a 2004 interview, "If the horse wasn't useful, you'd dispose of him. . . . A horse is something that has to be used. He has to carry a soldier, or has to compete, or whatever his mission is. If he can't do it, they don't turn him out, you shoot him." Jane knew the only horse ever retired by the army was Comanche, survivor of Custer's Last Stand. He lived to be twenty-nine at Fort Riley. Between ceremonial duties he was free to roam, grazing his choice of the greenest lawns on post.

The army had made its decision on Fitz, and for Jane to buck the order was contrary to her heritage. She had obedience drilled into her from Catholic schooling, military upbringing, and a stern German father. All army brats, when appealing to reverse parental decisions, had heard Kipling's lines: "Yours is not to reason why. Yours is but to do or die."

At the stable, Jane avoided seeing Fitz out of shame and sorrow. But she pleaded his case to anyone who would listen. There was condolence but not much sympathy for her argument to spare Fitz. Sitting on a bale of straw by the tack room, she covered her face and burst into tears over the finality that Fitz would be destroyed. Even worse, she felt it was her doing.

"Why don't you buy him?" one of the wives who rode at the stable asked.

"What do you mean?" Jane replied, astounded, and rose to her feet.

"Anybody can buy horses from the army. Price is the same for all of them. A hundred and sixty-some dollars. Army doesn't have to sell, but they might."

It had never occurred to Jane that the army sold horses and, even if it did, that the army might sell to anybody, anytime. Jane desperately and relentlessly begged Pop to buy Fitz. This caused immediate criticism in the Schofield Barracks community.

"If you buy that horse, you're buying your daughter's death warrant," he heard.

There was only one exception, and luckily for Jane, it carried considerable weight.

"Buy him," Colonel Van Deusen advised Pop simply. Then, seeing the befuddled expression on Pop's face, the colonel added, "His legs are sound, not a blemish on them. Hindquarters are built for jumping. Honestly, the horse has great possibilities." Colonel Van Deusen also said Jane didn't yet have the understanding to train the horse. In his opinion, she was an overenthusiastic teenager, but he allowed that she was dedicated and said the horse would teach her the patience she would need.

Pop had been a top wrestler at Lehigh and West Point. He actively sought challenge in his athletic and professional life and was not entirely comfortable with denying Jane the same opportunities. However, he considered owning Fitz to be a dangerously stupid idea. The best outcome could be that they would sell Fitz when the horse proved intractable. He didn't want to think about the worst case. On the other hand, Pop admired his daughter's disciplined commitment to riding and was proud of her success in the post horse shows.

Jane later wrote, "As any horse-crazy teenager can be, [I] was very persuasive." Ultimately, Pop yielded to Jane's pleas and agreed to inquire. The quartermaster offered to sell Fitz for $163.57, the government's standard price for purchasing a replacement (about $2,000 in today's dollars).

Pop became the reluctant owner of Fitzrada, just days before their departure. Jane was overjoyed, ran to the stable with the good news, and hugged Fitz's neck till her arms were sore. Fitz ignored her. Some at the stable shared her excitement. Others looked awkward, knowing she was doomed to fail.

"So now, I owned a horse, and it was up to me to prove that he was all I wanted," Jane wrote. "Secretly I resolved that he would show everyone, including the general, that he was the well-trained, beautiful jumper I had claimed he was."

U

On the morning of her departure, Jane said good-bye to Fitz in his stall. She told him she would see him soon in North Carolina, but she had her doubts. A lot could go wrong during the separation. Because of his rank, Pop was authorized to keep and ship one private horse at government expense. Luckily, the U.S. Army Transport *Meigs* was in Pearl Harbor, returning empty from the Philippines and bound for the United States in two days. Transport ships had decks for livestock. Horses and mules stood between padded stanchions to keep them upright during the ship's roll. Jane hoped they would pull his steel shoes and wrap his legs in shipping bandages.

Hitler had just invaded Russia, and the Japanese had consolidated China. The United States embargoed the Axis countries of Germany, Italy, and Japan and seized their merchant ships in U.S. ports. Few believed the United States could avoid war. Huge U.S. flags were painted on the sides of American ships so they might be identified as neutral to submarines. Jane worried that war might come while Fitz was at sea and that the flags would be highly visible targets. In California, Fitz would be transferred to a train. Unlike dogs, there was no quarantine for horses. A groom would accompany the carload of government livestock headed east. At the stops, the groom would top off the water barrel if there wasn't enough rain, muck out and replace the soiled bedding, and fill the hay racks.

Jane had visions of Fitz getting away in a rail yard and being hit by a train or, just as bad, getting misdelivered to God knows where or being forgotten in a huge freight yard, lost among thousands of cars, running out of water, and dying. More likely, he could go berserk or injure himself so badly he would have to be destroyed. Endless possibilities dawned on her, and safe arrival at Fort Bragg was the least likely.

As the tug pushed her ship away from the dock, Jane removed leis from her neck and cast them over the rail. *They say if you throw your leis into the water*, she told herself, *it means you'll return to Hawaii*. She never did.

6

LOST IN TRANSIT

On the afternoon of Fitz's expected arrival in North Carolina, Jane walked the several blocks to the Fort Bragg Transportation Office. She took the shipping inventory she'd been given in Hawaii. Empty packing boxes from their move waited on the sidewalk in front of their quarters, a new two-story stucco house on officer's row. It was identical to the houses surrounding it, reserved for families of battalion commanders, lieutenant colonels, just like Pop.

It was five months prior to the attack on Pearl Harbor, but the United States was preparing for the war already raging in Europe. Long formations of olive-drab C-47 aircraft passed overhead carrying paratroopers to Fort Bragg's drop zones, where the men jumped. They flew very low, and Jane could see the faces of helmeted soldiers standing inside the open doors. The airplanes were so prevalent that people on the sidewalks paid no attention except to suspend conversation under the din of their motors.

Jane was optimistic about working with Fitz at Fort Bragg. The post stables, where Fitz would reside, were just a mile away. The stables, paddocks, and riding ring were not as plush as Schofield Barracks. But to the east of the Fort Bragg stables, beyond the rifle ranges, riding trails crisscrossed a 200-square-mile training area of pine-forested sand hills. The town of Southern Pines bordered the other end of the training area. With showing, a harness-racing track, and a foxhunt, it was the most prominent center of horse activity south of Virginia.

At the transportation office, a clerk behind the counter took Jane's papers and searched through multiple drawers of a nearby filing cabinet. He came back with a puzzled look on his face, and Jane's heart sank.

"Sorry, we don't have anything," the clerk responded. "We used to get some advance warning on livestock. But railroads are jammed. Supplies and troops have priority over horses."

"Do you know if he made it to San Francisco?" Jane asked.

"No, but we wouldn't." He shrugged his shoulders. "Nowadays, stuff just shows up here."

Jane hung her head and straightened the dog-eared corners of the inventory. A lone carbon-copied line read, "1 each, chestnut gelding, 15.2 hands, branded US on left shoulder and 9J on left neck." She folded the paper gently. It was as close as she could get to touching Fitz.

Jane inquired daily about Fitz, and the answer was always the same: "Nothing yet. We'll let you know." By the time Fitz was two weeks overdue, Jane dreaded asking them, knowing the probability of bad news increased with time. At her request, the army placed a trace on the shipment. Tired of hearing hopeful words from her parents, Jane went to bed earlier and got up later each day.

Secretly, Jane thought the best-case scenario was Fitz had gotten loose and been stolen by some nice cowboy who had an eye for horses. She had a vision of Fitz on a North Texas plain, belly deep in prairie grass. Fitz nickered to an old unshaven cowhand who hobbled toward him and offered a drink from his cowboy hat. The scene in her mind shifted to winter. The old cowhand was long gone. Fitz's bony rump was turned into the howling wind to conserve body heat. He pawed weakly at the frozen crust of snow, trying to get to the grass below. A quick death would be a mercy.

Jane wept.

When Fitz was four weeks overdue, Pop got the call from the Transportation Office that his horse had arrived and was at the post stable. He immediately left his desk to pick up Jane at home.

"How is he?" she asked, getting in the car.

"I didn't think to ask," Pop said. "We'll see in a minute."

"When did he get here?" she asked.

"I don't know."

"Papa, can you please drive faster? What took so long?" she spat questions. "Think he lost a lot of weight? Did they have any trouble with him?"

Pop gave up on conversation with her.

A captain met them with shipping papers in hand, proud to have delivered Fitz safely, hoping for Lieutenant Colonel Pohl's praise and needing Pop's signature to finish the job.

"He's a fine-looking animal, sir." The captain led Pop and Jane down the long row of stalls, walking briskly ahead of them. "Not a cut or a scratch on him, sir. The army prides itself on shipping livestock around the world. Clean, healthy, and fit for duty."

The captain halted abruptly in front of a stall door, checked its number against his papers, smiled proudly, and gestured for Pop and Jane to look inside.

Jane peered over the Dutch door into the darkness. She saw a chestnut tail, and her heart filled at being reunited. She grabbed the door latch and swung the door open to throw her arms around him. The opening door lit his rump in sunlight. As the shadow from the door's swinging arc moved down his hind legs, her eyes followed it to where his chestnut coat turned to white. The horse in the stall had two white stockings. The only white on Fitz was a star on his forehead. Jane fled down the aisle sobbing.

"Damn it!" Pop wheeled on the captain, infuriated at the cruelty of what had just happened. "This animal is more than a month overdue. Now you want me to sign for the wrong horse?"

"Sir, I ah . . ." The captain stood at attention, red faced, unconsciously crumpling the shipping papers in his hand.

"No!" Pop yelled. "Tomorrow, you *will* report to me with the current location of my horse." Pop pointed at the inch of ground that separated them. "Even if the horse is found *dead*, I want the carcass delivered here for my inspection."

Jane padded down the aisle in tears, looking for a place to hide and cry alone. She saw a familiar chestnut head sticking out of a stall door at the far end of the stable. Anguish turned to joy. Gushing over him, she ran her hands down his legs. After determining that Fitz wasn't injured, she heard Pop chewing out the captain. She ran back part of the way.

"Papa, Papa," she shouted. "He's here!"

The trip had been hard on Fitz. His muscles atrophied from weeks of confinement, and his temperament was sour. Jane wondered if he remembered what awaited him at the end of his last trip by ship and rail and expected a fresh crop of soldiers intent on breaking him.

Jane brought carrots to the post stable and put one in Fitz's feed tub. When she came back to visit, the oats were gone, but the carrot remained, a hard orange testament to distrust.

Jane later wrote, "I gave him a rest of four months, and then started retraining him. Long walks through the sandy woods at Bragg, making him forget all his past experiences, letting him become free and easy in his gaits, and above all to have complete confidence in me. . . . My next desire was to break down the cold wall of reserve that was between us. I spent hours sitting on the side of the stall so he would become used to me."

She talked to him, stroked his neck and flanks, and tried to touch his ears, without success. Fitz remained eccentric and unpredictable. He could be jazzed as if in a panic, but then sometimes he acted oblivious as if in a fog, sometimes high strung and quirky, sometimes obstinate and malicious. If he had an agenda, it lacked consistency. Jane knew that both of them would have to suffer through this storm to reach the calm beyond. Ultimately, it would take five years for him to find his way again.

Jane was a "C" student in high school, and it wasn't for lack of trying. Relying on rote memorization of seemingly arbitrary rules, she crammed for grammar, French, and math tests, not seeing any structure that might bring comprehension. Homework routinely kept her up past her bedtime. She was lucky to get into Vassar, where Mother had graduated Phi Beta Kappa in 1922. Jane's four-year curriculum could be compressed into three years for the coming war, increasing the course load that she would have to carry each semester. Pop had graduated first in his class from West Point in August 1917. His curriculum had likewise been compressed into three years to rush fresh second lieutenants into World War I. Vassar was tough, and he had doubts about his daughter's being able keep up. Years later, Jane suggested that Vassar lowered the admissions standards for the war and facetiously maintained, "They let me in as part of an experiment to see how long the dimmer students might last."

Jane remembered long hours of her childhood at the dining room table being coached by Pop in math. Math was easy for him; he was an engineer and had been a math instructor at West Point. But his explanations at the dining room table were met with blank stares.

"What did I ever do to deserve such dumb children?" Pop teased, but he was genuinely frustrated by his oldest child's inability to grasp the concepts he labored to teach. While he believed attempting the improbable was a virtue, he considered attempting the impossible stupid. He reasoned that Jane would not last at Vassar, and then they would have to find another school for her on short notice.

"Look," Pop argued with his wife, "War's coming soon. I'll be overseas and won't be able to help. Why not send her to a small Catholic girl's college and be done with it?"

"Let her go to Vassar for as long as she can," Mother countered.

Like other disputes between Mother and Pop, this one turned into a standoff, and Pop did not speak to his wife for a week. Family meals during these feuds were icy silences. Jane felt particularly uncomfortable being the object of the conflict. Pop was a domineering German husband. He valued his wife's intelligence, but for her to challenge his decisions was insubordination. Duty was perhaps the only thing that held their marriage together. Love of his children was enough reward for Pop.

Stern upbringing by affectionless governesses led Mother to adopt curious maternal practices. She was charmed by her children, but she wasn't clingy or doting. In fact, she was not comfortable holding babies and found them interesting only after they were old enough to have opinions. She never forgave her own mother for not letting her stay up long enough to see Halley's comet. As a result, Mother would never deny a child the opportunity see anything new or rare and had incredible patience in those pursuits. She kept incidents from Pop that would cause him to punish a child. On the other hand, she had no patience for bad behavior. When Mother lost her temper at a kid, her verbal assaults were as sharp as a slap across the face, and she stayed mad for a day or two.

The coming war would give Mother independence from her husband. She looked forward to being on her own.

Luckily for Jane, war preparations were occupying Pop's attention. Hitler had consolidated Europe and was closing quickly on Moscow. The United States had not yet declared war, but everyone expected it very soon. Pop's command of the 96th Engineer Battalion required long hours in the field practicing bridge and bunker construction at Fort Bragg. Because the 96th was a segregated unit of black soldiers, he did not expect it to see much fighting and was worried about his career. He asked for an assignment that would place him closer to the impending war.

Orders arrived quickly from the War Department in Washington, assigning him to locate military airfield sites starting in Brazil, spanning Africa and southern Asia and ending in Samoa. With Hitler occupying Europe, the Allies quickly needed an air route around it. His mission was classified "Secret"; he was to proceed immediately and by himself. The orders authorized him to commandeer any air transportation available, regardless of whether it was military, commercial, or private. If necessary, he could kick everybody off an airliner, reroute it, and send the bill to Washington. That night at supper, Pop announced to his family he was leaving. He said he could not tell them where he was going, and he honestly didn't know for how long. He would write them when he could. The next morning, per his orders, he signed for a money belt full of gold coins from the post finance office and departed for Natal, Brazil.

With Pop no longer assigned to Fort Bragg, the Pohl family had to vacate their quarters on post. Mother rented a one-story bungalow in nearby Fayetteville not much larger than a cottage. The local radio station offered her a job writing advertising copy and satirical skits. She took it, highly unusual for an officer's wife. At night under a bare lightbulb in the attic, she sat at a card table and happily banged out copy on a portable typewriter in a haze of cigarette smoke. The skits became a series titled "Indigestion with Minnie." She played the part of Minnie, a housewife with witty, plainspoken opinions on local life, and enjoyed the job immensely. Experience as an amateur thespian on army posts had prepared her well.

Pop sent home boxes covered with exotic postage stamps from places like Khartoum and Mogadishu. The boxes contained carved African ebony and ivory art, undeveloped film he had taken of tourist attractions, a bas-relief plaque of General Mussolini liberated by the South African air force, malachite specimens, and other souvenirs. He was unable to receive mail, and Jane went to Vassar without further comment from her father. Since Mother could not take care of Fitz by herself, she agreed to send Fitz with Jane.

Jane loved being off on her own at college. She was five feet seven inches and a wiry 130 pounds. She took up smoking Camel cigarettes and felt sophisticated. Jane's roommate, Nini, was Dutch. Nini's parents had sent her to Vassar to get her out of Holland during the German occupation. Unable to return home during the war, Nini missed her family. Jane and Nini spent long hours studying together, with Jane helping Nini understand passages in English literature and Nini coaching Jane in math. They remained lifetime friends.

Fitz was stabled at Vassar, and Jane rode him several days a week. She started training him all over again, starting with the basics, so he might know her praise for the easier tasks done well before she asked him to reform bad habits. Jane wanted Fitz to have a long, earnest stride, carrying his head low on a loose rein, continuing in a perfectly straight line until she asked for a change of direction. When he had mastered the walk to her satisfaction, she schooled him at a trot. When he could maintain his tempo and heading without deliberate aids, she moved on to school him in large circles and figure eights.

She had apprehension about cantering. The Hale Kula Parade Ground runaway loomed in Jane's mind. She fought the possibility that she might be afraid of Fitz. At the trot she collected him carefully with her hands and steadied him with her legs. She was afraid that squeezing him would send him through the roof and was not sure how much leg would be too much. A disaster here could set them back weeks. She tenuously suggested with her legs that he move up on the bit and relaxed her hands, as if gently releasing a small bird. He broke into a collected, easy canter, and she heaved a sigh of relief. Jane savored the precise delicate beauty of finding him perfectly balanced between her knees and hands.

The slow work continued. When he grew tense, she brought him to a walk, put the reins on his withers, and let him pick his own path. After he settled, she tried to resume his training where they had left off. Sometimes he didn't settle, and she had to give up for the day. There were a few times when his mood turned mean. Jane knew she couldn't discipline him. She just had to wait him out, and it frustrated her. She wondered if she was teaching him that he could evade work by misbehaving.

At times when she got on him, she could tell he was eager to exercise hard. The problem was knowing why. Jane asked more experienced riders. Their suggestions were techniques aimed at improving show ring performance, the same types of drills that had caused him to come unglued at Fort Riley. They had little to do with correcting Fitz's temperament. She could see how each suggestion would improve his skill as jumper, if only he was willing. Even when he was enjoying his schooling over fences, he could suddenly snap, throw her to the ground, and run away. The next day, he would shiver when she got on him, like he was expecting to be beaten. He paid acute attention to her hands and heels, and she dared not make any sudden moves. It would take minutes of walking for him to relax into a working stride.

Discipline was another dilemma. Fitz had no tolerance for physical anger. Jane could scold, but she couldn't punish him. Hitting him in the mouth by snatching the reins or punching him in the ribs with her heels was out of the question. She had to use only her voice to let him know she was disappointed. Even with scolding, she could not harangue him. Jane had to show respect and give him credit that he understood he had erred.

For Fitz to improve, he had to be relaxed through the schooling jumps. "I spent weeks in the jumping ring making him forget that there ever had been heavy hands hauling on his mouth, hindering his easy way of going, and that tearing at a jump as fast as possible was the easiest way to get over it."

She was further frustrated by the need to expand her awareness to three places at once: *with* him in the rhythm of his movement, *ahead* of him in choosing a path through a course, and *above* him as a trainer gauging his capacity and mood.

At a trot he sometimes played with his feet, cutting a wide arc out from his shoulder as he brought a hoof forward. Jane wondered if he was bored and doing this to entertain himself. Other times he moved his legs straight and hard, with almost brutal intent, like racing trotters. It felt like he was trying to punish himself, deliberately flirting with injury, and it scared her. Jane continued to be baffled by his motivations. Was he just afraid of being punished, or could he feel guilt? She could tell if he was angry, playful, or tired. If she relaxed and focused, she could sense attitudes, like brittle, slippery, hollow, or thorny.

Brittle could predict he would resist learning anything new that day. *Slippery* could mean he was going to be evasive. *Hollow* might tell her his lights were on but nobody's home, like he didn't want to be bothered. Sometimes she sensed mild elation when he jumped cleanly. Surely he had memories, but what emotions did they provoke? What she really hoped was that he could someday feel loyalty.

Jane's ultimate goal was to reform her Thoroughbred as a recreational mount for afternoon rides through the countryside, foxhunting, and small local horse shows. Fitz and Jane shared common ground in their enjoyment of jumping, and Jane pursued it simply to build their connection. Any career for Fitz as a show jumper was beyond Jane's imagination, at least until his temperament steadied. When he was going well, he could neatly jump four feet, but Jane had no idea if he was capable of jumping higher than five feet and no interest in pushing him to do it. Even for a horse that was capable, that extra foot could take a year of training. Her short-term objective was to be able to set him up in a turn to a three-foot jump and let him go with no further instruction. She wanted him to continue the arc and the pace, straighten to jump square, and remain straight until she picked him up on the other side and turned him elsewhere. But even that was a pipe dream at this point.

She tried riding him in a double bridle, hoping to keep him on the bit. If he started to wander, she could easily collect him. This tactic worked slightly, but it took a very delicate touch. Once he felt the curb bending his neck, she could sense him bristle, and she had to back off. Jane tried trotting him through cavalletti (a series of evenly spaced ground poles), which encouraged him to collect himself with no input from Jane. Ultimately, she discovered that the secret was using less of her hands and more of her legs and seat to guide him. Eventually, when he bent his neck to each side to gaze at the scenery at a walk, with the correct application of her legs or slant of her hips, she could reshape him to maintain his line. After some weeks, she was amazed to discover he was holding his line without any input from her, even when walking along hillsides, where he used to drift to the bottom.

Foxhunting was available to Vassar students with the nearby Rombout Hunt. Because of his love for jumping, Jane thought Fitz could be a fantastic horse to ride over fences in a foxhunt. The hunt club's territory was the farms and woods in the Hudson Valley near Poughkeepsie. Her only hunting experience had been when she lived at Fort Belvoir. Jane rode an army horse on a hunt from George Washington's grist mill with the Belvoir Hounds. The field of riders followed the scarlet-coated master through the woods in single file. Most formal foxhunting clubs wanted a trail ride through beautiful country, spared from the gore of a kill. Few huntsmen bred their hounds for the kill. On the hunt, Jane had jumped small imitation chicken coops in the fence lines and listened to the hounds giving cry as they chased a fox. The sound built as more hounds joined the scent. It resonated in her chest as determined excitement and hinted at canine blood lust. As for Fitz, Jane knew Fort Riley kept a pack of hounds, but she had no idea whether he had hunted.

Jane was apprehensive about signing up to hunt at Vassar. If he exploded in close quarters, he might take another horse down with him. Injuring a hound was an unpardonable sin.

On the morning of Fitz's and Jane's first meet, hounds poured from the kennel to pack around the huntsman's horse, keen to find a fox in the autumn countryside. Fitz pranced in place and soon was in a lather of sweat waiting to move out. Jane was unable to get him to go close enough to the master for her to introduce herself, a required etiquette. The hounds moved off surrounding the master. Four whips (riders who assist in hunting the pack), also in scarlet, rode close outside the pack, keeping them bunched while passing through a farm gate. In a field on the other side, the hounds were released to cast for scent.

The field of other horses fell into line to jump the first fence in a single file. Fitz was so impatient he jigged in place, feeling for a way out from underneath her. She tightened her grip on his mouth, and he backed as fast as he could, and when she squeezed him, he started to wheel. Jane was embarrassed. The other horses stood calmly waiting their turn and trotted to the fence to jump it, allowing a safe margin from the horse ahead. Fitz's behavior was upsetting to the other members of the field and potentially dangerous. She pulled him out and turned him to the rear of the line. He hated being turned away from where the other horses were headed, and he reared. Jane grabbed his neck and stayed with him until he put his front legs down.

As the last horse in line, by the time it was his turn to jump, he was soaked in sweat from his pent-up exertion. Despite her efforts to make him trot, he bolted to the fence. She gave him his head to clear the jump, and he seized the bit, making a huge lunge over the obstacle. He almost landed on the rump of the horse ahead, who shied away in fright. The rider was jerked to the side of her saddle, managed to stay on, but lost her hat and glared at Jane.

Seeing other horses cantering ahead of him, Fitz was intoxicated by the possibility of speed. He acted like a green racehorse, plunging over his jumps, tearing to the front of the field of riders. Fitz and Jane blew right past the field master, who was too surprised to yell at her. In less than a minute, they had run up into the hounds, a serious breach of hunting etiquette.

"Can't you hold that horse?" a whip in his scarlet coat shouted at her. "Hounds can't do their work with you trampling among them."

Exhausted from fighting him, Jane turned Fitz's head away from the field of riders and strained to contain him while they passed behind. She blushed beet red and could feel them staring holes in her back. Spent and disappointed, she headed back to the stable. Without the distraction of the other horses, Fitz calmed to a determined walk, and she took off her derby to wipe her brow and sweat-smeared glasses. They crested a hill, and before them stretched farm fields rimmed with trees of red and yellow leaves.

"Oh Fitz, look at those colors. Three years in the tropics, and I forgot all about fall." She sighed, "We'll try again next week. That is, if the field master doesn't ban us."

A week later, she tried a standing martingale to restrict his head, hoping it would keep him from running away. As soon as she got on him, he went nuts. She had to jump off and hang on to the reins while he backpedaled to get away. The field of horses moved off while she was stripping the martingale from his neck. Fitz was still keyed up when she got back on him, and he pulled to catch up. He seized the bit, rushed the first fence, landed at a gallop, and streaked up through the field, just like last time.

Fitz picked a line between two horses walking ahead. The women were chatting with each other, unaware of what was closing on them.

"Watch out!" Jane screamed, but it was too late. The gap between the two women looked impossibly small. Scared, she squeezed her knees in to avoid clipping the women's legs. Fitz surged ahead as if he'd been shot. Jane's stirrup irons hit theirs, knocking their inside stirrups off their boots. Fitz plunged on. The field master yelled. She couldn't hear his words, but she knew their meaning. The same whip as last time caught up with her.

"Keep that damned orangutan back where he belongs!" he said hotly, and suggested that might be the school stable.

On the first Sunday morning of December 1941, the Japanese bombed Pearl Harbor. By that afternoon, the news had spread through campus. Jane's mind raced. *Were any of my school friends killed in Hawaii? Sergeant Mope? Belle, Pat, and the other horses at Schofield Barracks?*

The next day, Jane and her dorm mates huddled in front of the big mahogany console radio in the day room for the president's speech from the White House. They sat cross-legged on the rugs, pulled their socked feet up under their skirts, and leaned forward to hear. A senior delicately adjusted the tuning knob to make the signal less fuzzy. The room smelled of hot radio tubes and fear. President Franklin Delano Roosevelt's voice crackled: "No matter how long it may take us to overcome this pre-meditated invasion, the American people in their righteous might will win through to absolute victory. . . . I ask that the Congress declare . . . a state of war . . ." Several girls broke into tears. The words committed their brothers and boyfriends to fight to the death against the Axis. The future each girl had imagined for herself instantly disappeared. Jane worried for Pop. His last letter had come from Africa, postmarked months ago. She had no idea where he was now. The phones lines were tied up, and she could not get through to Mother.

The only one Jane could feel happy for was Nini. The Allies would try to free Holland, but Nini told Jane she was terrified. London was being bombed. Wouldn't the same be true for Holland from British bombers killing Germans there? Additionally, Nini felt morbidly re-sponsible and ashamed that American boys were going to die trying to push the Germans from her homeland. She shivered with visions of the boys whose framed pictures sat on her classmates' dressers.

Pop's orders took him to Brazil; across Africa, India, and Australia; and ultimately to American Samoa, staying south of the fighting, locat-ing and classifying airfields. The Allies needed a southern air route to Egypt, India, and China for ferrying heavy bombers and supplies. On the trip, Pop overslept and missed catching a scheduled flight to Ran-goon. When he finally got to the airfield, the clerk told him to wait for the next plane. Hours later, the terminal's loudspeakers announced the news that Rangoon had fallen to the Japanese. The plane Pop had missed was out of radio range by then and could not be recalled. The passengers were presumed to have been imprisoned or worse.

From phone calls to Mother, Jane heard a growing list of fathers shipping out who had been their neighbors at various army posts and boys enlisting whom she remembered from school. She was relieved when her younger brother, Richard, was accepted to West Point because it would keep him out of the war, at least until he graduated. Additionally, West Point was only thirty miles down the Hudson River from Vassar.

In the fall of 1943, Richard was a plebe and Jane a senior. Plebes were not allowed to leave the academy's grounds, so Jane signed up for a hop at West Point to see him. She made arrangements to spend the night with her aunt and uncle who were stationed at West Point. Jane boarded the bus from Vassar to the hop. It was filled with giggling college girls. Many knew she had lived at West Point and plied her with questions about what cadets were like.

"They get demerits for PDA," she answered. "It means 'public display of affection.' Anything from holding hands to kissing. So, even though they haven't seen a girl for a while, you won't be mauled on the dance floor."

"Personally, I like Princeton boys better," one girl confided. "Their canvas drinking jackets are nifty. Besides, after I find my prince charming and get married, I want to live in New York City, not on some dusty old Indian fort, heating my bath water on a wood-burning stove."

As the bus labored up West Point's Thayer Road, Jane spotted the family's old quarters next to the hospital. She remembered playing with Richard and Jennet in the yard. Mother read the Sunday comics to them on the porch after church as they looked over her shoulder at the pictures. The brakes groaned loudly as the bus halted among the military academy's gray granite buildings, their parapets reminiscent of castles.

Jane turned on the reading light and checked her brown curls and lipstick in her compact's mirror. Satisfied, she clicked it shut, stood in the aisle, and smoothed wrinkles in her dark blue taffeta cocktail dress. Waiting for the girls ahead of her to disembark, she fidgeted with her Mikimoto pearl necklace. *Boy, things have changed in three years,* she thought. She remembered admiring the necklace in the window of Gump's jewelry store in Honolulu with her girlfriends. Her jaw dropped when she opened her Christmas present from Pop. That was their last Christmas in Hawaii, the Christmas before Pearl Harbor, and just a few months before General Sultan asked her to ride Fitz.

Buses from other women's colleges emptied beside them. Richard stood among the eager throng of gray uniformed cadets searching for a familiar or pretty face. When Jane spotted him, she put her glasses in her purse, took him by surprise, and hugged him hard. He was taller and skinnier than she remembered.

"Sis, I'd like you to meet your date for the hop," he presented his classmate with a flourish, "Cadet McElvoy."

"Call me John," he said in a southern drawl and shook her hand, "Richard's told me an awful lot about you." He had a wry smile and an easy stance. Knowingly, he looked into her hazel eyes maybe a little longer than was polite.

Southern flirt, she stereotyped, and then scowled at her brother over the secrets he might have shared. But she immediately liked John's freckled, curly-haired good looks and imagined him as a boy, the spitting image of barefooted Tom Sawyer with a straw hat and a grass stem drooping from his teeth.

"C'mon we've got supper reservations at the Thayer Hotel. Better get moving."

"Where's your date?" Jane asked her brother.

"Sick. Couldn't make it," he shrugged. "It's okay. I'll go stag to the hop. Dance with more girls that way anyhow." He patted his stomach lovingly. "Besides, more food for the rest of us at the Thayer."

Their breath turned white in the crisp evening as they panted up the Thayer's steep driveway. Rich odors of steak and seafood strengthened near the top.

No war rationing here, Jane thought. *Remember to take Nini some cake made with real butter.*

After dessert, the two cadets leaned back in their chairs and unzipped their gray wool dress blouses from the bottom, a little higher up their abdomens, to make room for the meal. John bent over, pulled up his trouser leg, and removed a pack of cigarettes from the cuff of his sock.

Jane laughed, accepting a cigarette.

"Something funny?" John asked.

"Just remembered your uniforms don't have pockets."

"We wouldn't be so handsome walking around with bulging pockets, would we?"

Jane blushed.

"Richard tells me you've got an army horse that's quite a problem. How's that coming?"

"Sometimes not so good," Jane replied.

"When I graduate I'm going Armor," John said. "No horses for me. Want to be surrounded by thick steel when I ride through Berlin's Brandenburg Gate."

"What are you gonna be?" John looked Jane in the eye and smiled invitingly.

"I'm majoring in geology. Maybe I can find oil for your tanks. But my grades aren't so hot," Jane confessed and regretted it instantly.

"I wanna be a paratrooper," Richard piped up, saving her. "Jump out of airplanes."

"You're nuts," both Jane and John said simultaneously and laughed.

"Have you heard anything from Pop?" Richard asked his sister.

"No," Jane said softly.

"Jennet tells me he's going to Ireland." Richard said. "My guess is he'll be part of the invasion of Europe, when it comes." The speculation suddenly made Pop's danger more imminent in Jane's mind. It was worse than not knowing where he was.

"Jennet says he writes her all the time," Jane said, "but not me."

"Me either," Richard said. "Don't let it get under your skin."

"No more war talk, okay?" Jane asked. She worried about what the future held for Richard. He and John were too eager to get in the fight. Corpses of graduates were trickling into the West Point cemetery at an increasing rate. She remembered paratroopers pouring from planes at Fort Bragg. Her nightmare vision became her brother trapped in a burning plane he could not jump from. In less than a year, the lightly armed 82nd and 101st Airborne Divisions would parachute into Normandy in the dark to initiate D-Day. Their mission would be to delay German reinforcement of the Normandy defenses. As the first U.S.

troops on German-occupied French soil, the paratroopers were vulnerable to the point of being expendable.

Jane was hopeful that West Point would keep her brother out of the war for a few more years. Even though his curriculum, like hers, was shortened to three years, he wouldn't graduate until 1946.

"Well," John said, "that's what we do here. It'll be mighty quiet without war talk."

"Let's go to the hop," Jane suggested.

A few cadets and their dates milled on the front steps on Cullum Hall, smoking and laughing excitedly. Music spilled outside each time the door was opened.

"We're late," Richard said, breaking into a trot.

Inside, folding tables with red tablecloths and modest flower centerpieces surrounded the dance floor, which was in front of the bandstand. Richard, John, and Jane ambled to the enormous filigreed silver bowl of fruit punch. John filled their glasses from a heavy silver ladle, as tall as a canoe paddle.

Members of the big band wore dinner jackets and swayed behind their decorated music stands. The hall reverberated with "Two O'Clock Jump" and "Tuxedo Junction." Rich fat horns punched at the ceiling and smooth reeds tweaked a thin layer in Jane's chest.

"Let me see your hop card," Richard held out his hand to Jane, and she presented the little folded card with its miniature pencil attached by a delicate braid.

He opened it to the numbered lines representing each song of the evening and wrote his name and that of his roommates, taking up four of the lines.

"Hey, leave some for me," John protested. "The band's probably in the middle of the second dance already."

"I'll leave the last dance, 'Army Blue,' for you," Richard joked.

John snatched the card from Richard and started writing his name in the rest of the lines. Jane was flattered. He slapped the hop card into Jane's hand and whisked her to the dance floor.

She hoped John wasn't a good dancer and wouldn't be disappointed in her. Many of her friends, both boys and girls, took pride in their dancing. *I spend so much time thinking about how my body should follow a horse over a jump,* she thought now. *But I'm scared to dance.*

John slipped his arm around her waist. *Dreamy* was the word that came to her mind. When he danced, he tried too hard. But his enthusiasm was infectious.

They made the transitions from foxtrot to rumba, jitterbug, waltz, shag, conga, and Lindy. John spun Jane out and back, stomping out shifting patterns with a vengeance. Girls hiked their skirts for longer leg reach. The music magnetized them. Everybody's hair was wet from the hard work, but none cared. The only time they sat down was when the band took a break.

At the table their spirits floated. Jane modestly wiped her sweaty hands on a napkin under the table.

"My favorite for dancing is Benny Goodman. And you?" John looked to Jane for an answer, but in his lingering excitement continued without it, "Harry James and Woody Herman are a thrill. Miller and Jimmy Dorsey are too cute for me. Basie's got the rhythm. But dancing to one band all night, its gotta be Goodman, master of the black stick."

Richard and Jane laughed at him. He was possessed.

"Notice they didn't play a tango?" Richard asked his sister.

"You're right," Jane realized.

"Too lewd for West Point."

At the end of the break, the band leader tapped the microphone and announced a dance contest. John cheered, and Jane looked uncomfortable. He grabbed Jane's hand and stood.

"I think I'll sit this out," Jane offered from her chair, "Why don't you dance with my friend Betty, over there in the blue dress? She's really good."

"Nonsense," he ordered, "On your feet." It was a phrase sergeants used. Jane wondered if cadets were preoccupied with living to the hilt, knowing that they would be in combat within months after graduation.

By the end of the hop, Jane was happily tired, looking forward to a spending the night with her Uncle Buck and Aunt Kitty. Buck was one of Pop's younger brothers and had been a cadet when Jane was in grade school at West Point. During that time, he had been a regular visitor at their quarters for Sunday dinner and enjoyed playing with her. Shortly after graduation, Buck had been vaccinated by the army with a defective batch of serum and lost sight in one eye. As a result, his service as an officer in the field was finished, and he was assigned to West Point to teach math for the rest of his career.

On Buck's doorstep, John thanked Jane for a wonderful evening and lingered awkwardly. Jane could tell he was trying to decide whether to kiss her goodnight. She hoped he would and was puzzled that he was now shy after having been so animated on the dance floor. It was endearing. He waited too long and retreated but then turned back toward her.

"Will I see you tomorrow after chapel?" he asked.

"Yes, I'd like that," she replied, hoping she didn't sound too desperate.

At the breakfast table, Jane asked her uncle if he'd heard anything from Pop, hoping the war had caused the brothers to write. Historically, they only exchanged newsy Christmas cards penned by their wives. Buck had not heard from him but knew through the grapevine he'd been given command of an engineer group, a dream come true for Pop. He'd done a bang-up job in Africa and probably would have been promoted to brigadier general if he'd stayed to build the airfields he'd located. He could have stayed but requested reassignment for combat.

"You know your father," Buck said. "Duty, honor, country." Buck explained how Pop was now probably commanding five engineer battalions, as many as 4,000 men. It was a combat command, a plum assignment for an engineer full colonel. The Allies were massing in the British Isles for an invasion. Buck guessed that it would happen within a year and that Pop would fight through Europe to Berlin.

Jane felt suddenly sick. From growing up in the army, she knew combat engineers sustained the highest casualties. They were the ones that cleared the enemy minefields, and the minefields were covered by enemy artillery and machine guns.

After breakfast, Jane, Buck, and Kitty walked to Mass in the cadet Catholic chapel. Like most of West Point, it was made of stone but had a pitched slate roof that contrasted with the fortress parapets of the academy's other buildings, and it was dainty in comparison to the Protestant chapel that towered like a cathedral on the cliff overlooking the barracks and the parade ground.

Standing outside the chapel door on the granite stairs, Jane waited and listened for her brother. From her earliest childhood memories, she recalled the smell of incense, the sound of litanies murmured in Latin reverberating off white plaster walls, and the wrought-iron stand holding rows of votive candles at the offering. She remembered the first time Pop had given her a nickel to put in the box so she could light a candle by herself for the safe delivery of a deceased soul to heaven. She had asked Pop for a name to pray for, and he suggested his grandmother's. Jane had not known her, so she knelt and prayed for a family cat that had disappeared. She was sure God was listening to her small voice and pronounced her whispered words carefully.

Jane thought about how scared she had been walking up these same steps ten years ago. All dressed up in starched white crinoline and wearing her first veil, she held Pop's hand and climbed the steps to receive her First Holy Communion. Standing there now and waiting for Richard, she could not know, but she would descend these steps just three more times in her life. Each would be for a man she loved. Twice, she would be dressed in black and once in off-white.

Presently, from around the road bend came the crisp echoes of shoes marching and cadence calls to keep them in step. The formation strutted briskly into view and halted below her on the road. They were dismissed to storm the chapel steps. She strained to find Richard's smile in the herd of gray uniforms.

In the afternoon, Jane met John and he walked her to Trophy Point. Leaning on Civil War cannons, they soaked in the lofty view of the Hudson River. The wind gusted and chilled them.

"Coldest place I've ever been," he said inching closer to her. "Not like Savannah."

"Monument to Confederate marksmanship." He pointed to Battle Monument and waited for Jane to take the bait, but she knew the story and didn't. Battle Monument contained the names of over a thousand Union soldiers killed in the Civil War.

He started walking her toward Flirtation Walk. Jane knew where he was headed. It was a wooded path overlooking the Hudson River where First Classmen (seniors) could take their dates to hold hands or kiss without being punished for public display of affection. No such place existed for the younger classes of cadets, like John. In grade school, Jane and her playmates giggled over what might take place there.

"Aren't you afraid you'll get caught?" she asked.

"Where's your sense of adventure?" he teased her.

"Richard said you'd been in trouble," she replied.

"Pranks. None hold a candle to the cadet that blew up the water main."

"*What?*" She wasn't sure she'd heard him correctly.

"Yeah. Got in an argument with his engineering prof about water pressure in pipes. To prove his point, he flushed every commode in all the barracks simultaneously. Hundreds of 'em. Got his classmates in every cadet company to help him do it."

"What happened?" Jane asked.

"Geysers erupted on post from broken water mains. Cost thousands of dollars. No water in the barracks for a week. They busted him to cadet private. Spent every weekend for a year marching back and forth on the area with a rifle on his shoulder. Lucky they didn't kick him out."

Trying to act casual, John kept his eye out for First Classmen who would have him marching the area for his trespass. The rank on his sleeve would clearly indicate he was not authorized to be there. Jane was anxious for that and for another reason—they would soon come to Kissing Rock. Legend had it if you stood under the rock and didn't kiss, bad things would happen. *Probably concocted by a cadet who wasn't getting his way*, Jane guessed.

Under Kissing Rock, John reached out to hold her.

What if I get in trouble, she thought and stiffened. *Or word somehow gets to Papa. He'd skin me for being here knowing that John isn't authorized. To hell with him. I don't care if I do get caught.*

It was thrilling to be breaking the law in the longest kiss she could remember. A romantic charge rose within her. She wanted to melt, but Pop's conjured disapproval held her back, and the kiss ended formally.

"What happens when you kiss someone, and you know he's the one?" Jane asked Nini when she returned to Vassar. They worried the subject and speculated on John. Jane summed him up in one word: "Yummy."

But John didn't write or call. Jane felt disappointment and hurt and suspected she was in love mostly with being in love.

"It's just as well with the war on," Jane sighed. "Papa and Richard are enough to worry about."

Before the beginning of the next hunt meet, while the huntsman assembled hounds, the master and his whip conferred on horseback. Their scarlet coats glowed in the morning sun as Jane approached them.

"I'm so sorry for the way my horse has been behaving," Jane started.

The master smiled grimly, and the whip rolled his eyes.

"I want to keep hunting him, if it's okay with you."

The whip rose in his saddle and then bit his tongue because it was the master's place to speak.

"Young lady, I admire your suicidal spirit," the master teased, "and I'm not opposed to suicide. But I am against homicide. Give us clearer warning when you're bolting to the front."

"How 'bout wearing a cowbell," the whip muttered.

"We wouldn't be able to hear the hounds." The master chided his whip and winked at Jane. "We've got to encourage juniors or there won't be a hunt when we're gone."

Hunting every Saturday in the Hudson Valley farm country gradually established itself as a routine for Fitz. He initially tensed, pulled on her, and crow-hopped, shaking his head with his neck bowed. She yelled a warning to those nearby and readied herself for a buck, but it came less and less frequently. When the field checked waiting for the hounds to find a lost scent, Fitz started resting more and fighting less. Jane thought he figured out that by going calmly he wouldn't tire so easily, and he could stay up with the field better by saving his strength for the long runs. Nonetheless, the other riders gave Fitz a wide berth, and on occasion, he continued to give them cause.

But on those days when he eased up, it was sublime. Galloping across a yellowed field of straw after hounds, the bite of winter gusts stinging her cheeks, feeling his powerful hindquarters working in perfect rhythm, the excited beat of his heart between her knees—there was nothing like it. Jane hacked to the meets on Fitz with several other girls. They never left the barn on time and chattered about where on their route they might make up time by cantering. The first rays of daylight tinted the steel gray sky as they trotted down potholed dirt roads. Skim ice in mud puddles shattered under their hooves with the sound of breaking glass. Jane posted up and down with Fitz's beat. The air was so cold that it stabbed her teeth like biting into ice cream. If she exhaled in the wrong direction, her breath froze on the lenses of her glasses. Putting the reins in one hand, Jane swiped at her running nose and frosted lenses with the scratchy wool sleeve of her free arm. They slowed to a walk in the tall meadow grass, vigilant to avoid groundhog holes hidden by the stems. Fitz pushed his nose through the frozen grass, and a cloud of powdered frost exploded from its fronds. The suspended crystals glittered in the dawn's rays.

It was after these days that Jane lay awake under a stack of blankets listening to the steam radiator's clank. She stared at the darkened dorm room ceiling and smiled. She could not imagine anything ever occurring in her life that could feel so fine or right. A flow of warm happiness washed down to Jane's toes when she realized she was tasting the companionship she had wanted for so long. She and Fitz had finally lost themselves, if only for brief seconds, in something that neither one of them could get enough of.

"Oh my God," Jane said sitting bolt upright in bed. "I bet this is what falling in love is like." Her embarrassment over attachment to a horse was replaced by more questions. Unlike John's kiss, this feeling was not complicated by expectations.

A girl's esteem derived from the boys she attracted. The helpless feminine damsel in distress was the one who got rescued by the knight in armor. Jane liked to look attractive, but she couldn't feign helplessness or dependence. It was contrary to her dedication to competency. She welcomed being shown how to do something by a man, which fit nicely with the male role as an expert. But she'd practice until she'd mastered it and usurp the expert's role. Jane wanted to be praised for her effort and welcomed as an equal, but most young men found this threatening and did not come back for more.

As Fitz relaxed, Jane decided to see how he might do in the show ring. Vassar hosted an annual horse show, and Jane entered Fitz. In preparation, she schooled him over jumping courses they might expect and progressively raised the highest rails to four feet six inches, the highest she had attempted on Fitz. He bent his knees and rounded his back beautifully, qualities that are prized in jumpers and came instinctively to Fitz. If he knocked down a rail and felt like he wasn't being pushed, he'd try harder the next time. Even if he repeated his technical mistake, his desire to jump clean was evident. Jane started to believe he could learn more than she knew how to teach him. With a year's training he might be able to achieve five feet six inches.

Obstinancy was a problem, though. He did not like her adjusting his speed through the courses. He wanted to set his own pace and put himself at takeoff points of his own choosing. Over time Jane found he was receptive to her requests to speed up or slow down, but he always retained the right to disobey, and Jane had to accept it. Each came to respect the other's judgment. Generally, Jane picked the route, and Fitz set his stride. Mutual understanding of this delegation of responsibility knitted the beginnings of a team but hindered training. They were learning on Fitz's terms by trial and error.

The night before the show, Nini helped Jane get ready. Smells of shoe polish and glycerin saddle soap filled their dorm room. This would be his first show since Hawaii. Jane didn't think Fitz had a chance in the hunter classes. He wasn't that good looking, being skinny and long necked. Hunters were judged on conformation and manners. Besides, the judges came from the local hunt. Even if he went well, the folks that Fitz and Jane had mowed down would have a fit if he got pinned with a ribbon. But in the jumping classes, only height counted.

In the jumping classes, a horse named Weather Permitting, owned by Senator Alan Ryan, was favored. The horse was ridden by John Melville, the best rider in the area. Jane did not have any hopes of placing; she just hoped Fitz would go well and enjoy it.

The next morning Jane rubbed out Fitz and braided his mane and tail. He shone like a new copper penny. She painted his hooves with pine tar dressing to make them dark and glossy. The tar's bittersweet scent drifted among girls borrowing equipment and scurrying to groom their horses for the show.

A small set of bleachers filled with spectators, many of them students. The ring was surrounded by a single whitewashed rail. The locals pulled the noses of their cars to the rail and sat on the hoods for a ringside seat.

Although Fitz behaved himself in the hunter classes, he was not smooth and, as expected, did not place. Jane kept her fingers crossed for the knock-down-and-out jumper class.

The course of eight jumps was erected, and the bars were set at four feet six inches. Some half dozen horses were entered. While waiting their turn, Jane watched from Fitz's back as John Melville expertly piloted Weather Permitting through a clean round. Fitz entered the ring jigging nervously with his head high.

"Steady," Jane cautioned him.

Fitz rushed the first fence and set a pace that was too fast in Jane's opinion. But at the sixth jump, despite his speed, they were still clean, and Jane's hopes started to rise.

"Hope you know what you're doing," she said to Fitz as she concentrated on centering her weight with his.

On the penultimate jump, he went in too deep for Jane's liking. She gritted her teeth and gripped. Up and over he sailed in an exaggerated arc to correct for his error. She knew the moment he took off that they would clear it with inches to spare. *If he keeps this stride*, she speculated, *he'll have to take off way too early for the last fence. We'll crash land in the middle of the jump. What a finale that'll make.*

Fitz landed neatly with his ears trained on the last fence.

At least you're thinking about it, she thought as she held her breath.

Jane suddenly felt him loving the challenge that confronted him. With each second, the distance to the last fence closed, and opportunity for correction evaporated. Their fate would collapse into the placement of his last four hoof prints before the fence. With precise energy he fit the variables of speed and stride with the closing distance, softness of the footing that would rob his spring, and height of that last fence. Much to Jane's relief, he chose to chop his reach on each of the two strides going in. Neatly, he folded his front legs and launched free. He rounded his back, and Jane listened for a tick. There was none. She wore a broad grin as they landed.

A jump-off was required to determine the winner between Fitz and Weather Permitting. The bars were raised to five feet for the two of them, as high as Fitz had ever jumped, but Jane was not worried. She was still glowing from the joy she'd felt in him and the judgment he'd shown. When it was done, the senator's horse had two ticks, and Fitz knocked down a rail. Jane was elated to have lasted so long against the polished team of John Melville and Weather Permitting. She clutched her red ribbon proudly as Nini came running up to her.

"I was standing next to Senator Ryan," Nini gushed. "After you finished the course clean at four foot six before the jump off, he said, 'I hope she wins. That was beautiful!' And then, when you knocked down the rail in the jump-off, he groaned."

It had been over three years since Jane had started to work with Fitz in Hawaii. She had entered him in a few small local shows, and he had not placed higher than second. Jane's reward and pride was in his improvement.

Bobby Burke, friend of Jane's and Hall of Fame jumper jockey known for his tact with horses, was interviewed in 2004. He had this take on Jane and Fitz: "She had a lot of patience, and that's what it takes with a horse like that, that needs to be reformed. And some come around, some don't. Mostly, . . . it was [her] kindness [that won him over]. . . . He was one of those that wasn't gonna take it [being pushed], probably because he was more intelligent than most horses."

7

DROWNING IN QUICKSAND

At Vassar, despite Pop's misgivings and her own doubts, Jane maintained a C average. She chose geology as a major. Geology was a science she could identify with. Having lived in Hawaii, Jane remembered seeing Kilauea erupting. Searing lava oozed in cracks beside her feet. Across the crater, a mile away, sooty red blobs of lava the size of cars were ejected high into the air. Geology students from several colleges, including Vassar, attended Camp Davis, a summer field camp sponsored by the University of Michigan at a site south of Jackson Hole, Wyoming. Students lived in tents beside the Hoback River and mapped formations in the area. Jane fell in love with the panoramas of the Wind River Range, the Gros Ventres, and the Tetons. Jane was assigned to classify the geology of a ridge where she found a curious row of evenly spaced cobbles. She asked her professor to take a look. Recognizing the stones as dinosaur vertebrae and horrified that she might use her geologist's hammer, he shooed her away. She was miffed when he took full credit for the find, which went to a Michigan museum.

Jane graduated in 1944 with a curriculum shortened a year for the war. Her graduation occurred shortly before Pop landed in France a week after D-Day. He commanded 3,000 engineers in constructing infrastructure urgently needed for moving supplies from ship to shore and forward to the front. After the fight across France, he would become the corps engineer for General Wade Haslip's XVth Corps during the Battle of the Bulge. Jennet was in high school in Fayetteville, and Richard was a still a cadet at West Point with two years to go. Jane applied for work, hoping for a meaningful job in the war effort.

With the war in full swing at the time of Jane's graduation, the oil companies were frantic to locate and develop petroleum reserves. Jane applied for positions as a geologist. She dressed in a suit and rode the train down the Hudson River from Poughkeepsie to New York City for an interview with Standard Oil, where she waited in a smoke-filled room with a dozen male applicants wearing everything from dungarees to suits. She ignored their glances.

Jane wanted to smoke a cigarette, but as the only woman in the room, taking out a cigarette might appear to be an invitation. She wore gloves, clutched her pocketbook, and glanced at company photographs on the wall: U.S. bombers being fueled by Standard Oil trucks, refineries in Houston, oil wells in Oklahoma. Periodically, a side door opened, and a secretary called a name from a clipboard and ushered the applicant to his interview.

In time, the secretary fumbled in mispronouncing Jane's name. Jane stood to identify herself and was led through a maze of desks to an elderly woman wearing a gray suit and lace collar. Jane was introduced, and the elderly woman motioned for Jane to sit.

"I see you've graduated from a very good school," the woman opened. Jane seized the opportunity to bring up her thesis on Wyoming geology. The region was believed to have oil, and Jane's knowledge would have value in locating it.

"Well, that's very interesting. But before we get to that, your name is German isn't it? Do you have any relatives living in Germany?"

"Soon, I hope." Jane hissed at the implication. The woman looked puzzled. "My father is a U.S. Army colonel," Jane explained.

The woman pulled in her chin and asked about Jane's grades in English.

"I'm assuming you typed your thesis," she said.

Jane explained she was there for the geologist positions. The woman paused, considering Jane with a sad look, and stated the company couldn't possibly send a lady to the field with male crews, living in tents, bathing out of a bucket. Geologists had to supervise workers, and Standard Oil could not expect men to take orders from Jane. Jane argued that the company had females working men's jobs in refineries. That was different, according to the woman, because they were laborers and went home to their families at night.

"Senior management is always looking for educated women with poise and good diction," the woman said. "Do you know how to take shorthand?"

"They don't teach that at Vassar," Jane replied hotly.

The woman's mouth fell open. Jane regretted her flippancy but did not apologize. It cheered her slightly that she had the guts to refuse. Then, she flushed with embarrassment, stood, and excused herself before the woman could summon someone to show her to the elevator.

Disheartened by the same response from other oil companies, Jane returned to her mother's house in Fayetteville. Mother advised Jane that if she wanted to focus on Fitz, now was the time. With Pop's pay and Mother's job at the radio station, they were financially secure.

Jane thought about Fitz's form and how he might be able jump higher. He was fourteen years old, perhaps approaching the end of his physical peak as a jumper. The two of them were competent at four feet six inches. Jane knew that if she asked, he would attempt higher but might not know how. With the right technique and tact in asking him to attempt bigger fences, they might compete consistently at five feet, the upper limit of the amateur ranks and rare for women. Jane agreed with Mother: now was the time to try.

Jane was eager to move him to Southern Pines, North Carolina, a town with an active horse community and experienced horsemen who might be able to help her. While she could have borrowed a trailer and hauled him the twenty-three miles to Southern Pines, she decided to ride him and save the gas ration coupons. Jane and Fitz left the Fort Bragg stable late in the morning with a water flask and lunch strapped to her saddle. The ride could take six hours, but she was confident they would finish well before dark. They headed out of the garrison to Manchester Road. The dirt road spanned the post, running from the garrison, then beside the immense artillery impact zone where shells thudded and through the drop zones where paratroopers jumped from C-47s at low level and ran into the woods firing blanks. Jane wanted to stay off the road, as the hard ground might make Fitz sore. A carpet of pine needles on the shoulder and the shaded patrol paths provided softer footing. Fitz was glad to be away from the stable and the ring. He snorted at the new sights and smells. His small ears trained intently on a distant tree rustling in the light breeze.

While the day was still cool, she walked him for twenty minutes and trotted for twenty minutes, mindful of the mileage ahead. The rolling sandhills and their tall pine trees stretched endlessly into the haze. Occasionally, an army truck would lumber past them, stirring up billows of dust that hung in the air long after it had crested the next hill. At the bottom of the hills Jane looked for creeks. Once an hour she would stop and dismount, loosen the saddle girth, and let Fitz drink.

As it got hotter in the day, she could feel him tiring and did not trot as often. Closer to Southern Pines she saw a trail that seemed to offer a shady shortcut and decided to take it. As the trail went down a hill, she saw marsh grass among the pine trees below and thought there must be a creek close by. The soil looked wet but firm. Fitz was walking in ankle-deep black mud, and the trees were getting thinner. She thought nothing of it. Then with Fitz's next step, he sunk instantly to his knees and in reaction made a huge lurch ahead to pull his hooves free.

With this leap he landed mired up to his belly. Jane dismounted and sank to her waist. Unable to feel bottom, she realized that wading was impossible and, with the suction, that swimming would be impossible for Fitz. Fitz threw his head up and strained with his hocks, trying to free his front legs. The muck quivered like pudding. With each struggle, she watched in terror as the black plane inched up the saddle until only his neck and rump were visible.

Then, to Jane's amazement, Fitz stopped fighting and panted. She imagined reason creeping through her horse and took heart.

There was no way Fitz could turn around, so Jane floundered in a swimming crawl toward a hummock of swamp grass ahead. The root mat of the hummock held her weight as she tenuously pulled herself out and stood up on it. This would be moving Fitz in the wrong direction, deeper into quicksand, but it was the only direction possible.

"Come on Fitz, you've *got* to do this," she said, urging him to come to the hummock.

He struggled to push his knees forward until he was breathing in desperate gasps and his neck was lathered in sweat. Seconds passed between his attempts. The muck yielded only inches to each exertion. The intervals between his pushes were getting longer. His strength was ebbing.

We're not gonna make it, she thought, pushing back tears.

But Fitz finally got to where he could rest his chin on the hummock. Exhausted, he could do no more. Jane felt encouraged that he might not drown, but she had doubts that he would be able to haul himself up onto the hummock. She knelt and stroked his nose.

"Good boy." The fresh-bread smell of his exhales reassured her. "You're almost there . . . almost there."

When his breathing relaxed, she stood balanced on the hummock with the reins in both hands and bent over to look him in the eye.

"Okay Fitz, I know you're tired, but you've *got* to get up here."

She wrapped his slippery muddy reins around her hands and strained to pull him up to her. "*Come on.*"

He inched forward and pushed down into the grass with his chin. Fitz's knees gradually worked to the surface and the hummock's edge. The reins trembled in Jane's hands. Then he pushed with his hocks, pulled on his knees, and threw his head up, following it with his body. It seemed to Jane that this was happening in slow motion. As he scrambled up, it occurred to her that the hummock was not large enough for them both. She leaped off backward into the muck, hoping not to pull him in on top of her.

Waist deep in the mud, she looked up at him and laughed. Fitz looked ridiculous perched on this tiny island of grass with all four hooves touching each other, covered in mud, his back hunched, and his head down to her eye level. The expression on his face seemed to ask, *What are you doing in there?*

"We're not out of trouble yet," she said to him, "but we're a whole lot better off than we were."

She chose the nearest hummock heading back toward the solid ground they had come from and slithered toward it on her stomach. It was slow going. When she got to the end of the reins, she was only half-way to the next hummock. She turned, looked up at him, and clucked just as if she would in the ring when she wanted him to move forward.

Fitz looked apprehensively at the tuft of grass beyond her. He didn't want to jump, but he was tiring with all four hooves planted within the space of a doormat. The roots supporting him ripped audibly as he shifted his footing, and he hesitated. If he tore the roots too much, he'd punch through and be back in the soup again. Then he lowered his head, gathered himself, and jumped. As he flew past her, she threw away the reins so as not to hit him in the mouth. He landed short, scrambled up on his own, and turned his head to look backward at her wallowing to him. Another leap and he was on solid ground again.

Jane was euphoric for more reasons than rescue. She wrote, "I knew that I had gained this [his] confidence I had vainly sought for over a year. . . . Would a crazy horse have acted as calmly as this?"

They had to backtrack on the trail to Manchester Road and dragged into the Southern Pines stable at dark, long overdue. Mother was there with the sheriff, discussing a search when Jane and Fitz walked up. They eyed the horse and rider covered in black goop.

"Honey," the sheriff greeted Jane, "you must wanna hunt over here with Moore County Hounds awful bad."

Jane's bigger goal now was to improve Fitz's jumping. She hit the books to understand jumping in its component movements for both horse and rider, and she asked for advice from Pappy and Ginny Moss of Southern Pines, who owned and rode successful show horses. An outstanding athlete may be able to keep track of three separate things that occur simultaneously and act to improve all three on the next attempt. Most riders can concentrate on only one at a time, so Jane sought the one thing that would pull others into line, like feeling her collar with the back of her neck to keep her posture aligned. The problem was that riding is a continuum of motion, not a freeze-frame. She needed to correct deviations in Fitz before they occurred so as to arrive at the jump with the right impulsion, pace, and balance. Jane worked alone and settled on varying the type and spacing of the fences rather than their height, stressing fundamentals, and establishing a daily routine.

Jane's fault as a rider was not maintaining contact with his mouth over the jumps. As he rounded the top of the jump, her seat changed. She sat up and pushed her hands down and away, generating slack in the reins. Her seat was rock solid, but she threw his head away to prevent hitting him in the mouth. Fitz came to expect it and compensated. She focused on jumping four feet six from a trot to learn not to override the big fences by rushing them.

Sometimes when schooling Fitz, she became oblivious to all else. Her focus was so strong that she didn't hear people when they called her name. In her mind she could see herself on Fitz jumping a series of jumps, even an entire course. In the daydream, she put her hand on his shoulder, and it felt no different from touching the back of her own hand. Without thinking, she knew what would happen, when, and how. An indescribable joy filled her, but there was still one missing piece: reciprocity.

Then a long-awaited miracle happened. Jane marched down the stable aisle toward Fitz's stall to tack him for another schooling session. He heard her step, stuck his head out into the aisle, and nickered to her. She reached for the latch to his stall door, and he pushed his muzzle to her side. This was so different from his usual reserved behavior that she didn't know what to think, and then it dawned on her. In her coat pocket was a forgotten carrot, limp with age, waiting to be discarded when she got around to laundering her coat. She scrambled to fish it out, dust it off, and give it to him. Jane wrote, "No one else can know the pleasure in having him prick his ears up when I came in sight and push into my hands begging for a carrot." It had taken almost four years for Fitz to accept a carrot from Jane.

In the summer and fall of 1944, Jane entered hunter and jumper classes of shows close to Southern Pines. Fitz failed to win any jumping classes, but in working hunter classes he won five blue ribbons. He was settling and becoming accustomed to the commotion of horse shows.

Then, in a knock-down-and-out jumping class at Raleigh, North Carolina, several horses besides Fitz had gone clean at five feet, and the bars were raised to five feet six inches, a benchmark height for most riders, as jumping classes never got there, except in a jump-off, or in a skyscraper class, which consisted of one jump that was raised each round until only one horse cleared it.

She was nervous at the gate. "Neither one of us has jumped five foot six," she said to Fitz. "I feel like I've been goaded into a school-yard dare."

He stood absorbed, his ears pricked intently toward the ring.

"I guess you're right," she said to him. "Forfeiting would be a shame."

In the ring, Jane swallowed hard, braced in the saddle expecting the worst, and let Fitz have his head. He jumped in calm and measured control. His timing and distance were perfect. His spring, flight, and landing were purely efficient. She could feel his exuberance. Jane was so astounded at how easy it was for him to jump five foot six that she relaxed her grip and almost fell off.

"My God," she said to him afterward. "You could be right up there with the best jumpers in the country."

Over the next week, she pondered what had happened. *I'm sure he knew I had my doubts about five foot six. But it was as if he said, "Trust me, you're gonna like this." And he was right.*

They entered ten North Carolina shows in 1945. To Jane's amazement, he took the blue ribbon in every jumping class he entered, winning eight Jumper Championships (including Raleigh and Fayetteville, the two bigger shows in the state). She became conscious of Fitz anticipating and making up for her shortcomings as a rider. Jane wanted to believe an alchemy existed between them that could create magic in their sport. It seemed spooky, too good to be true, and skepticism crept toward Jane. But, on the other hand, he had the athletic ability, and there was no denying the synergy of fool's courage that swelled sometimes between them when they were jumping or hunting. Doubt would be a self-fulfilling prophecy, and she had to guard against it. Fitz was fifteen years old. There was not much time left to reach for the top.

U

In the late summer of 1945, Pop returned from Europe. For Mother he had a formal peck. She searched the jowled balding head of a stranger. In the four years he'd been gone, Jennet had accumulated a shoe box full of letters from him; the rest of them could count on one hand the letters each had received.

Home at Fort Bragg, he was awarded a bronze star for service as General Wade Haslip's XVth Corps engineer during the Battle of the Bulge, Hitler's last-ditch effort to stop the Allies short of Germany. The XVth Corps of 30,000 men was threatened by envelopment from a daring Panzer thrust. Pop was responsible for river crossings to prevent the Corps from being cut off. After the post commander pinned the medal on him, Pop saluted proudly as engineer battalions passed in review before him on the parade field. At the supper table he drank hard while answering excited questions from Jane and Jennet about his life during the war. Richard was at West Point.

"Go get the package wrapped in butcher paper by my bags," he ordered Jane. Pop unwrapped two exquisite prints of Frederick the Great's cavalry. He explained that the prints had been looted by his troops from a German barracks. He also had a Luger for Richard. The men gave them to Pop in thanks for letting them fight at the front. Pop landed in France a week after D-Day with the mission to improve port facilities. His troops wanted to see action. Pop made the arrangements and sent several dump trucks full of volunteers to the front for a week, on loan to the infantry.

"You never saw a bunch of guys so glad to get back on a bulldozer and push dirt," he said.

Jennet asked him if he was ever scared. Glancing at his wife as if appraising her, he asked for another bourbon. He turned back to Jennet and addressed her question, "I said a lot of rosaries."

After working on airfields from Brazil to Samoa, he went to Ireland and then France. He used to make his driver put the windshield down on the jeep. The wind was a relief in the July heat. One day he got in the jeep, and the windshield was up, but he was in a hurry, and they left it that way. Zipping down a dirt road in the woods, they heard a twang. It was a piano wire the Germans had stretched across the road, neck high. Neither one of them ever saw it. Jennet pried for another story. He looked down into his glass and hesitated.

"Out reconnoitering a route for a pipeline in France," his eyes turned steel gray, and he took another swallow of bourbon, "my driver and I were walking through a field. He stepped on a mine. Killed him." He closed his eyes.

Jane guessed what was going through his head. He'd been an engineer officer for twenty-eight years. Mines were engineer business. He'd served in World War I in France. He should have known just by the lay of the land where a minefield was likely to be. His family waited in uncomfortable respect.

The father Jane remembered from Hawaii had looked much like his wrestling team picture in his West Point yearbook. It was how she remembered him all through the war: broad chested, tight, and tan. Now his whiskers were gray, and his cheeks sagged.

The whiskey was taking hold when he broke the silence to describe the river crossings during the Battle of the Bulge, when his XVth Corps was running for its life. With the existing bridges destroyed, each river promised a formidable delay. Engineers launched rafts for ferries and erected floating pontoon bridges on the near shore while completely exposed to enemy fire from the far shore. After the far shore was secure, fixed bridging was installed to free the float bridging to move forward to the next river. Even in the best of conditions, it took days for the Corps to cross. Thousands of vehicles converged and waited their turn, sitting ducks for enemy artillery.

"We prayed for fog and laid down smoke screens, so enemy forward observers couldn't see. But when they knew where we were. . ." Pop was staring blankly into the tabletop.

No one moved. His eyelids slowly drooped, and he started snoring. Jennet pried the nearly finished drink from his hand, and they left him there at the table to go to their beds. None of them wanted to wake him back into his nightmare of American boys in long columns inching forward on muddy roads converging to a bottleneck at a bridgehead or a ferry site. The whistle of incoming artillery would begin, and there was nowhere to go.

The war scattered the people Jane had known in Hawaii. Colonel Van Deusen, a 1909 graduate of West Point, was too old to be deployed to combat for World War II. He spent the war at Fort Sill, Oklahoma, and at Cornell as professor of military science.

General Sultan's wartime mission was to retake the Burma Road from the Japanese. He commanded Chinese, Kachin Burmese, Nepalese Gurkhas, British, Africans, and U.S. Army Rangers. The terrain was impenetrable. He used elephants, Mongolian ponies, and Tibetan mules for pack trains on footpaths through mountains and jungles with 130-degree heat. Tibetan mules were too small for his 75-mm Pack Howitzers, so he requisitioned over 900 mules and horses from Fort Robinson. Sacks of rice and oats were airdropped to feed them.

Sergeant Mope's career is unknown. It is likely that he fought in the Pacific, where horrific losses were sustained in the majority of the island invasions.

The army did not deploy its horses to combat. Cavalry units were sent to fight as infantry, jeeps served as officers' mounts, and trucks did the hauling. The horses Jane knew at Schofield Barracks probably remained there through the war and were sold in 1947 at auction for recreational mounts or workhorses.

Part II

8

HONEYSUCKLE TO SKYSCRAPERS: FITZ'S DEBUT

Pop's new orders in 1945 stationed him in Washington, D.C. He had hoped to be promoted to brigadier general, but there was little chance with the war essentially over. Colonel Pohl was assigned to a desk in the Chief of Engineers Office, one more colonel among many overseeing congressional appropriations for public works. He and Mother purchased a twenty-three-acre farm on the west sloping face of Mt. Gilead, overlooking the Valley of Virginia and eye level with the Blue Ridge Mountains, ten miles away. They named it Mauka, the Hawaiian word for mountain.

The house began as a one-room log cabin in the 1700s, and each family owning it since had added on, making it larger than the rented Fayetteville bungalow the Pohls had moved from. Lightning rods tilted unevenly on the ridge of the black-tarred tin roof. Upstairs were three bedrooms, two fireplaces, and one bath. Conversation was overpowered there when rain drummed the metal roof, and until they learned the noises of the house, the Pohls mistook wind wrinkling the tin for distant thunder. Downstairs had a kitchen, dining room, den, living room, two fireplaces, and no bathroom. The result of the piecemeal additions was a step between each room. As the family unpacked in August 1945, curses punctuated the house as the Pohls banged their heads on low door frames and tripped over threshold risers.

The hand-dug well came complete with a dead cat in it. The well pump was run by an electric motor through a fan belt and pulleys that demanded Pop's frequent adjustment and oiling. Their telephone number was only four digits, and they shared a party line with a dozen other families on the mountain. The ring identifying the Pohl residence was one long, followed by one short. All the phones on the party line heard all the rings and could listen in on the conversations. Mauka had more than enough pasture for Fitz and a companion horse Jane might find. Massive timbers, joined by wooden pegs, framed the whitewashed bank barn. Under the barn and cut into the bank, hand-laid limestone walls provided a livestock pen. Aboveground were four box stalls, a grain room, and storage. Above that was a hayloft and a tin roof, tarred black to match the house. The ten-acre pasture was rimmed by a crumbling wall of limestone cobbles culled from the field. Sweet smells of honeysuckle and curing hay wafted up the mountain. Crows and blue jays argued over territory in the trees.

The closest town was Leesburg, population of 5,000, eight miles away. As Loudoun County's seat, it had the county's only newspaper and high school. The county had 500 dairies and orchards, supplying Washington and Baltimore with milk, apples, pears, and peaches. Jane and Pop went to Mass regularly at St. Francis Catholic Church, which was tiny and impoverished compared to the town's Episcopal church. Less frequently, Mother attended the Presbyterian services by herself. Jennet and Richard were away in college.

Pop's commute to the Chief of Engineers Office in Washington was forty miles, adding more than two hours to his workday, but in his opinion, Mauka's charm was worth it. Wild daylilies lined the driveway in orange, and the lilac bushes framing the front door filled the house with perfume. Sitting 800 feet above the Valley of Virginia, the temperature was noticeably cooler than steamy downtown Washington, where his office had only an open window and desk fan for relief. Pop planted a bed of spearmint beside the back door for his juleps and adopted a favorite lawn chair on the patio looking west to the Blue Ridge Mountains. In the summer heat, the mountains softened from the humid haze they were named after. When a large sun receded behind them, the higher clouds were painted the color of orange sherbet from below. Shrouded in rain, the mountain's wrinkles played like ghosts on the edge of visibility.

No other houses could be seen from the property. The closest neighbor was Rojah Chin, a dignified white-whiskered widower and black veteran of World War I. His log cabin was a five-minute walk beyond the stone wall of Mauka's pasture. Rojah lived without electricity or plumbing and quietly farmed vegetable produce on his steep plot with two mules. He wore wire-rimmed glasses and a felt fedora. At night, with the whip-poor-wills singing, Pop walked through the pasture and along Rojah's plowed furrows to visit. Sharing Rojah's homemade applejack, they would reminisce by kerosene lamplight about the "Great" war, Rojah's term for the war they had in common.

The road, identified simply as County Road 662, twisted past Rojah's place and Mauka, climbed and descended Hog Back Mountain, and ended at the Baileys' dairy farm, a mile away. If two cars met on the one-lane dirt road, one would have to back up to a space wide enough for both to pass. Only ten houses shared the road, so impasses were rare, but when they happened, news was exchanged through open car windows. It was how folks kept track of each other—at least those who didn't eavesdrop on the party line—and it was where the Pohl family introduced themselves to their neighbors. After some head-scratching, the place the Pohls named Mauka was recognized as "the old Porter place," followed by advice about living on the mountain. The family learned traveling to Washington, D.C., was "going down the country," and drainage was pronounced "dreenage." Potholes were reportedly terrible after the spring thaw. But, not to worry, every summer the state graded the gravel out of the ditches and used it to smooth the road. Snowfall predictions for the valley could be doubled for the mountain. It might take a week before the state snow plow came, only to have the road drifted closed that night by the wind. Trees felled by lightning or ice frequently knocked down the power line. After such advice, Pop tightened the lightning rods and their grounding cables. A bucket of water was placed permanently beside the commode to flush it if the power went out.

Mother bought two Dalmatians from the same litter and named them Sweetie and Snitch. Gifts from the neighbors included a mean tempered descented skunk named Charlemagne and a yellow cat named Christine, who promptly delivered a litter of six. The dogs ambushed delivery men, whom Pop reimbursed for their ripped trousers. Folks ribbed Pop by asking him to compare the amount of these "uniform expenses" to his as an army officer.

One morning in March 1946, Pop received a call from the sheriff of neighboring Fairfax County.

"Your Ford sedan's down here at the jail," the sheriff said.

Pop claimed the car was in his garage, but the sheriff explained two trustee prisoners had escaped from the Highway Department's work camp and stolen it. The sentences on the two were running out, and they wanted to renew their hitch. The work camp's bed and board was the best life they'd known, so they drove the car straight to the Fairfax jail to turn themselves in.

When Pop arrived to get the car, he discovered on the dashboard a note from the trustees apologizing for the trouble and a dollar for gas. Pop couldn't understand how the convicts got past the dogs. When he interviewed them, they told him the dogs had welcomed them while they looked through the house windows to see if the Pohls were occupied and then hot-wired the car. Pop's face turned red in remembering the trousers he had bought for delivery men and the profuse apologies he'd made. He had consoled himself that the dogs were reliable protection.

When Pop got home, he ranted about *Honor among thieves* and beat the dogs. Since the barn cats had been routinely terrorized by the Dalmatians, they came to the yelps, and a yellow tom took the opportunity to jump in. It whetted the tom's taste for revenge, and thereafter he perched concealed in the dense boxwood bushes by the house. As a Dalmatian ran past, claws raked the surprised dog. Neither Sweetie nor Snitch figured out to stay clear of the bushes.

Thompson Bailey had a whiskey still at the base of the mountain, hidden in the woods beside Goose Creek. He proudly shared his moon-

Jane stands with her sister, Jennet, and her brother, Richard, in the early 1930s. (Courtesy of the author)

At age sixteen, Jane rode in her first open jumping class at an army base horseshow. Riding against army officers and sergeants, she and her mount Pat took first place. (Courtesy of the author)

Fitzrada accompanied Jane to Vassar College, where he got his first taste of foxhunting. (Courtesy of the author)

Fitz and Jane made an impression at the Warrenton Horse Show when they won the "knock down and out" class. (Courtesy of the author)

At Middleburg in 1946, the pair won every class they entered. (Courtesy of the author)

Jane accepts a trophy for being "Champion Jumper" at Middleburg in 1946. (Courtesy of the author)

Fitzrada refuses to load the trailer, and the two lose the Handy Hunter class at the Keswick show in 1946. (Courtesy of the author)

Revealing his enormous talent for jumping, Fitzrada clears 6'6" at the Almas Shrine horseshow. (Courtesy of the author)

Loudoun Times-Mirror, Thursday, October 17, 1946

FITZRADA, Miss Jane Pohl in the irons.

Loudoun-Owned Horse Seen Strong Bidder For Top Garden Honor

By Major Larry Lawrence
Of the staff of the Washington Star, written expressly for the Times-Mirror.

In a box stall on a farm out in Mt. Gilead, near Leesburg, there is a little old 15:2 hands Thoroughbred, which this writer believes has an excellent chance of bringing to Loudoun the open jumping championship of America when that important event is decided during the week of November 4-9, at the National Horse Show, Madison Square Gardens.

This promising candidate for one of the highest honors in the horse show world is Fitzrada, a superior bit of horse-flesh owned by Miss Jane Pohl, daughter of Colonel Herman H. Pohl, U. S. Army. Under the expert riding of his owner, the 16-year-old son of Fitzgibbons-Parada has rolled up a record the past season which surpasses that of any open jumper in the East.

Fitzrada's sensational performances in the Virginia, Maryland and District of Columbia circuit where he has collected blue ribbons by the score and tri-colors in show after show, stamp the gelding as one of the best ever to represent this section at the Garden. Indeed, in his last five appearances Fitzrada has won four important championships, at the Hagerstown, Shrine, Forrestville and McLean fixtures.

The press had high expectations for Jane and Fitz as the National Horse Show approached. These are two of many newspaper clippings that Jane kept in her scrapbooks.

...ne Pohl, Dayton Horsewoman, Prepares To Rid... Jumper In National Horseshow

THE DAYTON HERALD
Wednesday, November 6, 1946

JANE POHL, highly regarded Dayton equestrienne, is pictured in New York's Madison Square Garden prior to her debut this week in the hunters and jumpers class of the National Horse show, which runs through Thursday. Miss Pohl, daughter of Col. and Mrs. Herman Pohl, now of Leesburg, Va., and granddaughter of Mrs. Reynolds Andrews, of Dayton, is entered from the Moore County (N. C.) Hunt club, and is riding an Hawaiian mount, Fitzrada. At right: In Hawaiian horse language, the youthful Jane tells Fitzrada she's counting on his co-operation: "It won't be long now ... there we are, at the National"; "Get that chin up, Fitzie, let's see our smiles."
(Acme Telephoto)

Jane was honored to show the prestigious horse Portmaker for one of the top show stables in the country. (Courtesy of the author)

Jane's worst habit while jumping: looking down at the fence. (Courtesy of the author)

Fitz stands for a portrait in 1947 at the age of 17. (Courtesy of the author)

Fitzrada was one of only a few horses that competed in both hunter and jumper competitions during his time. (Courtesy of the author)

Fitzrada caught the eye of noted illustrator Paul Brown who created several drawings of the horse and presented them to Jane. (Courtesy of the author)

shine with neighbors, then stayed for hours. Clothed in bib overalls and needing a shave, he'd arrive unannounced and serve his product from a half-gallon screw-top glass jug. The bottles had originally held deworming medicine for his family's dairy herd. Thompson liked the bottles because they had a finger hole in the neck for a secure grip. His slurred soliloquy on the nuances of distilling was that of a 4-H Club judge hovering over the pie entries with tablespoons in both hands.

Pop remembered folks going blind from bad liquor during Prohibition, so he sampled sparingly but complimented profusely, not wanting to hurt Thompson's feelings. At the end of the bout, Thompson gave the bottle to his reluctant host and asked to have the empty back when Pop was done. Immediately after Thompson left, Pop poured the shine down the sink. Only a week later, Thompson came back to find Pop's bottle empty, thought he'd discovered a kindred connoisseur, and forced two bottles on Pop, who felt obligated to pay. Thereafter, Pop put the full bottles on the laundry shelf beside the bleach and measured small amounts into the drain between Thompson's visits. Thus, Pop could demonstrate to Thompson moderate appreciation for his art yet delay buying more.

Jane mended the pasture's stone walls and cleaned the barn, thrilled at living where the best jumpers and hunters in the country were bred, trained, and shown. She was twenty-one, a year out of college, and bent on showing Fitz. As was the custom of the era, she was free to live with her parents until she found a husband or a job. Richard had less than a year to go at West Point, and Jennet was attending Marymount, a Catholic girls' college near West Point.

As it turned out, this mountain ridge would be Jane's home for more than forty years. Everything about it was to Jane's liking: a view that held her eye for longer than she intended, plain deep-hearted neighbors who stopped to ask after her family and speculate on local horses as avidly as on professional baseball, and endless rolling country to ride over. Calcium-rich limestone soils bore grasses excellent for milk in dairy cattle and bone development in foals. On still fall mornings, she would hear hounds giving tongue while running a fox through the dozens of dairy farms whose white silos dotted the Valley of Virginia below her. Many farmers bred, bought, and sold horses and ponies as a sideline. They put their children to work breaking, hunting, and riding their home-grown stock in the local horse shows to advertise them for sale.

In a 2006 interview, Barbara Graham, a race horse trainer in her sixties with over fifty horses in training and still riding, recalled, "My father made me ride four horses every day before school." The county 4-H Club offered a kids' program specific to horse husbandry.

While in this end of the county the horse industry was grassroots, a little further south down the valley toward Middleburg and Upperville, horses were objects of opulent worship. In the 1920s rich folks shipped their horses there by rail from New York for weekends of hunting. They'd rent the entire Red Fox Tavern in Middleburg, hunt all day, and party all night. Paul Mellon, Ogden Phipps, and other captains of industry fell in love with the country and bought thousand-acre parcels to build lavish facilities for upward of seventy horses. The horse farms had indoor riding halls, stable managers, trainers, exercise jockeys, grooms, gardeners, and farmhands all focused on winning horse show championship titles.

Marie Greenhalgh, whose family founded Libbey-Owens Glass, was perhaps the most dedicated breeder of show hunters in Virginia. Her Springsbury Farm in nearby Berryville had a fantastic winning record at the national level. Dr. and Mrs. Alvin I. Kay of Kay Jewelry stores entrusted their horses to Springsbury. Liz Whitney, a gutsy and glamorous model who married the heir to Standard Oil, built a show barn in the shape of a horseshoe near Upperville, bred gray hunters, and showed them herself. Stables from as far away as Missouri came to compete here. August Busch, Budweiser's heir, and Max Bonham, owner of the Hathaway Shirt Company, were among them. Professional horsemen, the most famous of whom was Cappy Smith, relocated to Middleburg after the war to train, show, and sell horses to the rich. For Jane's one-horse backyard stable to compete in this league, she would need to overcome the unlimited resources of the wealthy stables, and she would have to do it without apology for mucking Fitz's manure by herself.

The Warrenton Horse Show in September 1946 attracted entries from Virginia, the District of Columbia, and Maryland. At the last National, five years ago, horses from these states won every division championship entered, except conformation hunter, taking reserve champion there. Warrenton was a clear step above the local shows in North Carolina, where Fitz had won an unbelievable eight Jumper Championships in ten shows.

Since arriving in Virginia, Fitz had won the Jumper Championship at Fairfax, a local show, and Jane was eager to see how he compared against stiffer competition. With the National Horse Show at Madison Square Garden only two months away, the newspapers followed Warrenton class by class, predicting contestants for the first National to be held since the war.

Warrenton's show grounds were just an hour's drive from Mauka Farm. The grandstand gave a lofty view of the mowed grass show ring. A massive roof shaded the seats from a searing sun. On the other side of the ring, spectators fanned themselves with folded programs and pressed to the white rail for a better view. Beyond them, groups of people stood on the hill or sat on the hoods of parked cars to see over the heads of those in front. In a field behind and above the cars stood the huge new post-and-rail fences of the mile-long outside course for hunters.

Jane's big knock-down-and-out class for open jumpers came at night. Any horse knocking down a bar would have to leave the ring. The class would be won by the horse jumping the most fences before a knockdown. Sixteen horses were entered. Among them were the well-known champions Captain D'Arcy, owned by Jane Weaver; Dr. and Mrs. W. H. Lowe's Sanjo; and Ballantrae Farm's Irish Lad.

Strong spot lights on the grandstand roof bleached the show ring. Freshly painted white poles on the jumps glared sharply against the surrounding darkness. Bats cut back and forth through the insects swarming to the bright lights. When the crowd held its breath in empathic strain for a horse to clear a fence, the background noise of crickets and katydids was audible. Jane saddled Fitz under a bare lightbulb at the show-ground stable, located beside the grandstand, and walked him to the practice ring to warm up.

The practice ring was crowded with sixteen horses schooling over jumps. Riders called out the height they wanted on a jump, and grooms and trainers made the adjustments to the bars. "Steady, steady!" a trainer warned a man who was rushing his horse into a jump. After the jump, the trainer motioned for the rider and advised him in hushed tones, but Jane could tell from the trainer's gestures that he was impatient. Nearby, a razor-fit jumper jigged in place, collected by its rider into a tight ball, lathered in sweat and foam, wanting to dash for the fence ahead. Some of the open jumper jockeys rode roughly, snatching and spurring in the pause between fences to keep their horses keyed up. When the rider wanted to negotiate a tight in-and-out that demanded slower speed, he held his jumper in as they inched toward the first jump prancing at the boiling point. Jane stayed out of the melee, cantering Fitz around the outside of the practice ring to loosen him up.

The knock-down-and-out class was announced, and Jane walked Fitz to the show ring. She was lucky that five entries would go before her so that she could watch them and learn. The first horse went into the first fence way too deep, reacted by launching steeply, cleaned out a bar on the way up, and exited the ring without proceeding further. Same with the second horse and the third. Jane was perplexed. She couldn't see a reason and needed to know so that she might avoid the same pitfall.

"It's the lights," Jane overheard a defeated rider say leaving the ring.

She crowded Fitz up closer to the ring rail and watched carefully. The first fence had a three foot gap between the grass and the bottom rail. The next horse bowed its head, took off early, and landed in the fence.

Fitz squirmed, chomping his bit, infected with the bustle around him. Without taking her eyes off the first fence, Jane quickly tugged a rein and squeezed a leg to confine him. He moved to turn away in the opposite direction, and she wrestled him back. Her hairnet was hot on her neck and under her derby. Sweat beads ran down her forehead. Under the riding coat, her blouse sopped to her back.

"Hold still," she ordered Fitz. "Gotta figure this out." Her eyes searched down the first fence's bars, and then she guessed.

Shadows, she told herself. *Rails are casting shadows. Looks like black slats in the grass. Just like a cattle guard in a road.*

The only time Fitz and Jane had jumped with lights was a few weeks earlier at Fairfax. The show was a local event held in a pasture beside Bailey's Crossroads. The feature jumping class ran through sunset, and a jump-off was required. In the dark, the riders and judges agreed to finish the class with the course illuminated by headlights of cars surrounding the ring. The white bars of the jumps were dimly suspended in space with scant reference to objects on the ground for the horses to judge distance and height. It was a gutsy expedient, inconceivable by today's safety standards, sixty years later. Jane had misgivings, but Fitz had jumped the same course splendidly in the fading light. In the headlights, he went as if on a wire, and they won the Jumper Championship. However, car headlights did not shine down from above to cast confusing shadows on the ground.

Fitz wrenched under her. He'd run out of patience with standing still and was preparing to buck. Jane let him move off at a brisk walk, hoping it wasn't too late. But now she had another problem to worry about.

"Look at the bar, not the ground," she told him as they passed through the entry gate into the show ring.

Should I take my time, circle before the first fence, she asked herself, *and let his eyes adjust to the lights? No! Don't want him to see details on the ground, just those big white rails.*

"C'mon, straight at it," she said to Fitz.

She was conscious of the thud of Fitz's hooves and his elastic body moving under her. She felt him chop his stride. He'd seen something and was adjusting. A twinge of dread seized her, and she shifted her focus from the top rail down to the shadows.

No! she told herself. *The rail.*

His familiar rhythmic canter quickened. Her eyes clutched an infinitely small point in the center of the top rail. The brilliant white of it dazzled her as it came closer and closer. And then, he took off.

In flight, it seemed to Jane that the jump was heading under Fitz in slow motion. She held the spot of her concentration to see it pass under his front hooves. The moment was dead silent, eerie. She waited for the hollow clunk of a rear hoof hitting the rail or the ripple of its shock in his body.

Jane heard a communal cheer, and it startled her. She had forgotten the crowd hidden in the dark. The cheer meant one thing. Out of the six entrants so far, Fitz was the only horse to make it over this first fence.

Quickly, where's the next fence? Get back on track, she ordered herself.

The crowed cheered four more times. On the sixth fence, with only two more remaining, she heard a resounding thunk, a pervasive audience moan, and the echoes of the rail bouncing off the ground. She pulled up and trotted out of the ring to excited applause.

Larry Lawrence, a horse show journalist who followed the circuit for the Washington area newspapers, reported on this class: "Poor judgement was shown in placing the first jump in a position where the lights cast shadows. The shadows confused the horses in choosing where to take off. Consequently, thirteen of the best open jumpers in the East went out at the first fence; none completed the tough course. The event was finally won by Fitzrada owned and ridden by Jane Pohl."

Fitz did not do well in any of the other jumper classes. Jane was not disappointed. This show was his debut against professionally trained competition, some of whom were already entered for Madison Square Garden. Winning the knock-down-and-out class fanned her hopes, but she needed confirmation.

The week after a dismal performance at the Maryland Hunter Show that September, Fitz displayed a tendency that plagued Jane for years to come. Before dawn, she loaded the tack trunk for the Keswick horse show near Charlottesville, Virginia, allowing three hours for the drive. As was their custom on long trips, Mother came along to share in the driving and to hold Fitz while Jane worked on him at the show. Mother's old broken ankle would never allow more. But when Jane led Fitz to the trailer, she walked up the trailer's ramp, and he stopped at the bottom with his nose over the ramp. She tugged his lead shank, and he pulled back. Jane knew he wouldn't be forced and thought it had been a mistake for her to tug. She jumped off the ramp and led him in a circle where he moved freely. Keeping his momentum, she again walked up the ramp, and he refused to put a hoof on it. There was nothing to do but wait. Jane stood at the top of the ramp with him at the base, holding his shank for almost two hours until he got bored enough to follow her into the trailer. They arrived late but in time to make the handy hunter class.

"Oh no," Jane groaned when she saw a horse trailer in the ring among the jumps. Loading onto a trailer would be one of the required tasks of this class, designed to test the obedience and utility of a horse used for foxhunting.

Fitz went beautifully in the class, clearing bizarre jumps designed to spook horses, opening and closing gates, right up until the trailer, where he would not load and was disqualified.

Not wanting to drive back from Keswick in the dark, Jane and Mother decided to spend the night and leave early the next day. Hoping for a 7:00 A.M. departure, Jane bandaged his legs and led him to the trailer at 4:30 in the morning, allowing more than two hours for him to load. He walked up the ramp into the trailer without breaking stride.

"Why couldn't you do that *yesterday?*" Jane asked him. She drove to the motel with Fitz to wake Mother, who had been expecting to sleep for another two hours.

Days later, the photos Jane ordered from the show photographer arrived. One captured Fitz balking at the bottom of the trailer ramp in the handy hunter class. Jane stood in the trailer holding his reins with a sheepish expression on her face. She captioned the photo, "Losing the handy hunter class—which was his 'til *this*," and pasted it in her scrapbook. It was the end of September, little more than a month until the National, and Jane was no closer to knowing if Fitz was worthy of competing in the top league.

The first time Jane entered Fitz in a skyscraper class was at Hagerstown, Maryland. The outcome would weigh heavily in Jane's decision whether to enter the National. With the war over and a beautiful fall weekend, the two-day show in October 1946 was the biggest success in its twelve-year history. From an uncredited newspaper article in Jane's scrapbook: "Largest Number of [equine] Entries in Local History Reported at [Hagerstown] Show; . . . between 2,000 and 3,000 persons saw the show . . . all bleacher and box seats filled with many hundreds standing around the rail of the ring. . . . Some of the finest horses ever seen in a local show performed. . . . The competition was keener than ever with horses coming from several states. . . . Horses were housed in stables under tents and an overflow had to be placed in a large cow barn nearby." That year, the show initiated harness racing. On Saturday, a trotter fell on the tanbark track throwing his driver and breaking his tack. The horse quickly got to his feet, and the driver made hasty repairs, jumped on the sulky, and continued to catch up with the field and win with the crowd cheering wildly. The publicity boosted attendance for Sunday, with the skyscraper class as the feature event.

The packed grandstand was decorated with American flags and sheltered from the sun by a red and white striped canvas awning. The skyscraper class began by requiring each entrant to clear a single fence, a solid white panel, four feet six inches high with bars above. Bars would be added until all horses but one were eliminated. The panel had wings to funnel horses into the jump and prevent them from running out to avoid it.

Fitz jumped flawlessly at five feet and then again at five feet six inches. When the bars were raised to six feet, additional wing boards were nailed higher on the stanchions to discourage horses from jumping over the wings, which were lower than the jump.

What are we doing? Jane asked herself. *He's sixteen years old.* But he cleared six feet and then six feet six inches effortlessly. The bar was raised to six feet ten inches.

"Any horse clearing this height," the announcer said through the loudspeakers, "will establish a regional record." Earlier that year, Cateer, with owner Dave Martin aboard, jumped seven feet in the District of Columbia. But the record was disallowed because the bar had been tied to the stanchions, preventing it from falling.

Little errors in either the rider's or the horse's form or the horse's conformation had disastrous consequences at this height. None of Fitz's hooves could skid as he set up for the jump. A slip of a front hoof would put him in too tight so that he might jump up into the bars. A slip of a hind hoof would rob him of the height he would need. If a hind leg hung on a bar, he could flip and land on Jane. But Jane reasoned he had jumped out of this very pit the preceding four times, all the way through six feet six inches. She turned him to the six-foot-ten-inch jump.

He cantered into the pit between the wings with his ears forward, seeming confident. *My God*, she thought as the fence came closer and grew enormous, *it's more than a foot above his ears.* Jane's legs asked nothing, waiting for him to make the decision. He paused at the fence's base. *If you don't want to do it, that's perfectly okay with me.* She was glad to be off the hook.

Then he rocked back on his haunches. A pang of terror grabbed Jane's stomach. The crowd gasped. *He'll never make it, jumping from a dead standstill.*

Fitz launched for the top, and Jane wasn't ready. He would jump out from underneath her, and she would be left behind. She grabbed to hook her fingers in the braids of his mane, stood deep in her stirrups, and pulled her weight forward, squeezing her knees for grip. From the power of his thrust, she felt hairs of his mane tearing free from his neck in her fingers, but she hung on. It was a long ride going up. She was sure she had hindered him in pulling herself forward, adding to the weight he was lifting.

Jane saw the top bar pass under his front legs, felt momentary relief, and then clenched her jaw hoping his hind legs wouldn't strike the bar and topple him forward. At the apex he kicked to clear his hind hooves. Fitz plunged with his forelegs straight down and kept his head high to take the coming shock.

Damned long way to the ground, she thought. If he stumbled, he would collapse. But, as his front hooves hit, his chin came down almost to touch the ground in absorbing the landing. He kept his footing and cantered off. Except for the strain he showed in clearing the jump with his hind legs, it appeared easy. The crowd leapt to its feet, cheering and applauding. Jane was too dumbfounded to smile. No other horse cleared six foot ten inches. Being small and light had its advantages. Fitz won the skyscraper class and the Jumper Championship.

Fans and a few reporters walked with Jane and Fitz back to her trailer, asking questions. They passed by well-dressed owners, lounging in varnished studio chairs beside their vans, sipping cocktails from silver stirrup cups. A crystal vase of fresh-cut flowers was the standard centerpiece among trays of sandwiches and iced shrimp. The light breeze fluttered recently won ribbons prominently displayed on the side of each van. Grooms hobbled, carrying in each hand a bucket monogrammed with their stable colors and sloshing water over the rims onto their khaki trousers.

The retinue following Jane and Fitz asked, "Were you scared?" "How old's he?" "I see there's a U.S. brand on this horse's shoulder." "Is he for sale?" "How long have you been riding?" "Has he jumped this high before?" "When did you know he was so good?" Jane was swollen with pride and giddy from the recent danger of the big jump, but she was intimidated by the onslaught of attention, and the question she didn't answer was, "Are you going to Madison Square Garden?" She was flattered that Fitz's performance seemed inspirational to these people. It was clear they had been riding in her boots and had felt her same terror, relief, and elation.

The questions subsided when Jane stopped Fitz beside the family sedan hooked to the one-horse wooden trailer. The door of the Ford creaked loudly when she opened it to throw her coat, blue ribbon, and saddle on the back seat. She had to slam the door twice to latch it.

"How many horses do you have?" a reporter asked.

She rolled up her shirt sleeve and prepared to wash the old horse, who stood patiently, saddle marked with sweat, swishing his tail randomly at flies.

"Just Fitz," she said.

In 1946, women populated the hunter division of horse shows, but in the jumper division, Jane was unusual. While a woman occasionally entered an open jumping class, few women were campaigning, show after show, in the jumper division. Jane's persistent entry in these classes was unique, and her wins were newsworthy. Tully Rector, a large-scale show horse importer and owner, recalled in a recent interview, "Jane caused quite a sensation being the only woman in jumping classes of fifty or more men, many of them professionals. It marked the beginning of the great postwar era of show jumping. Those classes were box office sellouts."

However, Jane did not see herself as a maverick. The jumping classes she entered were defined as "open to all." There were no ladies' tees in this sport. From her childhood, Jane had seen equal opportunity practiced in the army when men from humble backgrounds were promoted to high rank based on their performance. She embraced the virtues of sportsmanship and fair play, particularly the saying "Let the best man win" or, in the case of the open classes, "Let the best person win." Jane was somewhat amazed by her success and flattered to be welcomed by her male competitors, especially the professionals. Although it would have been ungentlemanly for them to treat her otherwise, she felt their acceptance was genuine.

Preceding the 1946 National Horse Show, the Washington-area newspapers weighed potential contenders. Fitz and Jane made heartwarming copy as an outlaw tamed by a woman and a threat to male domination of the sport, but Jane deferred the decision to enter. Two weeks after Hagerstown, Cateer reclaimed the regional skyscraper record from Fitz by jumping seven feet, this time without twine securing the bar. Since 1946 was the first show season in five years, the record of any horse on the circuit was unproven; however, there was little dispute over the best trainer/rider. Before the war, Cappy Smith won the Jumper Championship at Madison Square Garden three out of four years. In 1940, he rode his horses Bartender and Intrepid to win *both* the Jumper Championship and the Reserve Jumper Championship at the National, the first and second places of the competition. In a huge gender upset at the 1941 National, Cappy lost to Maggie Cotter. Originally from Connecticut, Cappy moved to Middleburg after the war, and the Washington-area press embraced him as a native son. In 1946, Cappy's best jumper was a paint gelding named Chamorro, a full hand (four inches) taller than Fitz and a lot more powerful. Chamorro was in his prime at age twelve, compared to Fitz at sixteen, and favored to give Cappy his fourth title as jumper champion of America.

As the story spread through Leesburg of Fitz's rogue past and recent wins, strangers stopped Jane on the sidewalk to ask about the horse. In the drugstore, the pharmacist summoned her from his elevated prescription counter. The collar of his starched white jacket was casually unbuttoned. On the wall, hanging beside his diploma and pharmacist's license, was a framed photo of a racehorse in the winner's circle at nearby Charles Town, West Virginia, where there were two tracks, one for day racing and one for night. The horse's name was recorded on the photo in large print, followed by details of the race. In the track photo, the pharmacist wore a dark suit and stood proudly beside his racehorse.

"Here," he said peering down at Jane over his black-framed glasses. He pushed a brown bottle into her hands. "This is something I made up myself. It'll keep Fitz's legs from stocking up with fluid on long trips in your trailer. Mix it in his feed the day before."

"Thank you," Jane said, taken by surprise. "How much do I owe you?" reading his name tag and adding, "Dr. Pulliam."

"Name's Matt," he corrected her. "Nothing. Just bring back a blue ribbon from the National in November."

"The National? Ah," Jane fumbled. The possibility confronted her with a witness. It had been her pipe dream since childhood. Despite the encouragement, she fought with herself to be realistic. Fitz was sixteen. Most top jumpers came into their own before eleven. The jumper division at the National had eight classes, and each one had an average of fifty horses entered. Over half were professionally trained, and most of those would be ridden by professionals. The odds against her were enormous.

Dr. Pulliam winked at her and turned to his next customer.

Pasting recent articles into her scrapbook, Jane reviewed the favorable evidence. From the Almas Shrine Show after Hagerstown: "Jane Pohl's famous open jumper, Fitzrada, brilliantly ridden by his Leesburg owner, tied in the Skyscraper at 6 feet 6 inches." From the McLean Horse Show: "The little Fitzgibbon-Perada gelding fenced faultlessly in his usual dashing style." She persuaded herself to fill out the entry form for the National and entered him in six of the eight open jumping classes, based on how much exertion she thought he could handle. Each class had a morning qualification to cull the field to twelve for the evening class. Jane entered Fitz in one class each day Monday through Wednesday, two classes on Thursday, followed by a rest day, and his last class on Saturday. If he qualified in all six classes, he would go through an open jumping course a minimum of twelve times.

Just as Jane put up the red flag on the mailbox, the mailman's tires crunched on the gravel announcing his arrival. His name was John Royston. He had a crippled arm and wore a big blue star sapphire pinkie ring on his good hand. Like the pharmacist, John kept a racehorse in training across the Shenandoah River at Charles Town. In fact, many local working men—including farmers, the plumber, the barber, and the grocery store clerk—had a horse (or a share of one) running there in the spring and summer and on the local county fair circuit in the fall. It was something to root for. John Royston pulled Jane's envelope out of the mailbox and read the address: The National Horse Show Association, 90 Broad Street, New York.

"Was wondering when you'd get around to it," he said, grinning.

"Well John, I don't know . . ." Jane bit her fingernail uncertainly during her stock reply. John offered her advice about training racehorses to change leads, which would help Fitz negotiate turns on a jumping course. Jane nodded tentatively.

The trash collector was Jesse Randolph, a black man who kept a horse or two at the local track. The week before the National, he finished emptying Mauka's garbage cans into his battered truck and climbed the back stairs to the kitchen door.

"John Royston told me you entered the National, and I've been following the papers," Jesse said. "You 'n Fitz teach that fancy Middleburg-Warrenton crowd what we're all about in Leesburg. Have you got any rubber reins, like we use on the track? They won't slip in your hands no matter how lathered Fitz's neck gets."

From childhood, she remembered Pop listening to sports radio broadcasts from the Madison Square Garden, the home of the New York Rangers and the New York Knicks and the site of world-title prizefighting bouts. Appearing there was so intimidating that many star athletes suffered from "Garden-itis," the sports equivalent of stage fright.

In the weeks leading up to Madison Square Garden, Fitz won four Jumper Championships in five local appearances, but Jane's anxiety mounted with the acclaim. She dreaded reading Larry Lawrence's articles published in the *Washington Star*: "Loudoun-Owned Horse Seen Strong Bidder for Top Garden Honor": "In a box stall on a farm out in Mount Gilead, near Leesburg, there is a little old 15.2 hands Thoroughbred, which this writer believes has an excellent chance of bringing to Loudoun the open jumping championship [at the National Horse Show] . . . the 16-year-old son of Fitzgibbon-Perada has rolled up a record season which surpasses any open jumper in the East."

Jane was superstitious about optimism. Too much gushing invited disaster. The Garden would be the first time that Fitz performed indoors under lights or on a springy steel floor covered with artificial soil or with sudden outbursts from 15,000 spectators. Fitz was used to jumping from firm natural ground. On the spongy tanbark footing, he could underestimate the effort required to clear his fences. The oscillations of the steel floor under the tanbark could spook him. She had no way to prepare him for any of these conditions. Whenever she was asked for an opinion on how they would do, Jane said, "As the saying goes, 'You pays your money and takes your chances.'"

In his last article before the Garden, Larry Lawrence picked Fitz to win: "Van loads of aristocratic hunters and sensational jumpers from Maryland, Virginia and the District will be on their way this week to New York City. . . . Under the skilled hand of his owner, the great gelding [Fitzrada] is a most consistent performer and it takes consistent blue ribbon winning to win top honors at the National. As reserve we pick Chamorro, mostly because of 'Cappy' Smith's expert riding than the flashy gelding's ability. But if steady old Cateer gets hot and takes to the tanbark, put your money on Dave Martin's gray champion."

Jane had a hard time sleeping during the nights leading up to their November 3 departure for Manhattan and the country's highest test. Jane hand painted "Leesburg, Va." in big white letters on her tack trunk in appreciation for the local folks who had encouraged her, lent their hard-won secrets and equipment, and were rooting for Fitz. She hoped seeing the letters in the basement of Madison Square Garden would bolster her courage.

9

AGAINST ALL ODDS: THE 1946 NATIONAL

At 4:30 A.M. on Sunday, November 3, winter was in the air. A brisk wind oil-canned the barn's tin roof as Jane wrapped Fitz's legs in sheet cotton and shipping bandages for the trip to the National. He stood patiently under a bare bulb in the barn aisle. Jane noticed his breath condensing and guessed it was near forty degrees here, probably below freezing in New York. She adjusted his heavy wool horse blanket for a tighter fit. The canvas-topped trailer wouldn't offer much protection against the cold.

Mother slid into the seat beside Jane, and they left Mauka at 5:00 a.m., on time. No others from the family could attend. Pop had urgent work, Jennet was in college, and Richard was a second lieutenant at Fort Bliss, Texas. In a way, Jane was grateful. The pressure would be bad enough without them watching. The backseat of the car was crammed with suitcases and supplies. Days before, Jane had packed her tack trunk with buckets, brushes, a curry comb, a horse blanket and sheet, bridles, girths, her saddle, saddle soap, a hoof pick and paint, mane-braiding yarn, liniment, leg bandages, and many other items. With paranoid rigor she had emptied, verified, and rearranged its contents against her list.

With the car's motor laboring under the load, they pulled the wooden one-horse trailer north for nine hours to New York. They pulled the trailer up U.S. Highway 1 through Washington, Baltimore, Philadelphia, and Trenton. Rarely able to go more than forty-five miles an hour, they were careful not to tailgate. If a car ahead halted quickly, they would need plenty of room to stop.

Jane was sure she had forgotten something critical. She checked Fitz when they stopped for gas. He seemed content standing with his legs bandaged in sheet cotton, pulling hay from a net hanging in front of his nose.

"Have we got a jack, in case we have a flat?" Jane asked Mother before they reached Baltimore.

"In case you forgot, your father is an engineer. Probably greases it monthly and documents the maintenance."

As Jane twisted the knob on the car radio, searching for a weather report, a rope holding the tarp on the top of the trailer broke. Jane looked in the rearview mirror and saw the tarp's corner whipping freely. She pulled over and climbed the side of the trailer, threaded the rope's pieces through the tarp's grommets, tied knots at the breaks, and lashed the tarp to the cleats on the trailer's wood siding.

"I hope Fitz's legs don't swell—a whole day of standing in the trailer!"

"Did you give him the pharmacist's medicine?"

"Chrikies, I can't remember," Jane said.

They drank coffee from a thermos and ate sandwiches Mother had made and wrapped in wax paper. On the rare occasions where Jane caught herself *not* worrying, she feared it was a sign of a jinx.

North of Philadelphia, Jane found an open lot where she could unload Fitz and walk him around to promote circulation in his legs.

"Remember what happened when you tried to load him at Keswick," Mother said.

"I'm gonna chance it," Jane said.

Fitz was a bit stiff but seemed to loosen after five minutes of walking on a lead shank. Jane let him graze for another few minutes and then led him back to the trailer's ramp. He balked.

"Not now," Jane said loud enough to startle Fitz.

Get a grip, she told herself. *It's just a horse show.* But she knew better. The eight classes in the jumper division had drawn 341 entries, the largest number in the show's history. Jane circled Fitz again to the trailer ramp, and he loaded. She apologized to him under her breath.

The Sunday afternoon sky was overcast when they drove up Manhattan to Madison Square Garden on Eighth Avenue between

49th and 50th streets. A policeman blew his whistle angrily, pointed for them to park at the curb, and motioned urgently for the clogged traffic to bypass the horse vans and trailers. Jane and Mother opened the car doors to the cold nip of New York's autumn. Mother went to sign for Fitz's stall, and Jane unloaded him in the dimming light between gray buildings. Groups of pedestrians, holding their overcoats closed with hands in their pockets, paused to watch the arriving horses. Infected with the excitement of being at the National, Jane forgot the weariness and anxiety of the trip. Fitz, too, perked up at the bustle of Manhattan. Honking car horns reverberated off the buildings. His ears flicked in chasing their echoes.

Fearful of Fitz spooking and getting away from her in the city, Jane ran the chain of the lead shank through his halter and over his nose for better control and backed him down the trailer ramp. Steam rose from a metal grate down the sidewalk. Fitz eyed it cautiously and flared his nostrils. The acrid smells of burning coal and car exhaust enveloped them. His steel shoes clicked on the concrete as she led the old horse on the sidewalk, but the sound was muted by the pervasive grind of city traffic.

"We're not in Kansas any more, Toto," Jane told him.

Passing through the side entrance into the Garden, then under the steel beams supporting the seating above, Jane followed other horses led by grooms toward the ramp leading down to the basement stalls. Street sounds and smells were replaced by hammer blows, sawing, and the clean odor of fresh paint in the hurried completion of the promenade and box seats surrounding the 90-by-200-foot show ring. Earlier that morning, a fleet of dump trucks and twenty-five men had spread 900 tons of tanbark over the ring's floor. The mixture of loam, sand, and clay made a shock-absorbing carpet ten inches deep. The earthy aroma of moist tanbark reminded Jane of the smell of newly tilled furrows back home. It should have been a comfort but seemed foreign in the cavernous steel-girded building. Jane winced at the ramp's springy bounce from the jostle of descending horses. It didn't feel entirely safe, but Fitz unquestioningly followed the horse ahead.

Mother and Jane set the white-lettered "Leesburg, Va." tack trunk in front of his basement stall. A stable boy sprinted past them, down the aisle, to where the blacksmith shop and the veterinarian's quarters were being finished.

"Doctor! Come quick," the boy yelled to the vet. "Horse's flat on its side, moaning like all hell."

The aging vet grabbed his black bag and trotted through the maze of aisles, puffing to keep the fleeing stable boy in sight. Jane followed out of curiosity. When they arrived, the mare's groom was leisurely sweeping the tack room floor.

"Oh," he said to them, "don't pay her no attention. Acts like this after every trip in the van."

For the horse show, Madison Square Garden held 15,000 spectators. Because the show ring took up much of the floor space, the seats were right on top of the action, whether in the lower stands, the mezzanine, or the balcony. No New York event required more preparation, and unlike other entertainment spectacles, the National Horse Show never had a dress rehearsal. The production cost in 1946 exceeded $300,000, an enormous expense for those days. The net proceeds were donated to the American Red Cross.

Preparation of the Garden for the horse show had to wait until the close of the preceding event, typically a title prizefight or a convention. With only four days before the show's opening, Ned King, manager of the National Horse Show since 1932, began construction of the stalls, bandstand, promenade, and the show's traditional nine- and six-seat boxes.

Providing stable space for 500 horses in the middle of Manhattan was a feat. Since the basement of Madison Square Garden had space for only 394 stalls, some of which were used for tack rooms and grooms' quarters, ninety more stalls were erected in the "Squadron A" National Guard Armory, fifty blocks away at Madison Avenue and 94th Street. The Canadian Mounties' drill team used the parking lot behind the Garden as a corral.

Horses began arriving in the predawn of Sunday morning, nearly twelve hours before Fitz, some in tractor-trailer vans carrying eight or more. They came from all over the United States and Canada. The Mexican and Peruvian military jumping teams, invited by the U.S. State Department, made the voyage. In years past, Britain, France, and the Netherlands had sent military teams, but this year, war recovery precluded their attendance. Walter B. Devereux, president of the National Horse Show, wrote in his November 1954 article "New York Again Hails the Horse" for *National Geographic*, "Entries at the National vary from people with means to maintain large stables having several grooms to those who enter one horse they care for themselves. Exhibitors ship and board their horses entirely at their own expense. A typical exhibitor ships 5 horses, a manager, groom, rider, and sometimes a mascot [companion for the horse]. The mascot is usually a dog, sometimes a cat, goat, donkey, or even a monkey. A loose goat once got to the arena and ate name placards off the box rails."

As soon as Jane finished bedding down Fitz, she walked up to see the arena. National flags of the military jumping teams were suspended from the rafters. On the catwalks high above, electricians trained spotlights where the big fences would be placed for the jumpers. The lights had to be precisely right—jumping five feet is difficult and dangerous enough in daylight. A network of field telephones was being connected between the Garden basement, the announcer, the ring clerk's small shanty, and other strategic points. Meanwhile, the jump crew sorted poles, imitation stone walls, and potted trees and shrubs. Jumping courses in a dozen different variations had to be erected between classes with the haste and precision of a race car pit crew.

Parked just outside the arena was a white horse ambulance lettered "American Society for the Prevention of Cruelty to Animals." It would evacuate injured horses to veterinary surgeries. Rarely, a horse broke a leg in the ring. When this happened, the veterinarian signaled to extinguish the lights and strike up the band, in an attempt to hide the horse from view and distract the crowd. The vet administered a lethal injection. In less than three minutes and under cover of darkness, the body was rolled onto a tarp and pulled from the arena.

At 6:00 p.m. on Sunday, after the tanbark had been watered and rolled smooth, the arena was opened to horses for exercise. Jane was eager to get the blood circulating in Fitz's legs. She saddled him and worked him briefly through extended trot and hand canter. She was relieved to find him sound and moving well. By 9:00 p.m., Jane and Mother were in their room at the Hotel New Yorker looking forward to hot baths. Tomorrow would begin with the qualification round for Fitz's first jumping class, the feature event of the National Horse Show's opening night. From the program, she knew Cappy's Chamorro and Dave Martin's Cateer were among the fifty-five of the nation's top jumpers entered in the open jumper class. Only the best twelve would survive the morning elimination to compete in the evening.

Jane sat in bed and studied the course diagram while Mother slept. *Eight fences*, she said to herself, tracing the route with a pencil. *Brush, three foot six; picket fence, four foot three; hundred and eighty degree turn to the right; single rail, four feet; . . . can't tell how much distance between fences. Last one looks like the worst, four-foot-three-inch triple bar with a six-foot spread.*

When Jane felt she had it memorized, she turned off the light and tried to visualize each turn and fence in sequence. Her thoughts drifted to worrying about the noise, the lighting, the crowd, the footing, and the flashbulbs. She turned the light back on to study the course diagram again. When the alarm clock went off that Monday morning, it was still dark outside. Jane woke with a jerk to find the diagram in her lap and the light on. She and Mother went downstairs for breakfast, but Jane could only stomach a piece of toast, coffee, and a cigarette as she read the morning paper.

"Cappy's at it again," she told Mother. "He bet Alex Aitkins $1,000 that he would 'run away with' the Jumper Championship of America. A thousand dollars. Can you imagine?" In comparison, the purse for that evening's jumping class was $250, a hundred going to the winner and the remainder graduated among the next three places.

At 7:00 a.m., the ring was cleared for saddle horses to work at the rack and slow gait or to practice standing properly, looking noble in the center of the ring. Then came fine harness horses. With eighty buggies trotting in the ring at once, wheels sometimes interlocked, resulting in a skid and a spill. Schooling jumps were erected for hunters and jumpers to practice between 8:30 and 9:30. Riders wore jeans and flannel shirts, contrasting with the black coats, yellow breeches, and silk top hats they would wear in the formal classes at night. They told the assistant ringmaster which classes they had entered, and he pointed to the line waiting for the appropriate jumps. Jane warmed Fitz up and was nervous about working in such close quarters. When a horse refused a jump, the following rider rode into the stalled horse. Tempers flared.

Next, the fences for the open jumping class were erected for the morning elimination round. Jane and Fitz queued early among the fifty-five horses attempting to qualify for the evening class. Half the entries were trained and ridden by professionals. Fitz had jumped against some of them with mixed results in the shows around Washington, D.C. Four represented the U.S. Army Equestrian Team from Fort Riley, Fitz's old home. Only four of the fifty-five riders were women, all amateurs, each riding her own horse.

Fitz was unsettled and flinched at echoes in the indoor arena. After watching the entries go ahead of her, it was clear to Jane that only a clean round would ensure qualification. Jane prayed that Fitz would ignore the distractions.

"Stay the course, Fitz," she said to him, trying to relax at the head of the line. "Steady and sure. All except for that last fence with the six-foot spread." He would need some steam to clear it.

They were next. The assistant ringmaster called Jane's number, and the gate yawned open before them. Through the gate, she bent Fitz to the right, urging him to a canter on his right lead in as big a circle as she could scribe, and straightened for the first fence, the brush. They sailed over it easily. Stride, stride, stride, he was building speed to the big stark-white picket fence.

Slow down, she thought. *Gotta turn right after it to jump the single rail.*

He landed neatly and leaned to change direction. Halfway through the turn, he felt for the bit. It was a reassuring to Jane. *Got the single rail*, he was telling her.

She relaxed and shifted her focus to the next jump, the highest of the course, a four-and-a-half-foot-high pole over a target panel. He cleared the single rail and surged for the big panel.

Easy, she thought. *Got to reverse direction after the target panel.*

He checked his pace, and it relieved Jane. Then clean over the target panel. Turn. Clean over the gate fence. Stride, stride, stride. Clean over the drums.

Last turn. A tight one. Then the double-crossed poles. Not high at three foot six. But don't get confident because then comes that nasty last fence, four foot three with a six-foot spread.

Out of the turn she felt him looking through the crossed poles in front of him and recognizing the spread fence beyond. *He's got it figured out*, she thought. *Now look beyond that last fence and think right turn so there's no doubt what we're gonna do when we land the last fence.*

He carefully increased momentum through the crossed poles and up to the last fence. As soon as he launched for the spread, she knew it was good.

As he settled back to a walk, she patted his neck excitedly over his clean round. Once they left the arena, Jane slouched in the saddle, feeling like she had held her breath through the entire course. Rather than endure the long wait through the other horses' rounds to see if they qualified, Jane took Fitz back to his stall to rest him. Mother remained at ringside to tally the results. If too many horses went clean, the judges would call Jane back to the ring for another round.

Jane stripped his tack and sponged his coat of the sweat marks left by the saddle and girth, but her mind was upstairs. To kill time over the next hour, she rubbed Fitz's legs with liniment, precisely trimmed his fetlocks with fingernail scissors, and brushed his tail, knowing it wasn't necessary. There was no call over the loudspeakers for her to return to the ring. Mother arrived later with a pencil marking the place in the program where she had written the names of the qualifying horses. From the smile on her face, Jane knew Fitz had made the cut. Jane was flooded with relief.

"Fitz and eleven others qualified with clean rounds," Mother said opening the program and looking at her notes. "Among them are Cappy, Alex, and one of the Army Horse Show Team members. Cateer didn't make it."

Fitz and Jane's shot at the big time had arrived. Nine of the twelve surviving horses were professionally trained, and eight were professionally ridden. Only two of the twelve riders were women.

It was impossible for Jane to relax. She worried about the noise from a full house on opening night. "You could try stuffing his ears with cotton," Mother suggested. "Army does that for parade horses marching in front of the band." Jane discounted the suggestion. He could be funny about her fooling with his ears. She remembered hearing about a horse at a previous National that refused to go into the ring. In desperation, his owner had a blanket thrown over the horse's head while the horse was led in blind.

$$\bigcup$$

After lunch, harrows smoothed the tanbark, a magnet rolled over the ring to pick up nails, and a tanker watered the dark mixture to tack the dust. At 1:30 the lights went up, and a half hour later, "Honey" Craven, ringmaster for eighteen years, walked to the center of the arena in the red coat and black silk top hat of a coach guard for Royal English Mail, raised a long brass coach horn to his lips, and blew the call. The 1946 National Horse Show was officially under way.

Military teams formed up outside for their grand entrance in the opening ceremony. At the head of the column stood the First Army Band. The house lights dimmed, and the spotlights focused on the show ring's entrance. The crowd hushed. In the box seats, a top hat's brushed silk shimmered, a white orchid bobbed, a diamond earring glittered. The gates to the ring opened, and the band issued a booming brass blast, stepping off for their march, playing "The Dashing White Sergeant." Behind the band, the glistening chargers of the military jumping teams skittered, alarmed by the sudden noise, regrouped, and followed the band. The audience rose to their feet in applause.

A New York City mounted policeman rode on both flanks of every team. One policeman carried the orange and black colors of the National Horse Show, and the other policeman bore the team's national flag. The teams wheeled their horses to face Mr. Whitney Stone, president of the National Horse Show, who accepted their salute. As the band played the national anthem of each team, the team moved forward one pace and saluted again. At the end, the standing audience cheered and the classes began.

A little after 7:00 p.m., the ring emptied of the preceding hunter class, and the jump crew scurried to set up the open jumper course for the evening's feature. As the class began, Majors Delton Wilkins and Rye Yandle stood side by side, watching from the promenade. One of their fellow Army Horse Show Team members was entered. When Jane passed through the gate into the ring, both officers recognized Fitz, confirming him as the same rogue that injured Del and others at Fort Riley before the war.

At the completion of the order of twelve for the open jumping class, four horses had gone clean and were tied for first place. Among them were Chamorro and Fitz. The army team horse was out of contention, having finishing the course with one fault. A jump-off was required to settle the first four places. The jump crew raised the bars six inches for a second round.

Jane bit her lip and adjusted her coattails to cover the split in the back seam of her breeches, which had ripped open fifteen minutes ago over the first fence. She worked her prescription sunglasses firmly onto the bridge of her nose. *Can't believe I lost my regular glasses*, she said to herself. Without the dark glasses, objects beyond Fitz's ears appeared blurry. With them on, contrast was dimmed, and the shadows cast by the lights on the tanbark from the jumps were not discernable.

"Miss Pohl and your old buddy, Fitzrada, did good, didn't they?" Rye asked his friend.

"Did *well*," Delton said tersely. Rye did not respond. He understood the dig was motivated by mourning. Horse cavalry was obsolete, replaced by tanks. The Army Horse Show Team probably wouldn't exist a year from now, ending the life the two officers had known with horses. In representing the United States in international jumping since 1912, the team had advanced the technique of forward-seat jumping, put the United States on the map in breeding and training sporting horses, and won Olympic medals. Rightfully, it was the highest authority on horsemanship in the country. Losing to a girl, riding a horse the team couldn't handle, was a final indignity.

Fitz and three others assembled in the aisle waiting their turn to decide the first four places in a jump-off. Never had Fitz attempted a course where six out of eight fences were at least four feet six inches high. Jane and Fitz stuck out like a sore thumb as the only woman and the smallest horse. Less obvious, they were the only owner–rider combination and the sole amateur backyard stable. Cappy was riding Chamorro for his client Lieutenant Commander Rives, who had purchased the horse from Cappy. Alex was riding Irish Lad for Harry Newman's Ballantrae Farm, a large show stable near Washington that brought six horses to the Garden. The fourth survivor was Jim Dalling on Albrurae Farm's accomplished gray mare, Princess Peroxide. Albrurae Farm was owned by Raymond Lutz and located in Wilton, Connecticut, a rural community within commuting distance of Manhattan. The mare was a hometown favorite against the three horses from Virginia.

Jane looked at Cappy, astride Chamorro, waiting his turn for the jump-off. His elegant posture told everybody he felt victory was a foregone conclusion. Going through the course again was a mere formality.

Jane vied for dominance over her butterflies. She took a deep breath, aware of the crowd, the murmur of its conversation and shuffling, and the smell of her own sweat. Intermittently, this scene seemed thankfully distant to her, as if she were viewing it on a movie screen.

On the course, Chamorro finished with one tick for one-half fault. Irish Lad knocked down a bar for three faults. A clean round could win it for Fitz and Jane.

Fitz and Jane entered the ring as the announcer called their number. When she squeezed him toward the first fence, her anxiety meshed with focus. It was a part of jumping that she dreaded and lived for at the same time. Because of the immediacy, it was impossible to think about anything but the task at hand. Their commitment to the first fence had to be unequivocal. For Jane it came as an acceptance that it was too late to turn back, a resignation to her fate over the next fifty seconds of eight successive jumps.

Fitz went splendidly through the first three fences. His jumping was as quick and light as a suddenly inhaled breath. Their path and flights seemed predestined, agile, and unconscious. But then he ticked a rail on the fourth fence. It came as a surprise to Jane, and she winced. At the same time, the crowd groaned in disappointment. The distraction interrupted her concentration and put her behind in visualizing a path through the turn to the fifth fence. Exiting the turn, he was tight into the fence on takeoff and ticked it too. The crowd groaned again, and it seemed louder to Jane than before. She fought to put the faults out of her mind and stay ahead of Fitz on the course. He corrected his stride for the next fence, and they returned to a single consciousness for the remaining three fences, finishing with one fault. Jane was relieved it was over but regretted the mistakes and played them over in her memory, unable to find a cause for the first tick. She blamed herself for the second.

Next up, the big gray mare, Princess Peroxide, took the ring. Fence after fence passed under her without the sound of a hoof touching a rail. The crowd was straining for them as they neared the end. When Jim Dalling cleared the last jump, he twisted sharply in the saddle, looking over his shoulder at the fence, but there was no cause for worry. The crowd burst into applause for their clean round. It was done, and Fitz had taken third, ahead of Irish Lad.

Jane was beside herself with joy that Fitz had acquitted himself against the best in the nation. To take third in his first class at the National Horse Show was beyond her imagination. They finished only a half fault behind Cappy Smith, the best professional in the world. When the judge approached to pin the yellow ribbon on Fitz's bridle, she felt goose bumps rise on her flesh. Jane raised her face to the mezzanine of Madison Square Garden and soaked it all in.

"All those years of hard work and faith," she said, patting the little horse on his neck, feeling tears brim in her eyes.

To preserve modesty in dismounting with the seat split in her breeches, she put Fitz's left side close to a wall and slid off of him with her buttocks against it. She hoped she had brought needle and thread to sew the breeches together for Fitz's next class tomorrow morning.

As Jane walked down the hall to her hotel room with Mother that night, she danced on breaking waves of joy. In her mind, she jumped the course with Fitz again, remembered finishing the class and cooing praise to Fitz. In retrospect, she felt her excessive display of affection was inappropriate in front of 15,000 spectators at the most exclusive horse show in the nation. Then she felt indignant about her embarrassment. No one who knew their story could deny they had earned that moment.

For the 1946 National, Jane entered Fitz in three other evening classes and two matinee classes, all in the jumper division. He made it through the morning qualifications for two of these classes but did not place in either class. As far as Jane was concerned, taking third in the open jumping class was incredible. Despite his small size, advanced age, and outlaw past and despite her being an amateur, for one evening Fitz placed among the three best open jumpers in the country. Jane and Fitz had been competing against top horses in Virginia for a year. The professional men who trained and rode them had been winning ribbons at the National for a decade. She could not have hoped for more.

Cappy won his much-publicized bet of $1000 with Alex that he would "run away" with the Jumper Championship of America. As Jane and Mother were packing the tack trunk in the basement of the Garden, Cappy approached them. Jane stood meekly in the great horseman's presence. After a curt introduction, he got right to the point.

"Bring your horse over to my place next week," Cappy ordered. Jane hesitated, wondering if Cappy wanted to purchase Fitz. He read the consternation in her face and added, "I don't want to buy him. Too small for me."

Jane realized he was offering to help her. She didn't search for further motive, thinking how fortunate she was that Fitz had caught his attention. Learning from Cappy could be a fantastic opportunity. But his interest wasn't a whim. Cappy was inclined toward underdogs. Sweat equity demonstrated discipline that was disappointingly temporary in his moneyed clients. Besides, helping the rare female to rival him in open jumping would make great copy in the papers and might bring him some business.

On the Olympic front, opportunities were stirring. It was public knowledge that the army would give up horses in favor of tanks. Although the dissolution of the Army Equestrian Team had not yet been announced, it was believed civilians would represent the United States in the London Olympics, less than two years away. If a civilian team was formed, Jane had hopes of making the team with Fitz in stadium jumping, one of the three Olympic events.

The Olympics were restricted to amateurs. Curiously, the military officers who trained exclusively for competition were considered amateurs because their duty was to command soldiers, not take care of horses. Since the best civilian riders in the country were professional horsemen, like Cappy Smith, the United States was at a distinct disadvantage.

Jane believed that Fitz's alacrity, small size, and build were ideally suited to stadium jumping. As for the riding, Jane had been taught to ride in the army mold, which was derived from Olympic competition. If selection of a civilian team was based on ability, she thought they had a good chance.

To introduce Olympic events in the United States and stir up interest among its civilian riders, Olympia classes were offered at horse shows. These classes were usually judged by members of the army team who were the only Americans experienced with Fédération Equestre Internationale (FEI) rules governing the Olympics.

Olympic equestrian events were created to test the skill and courage of military couriers delivering messages quickly and reliably over miles of obstacle-ridden terrain. Unlike open jumping classes, Olympic stadium jumping was timed, so there was no pausing between fences on the course. Touching a fence had no penalty. Only knockdowns counted. Thus, there was no incentive to clear fences by a large margin as open jumpers were trained to do. Compared to open jumping, the emphasis was on speed as opposed to height. While an open jumping class might consist of eight jumps, Olympic stadium jumping might have twelve to twenty, and two separate rounds were required for a score. The additional jumps and the uninterrupted pace demanded stamina not required for U.S. jumping.

Jane rode Fitz through the open jumping courses in the same smooth, uninterrupted manner necessary for stadium jumping. Schooling would be required to polish him, but in Jane's opinion, he had already mastered the basics.

However, the FEI excluded women. From the perspective of cultured societies, a lady would never accept the risks inherent in military sports. Per this paradigm, Jane and the other women riding to big fences were freaks.

With the 1948 games fast approaching and amateur women beating professional men in open jumping, the press lobbied for change in the FEI gender rule, sparking controversy. If the United States wanted to win medals, women would have to ride. In a 1949 article in the *Sunday American*, "Girls Risk Limbs for Show Honors," Jeanne Hoffman asked, "Why are girls such good riders? 'Potentially they're better than men because they're more sympathetic, have lighter hands, are lighter weight on a horse's back, and gentle and kind,' reasons Ethel Beck. . . . 'Horse and [female] rider usually develop a very close affinity.'" Jane and others agreed with this explanation. But conservatives thought it unchivalrous to allow the fairer sex into harm's way. Further, it would be insulting to ask foreign military teams to compete against women. Yet everybody knew that horse cavalries were obsolete and that other countries would disband their military teams. With the demise of the military teams, the gender rule would also become obsolete.

The new Olympia classes were opened to women in anticipation of the rule change. A 1949 headline in a Dayton, Ohio, paper read, "Jane Pohl Rust Helps Prove Why Women Should Ride in Olympics."

10

THE "YOUNG GIRLS"
TAKE ON THE PROS

In 1946, Cappy's farm was beside the stucco-walled settlement of Leithtown, near Middleburg, only twenty minutes from Mauka. Cappy derived his living from training and selling show horses. As such, he was a member of the Professional Horseman's Association. In the show horse game, unlike the racetrack, the professional trainer did all the riding and showing. His staff consisted of grooms, one of whom might double as an exercise jockey. A professional in Cappy's league might have a dozen of his own horses at various stages of development and more that were brought to him by private owners. All his horses were for sale, and as they won, the asking price went up. Before the war, Cappy profited handsomely, selling his three-year-old champion, Bill Star, for the highest price ever paid for a show hunter in New York. During the war, Cappy served in the cavalry, breaking horses at Fort Robinson.

Cappy's clients were the wealthy who rode their professionally trained horses as amateurs, or they campaigned on the show circuit as owners with their own jockeys, sometimes hiring Cappy to ride. Unlike his contemporaries with flamboyant and unorthodox riding styles, Cappy breezed through the jumping courses, oozing quiet control. No matter how tight the turn, how little room to the next hurdle, he found reserve. Spectators winced in anticipation that his confidence had surely deluded him, only to feel their scalps tingle when he made it. Then came disbelief, respect, and mild humiliation that they had doubted him.

Jane schooled Fitz in Cappy's ring while he trained his own horses and simultaneously kept an eye on her. His advice was delivered with the same tact of the cavalry sergeants she remembered. Those who first met him said he was gruff. Those who knew him said he was the most self-confident man they ever met. When Jane asked questions, he amplified with condescendingly terse logic. Cappy had turned down college to learn his trade the hard way and didn't relish debate with Ivy Leaguers.

"He's bigger than you are," Cappy scoffed at Jane. "Don't try to lift him over the jump with your legs. If what he does best is make his own decisions, then *trust* him."

Cappy sometimes wore roweled spurs, and some horses' flanks were marked when they left his schooling ring. However, a horseman's business is to know how hard to train without souring a horse by demanding too much or wasting time by asking too little. Some people thought his horses went so well for him because none dared to disobey him. He preferred Thoroughbreds, but regardless of breed, horses were infected by his confidence. In showing his horses, his riding style exuded bravado, yet it was casual, masterfully relaxed. It promoted the same synergy of fool's courage that sweeps away caution among boys facing a school-yard dare, and Cappy's horses were seduced to try. He bought diamonds in the rough, spent a month or two on them, rode them to victory, and sold the good ones for sums rumored to be ten times what he paid. Having ridden his horses to win the Jumper Championship at the National Horse Show three out of four years just before the war and most recently in the first National Horse Show after the war, Cappy was king. To this day, some considered Cappy to be the best horseman America ever produced.

As a professional, he was a working man not of the same class as the heirs who bought his horses. He wore clothes of their taste, cutting a better figure than they did, but kept a distance worthy of his celebrity. As a competitor, winning was everything, and he left the sportsmen trust-fund captains in the dust. He constantly watched the other entrants and decided how their rides could have been smoother, more secure. Then he conceived tricks that never occurred to Jane, made perfect sense, and worked.

At a horse show, Jane witnessed two jump crew attendants flanking a fence during Cappy's round yet sitting on their wagon for everybody else's round. At his farm, she had seen him use his own men to haze this horse into jumping a similar fence. She wondered how he induced the show's crew to stand by the fence, but to ask him would imply that he had cheated. Yet Cappy was liked by those he trounced and generous with his critique of those who sought it. Jane thought he gave away his secrets to keep the game interesting.

"Stop looking down when you're over a fence," he barked at Jane in the ring. "You've already jumped it."

At night, she would diagram his advice in a spiral notebook. One page had an aerial view of a horse with jumps laid out in a curve. She captioned it "Stay ahead of your horse as *far* as you can" and traced an arrow directly from the rider to the last fence in the arc. Despite her notes, interrupting her concentration by looking down at a fence to see it pass underneath was a habit she never fully overcame.

Cappy's tips weren't always about riding. Another penciled diagram showed a side view of the front half of a horse at the bottom of a trailer's loading ramp. A stick man stood at the top with the lead shank in one hand and a buggy whip in the other. It was captioned "Flick the back of the horse's knees until he gets irritated (thinks it's flies?) and steps forward."

But sometimes Cappy's advice was more abstract. "What are your goals with Fitz?" he asked.

"I've lost plenty of classes where I was thrilled with his performance," Jane replied. "So I guess I'm more concerned with how he goes than where he finishes."

"That's a luxury amateurs can afford," Cappy said.

Jane worried about Fitz's age, and Cappy countered by naming a few horses in their twenties who had been top jumpers, and just like Fitz, they started late. But Cappy added that regardless of how young or old, not many stayed on top for more than five years, and not all of those quit for injury. Cappy thought they got bored. "If you don't keep it interesting for Fitz," Cappy said, "he's gonna *make* it interesting for you. He's not going to enjoy posing for pictures in retirement with grandchildren perched on his back."

Cappy said Fitz could do it all and advocated entering him in both the jumper and the hunter divisions. In the jumper classes, his small size allowed sharp turns at the right pace for the big fences, suggesting an ideal candidate for Olympic stadium jumping. In the hunter classes, Fitz had twice the jumping ability of the show hunters, his style was just as pretty, and his conformation was refined and classic enough to place in the working hunter and the light hunter classes. Jane had doubts. In her lifetime, less than a handful of horses had ever been successful in the hunter and jumper divisions simultaneously.

"You only get one good horse in a lifetime," Cappy replied. "You better get busy."

Driving home after working with Cappy, Jane realized that Fitz's attempts on five feet and above that day should have been tensely focused, as they had always been, but instead the jumping was confident, and then she understood how her frame of mind increased the chances of winning. However, some of Cappy's tactics were beyond Jane's capability. Even if she had the means, she didn't have the guts. Lined up before the entrance gate of a class, Cappy sometimes bet his horse against the horse of his closest competitor, adding with an offhand shrug, "If I don't win on this horse, I don't want him anyway." Those taking the bet thinking Cappy was kidding were mistaken. Cappy led away more horses than he gave up, and he never looked over his shoulder when he lost, even if it was a good horse. Much to the delight of the press, when these bets involved money, the amount approached the price of a new car. Jane never wagered more than she was willing to lose. The maximum was five dollars, her annual loyalty bet on the Army–Navy football game.

The time Jane spent with Cappy wasn't always confined to the ring.

"Come with me over to Upperville," Cappy said one day. "I need to see a man about a horse at Liz Whitney's barn." Jane knew the place's reputation as the most lavish show barn in Virginia.

"What's the story behind the horse?" Jane asked. She didn't know why Cappy asked her along but figured he had a reason.

"When we get there," Cappy said, ignoring her question, "look at the horse briefly, then stay away from us."

It was a rebuke to be excluded from the conversation, but Jane was happy to repay him for his help with Fitz. Horse dealing was a refined genre in the art of caveat emptor, and Cappy's livelihood relied on buying low and selling dear. She thought her presence there somehow played into the smokescreen of feint, innuendo, and hubris that are inherent in horse trading. Whatever the price and no matter how the horse panned out, gossip would judge it to be robbery for one side or the other. So the less known about prices, the better.

Liz Whitney (Tippett) married into money without end through a string of husbands. She was a glamorous model for Pond's face cream in magazine ads. At her farm, named Llangollen after a district in Wales, Liz bred her own gray hunters and had a full staff that included a stable manager and a trainer who shared the riding with her in the hunter division at the top shows. In the hunt field, Liz rode to big fences and was proud of it. At parties, she dressed in designer gowns, wore gems so exquisite that they were known by name, and drew a crowd of men who tried to keep up. She had a pet monkey and kept a herd of Great Danes underfoot. Carol Miller in a 2006 interview remembered Liz's house littered with their manure, yet Liz forbid the house staff from removing the piles and preserved deceased dogs in a giant freezer in her basement.

In a recent interview, Jackie Burke, author of the book *Equal to the Challenge* on horsewomen of the era, remembered Liz and a few others as "those glamorous, whiskey drinking, cigarette smoking, women who rode the show circuit." Burke recalled Betty Bosley (Bird) supposedly called in a false alarm. When the fire engine arrived at her farm, she explained, "I don't drink alone." Theodora Randolph owned the Piedmont Hounds and took them home if she didn't like the way somebody was dressed at a hunt meet, ending the day for everyone.

Liz had built her show barn in the shape of a giant horseshoe. Jane wandered through the barn astounded, not just at the quality of horseflesh. The stalls opened toward the center, where the horses had a view of manicured boxwood hedges and plots of iris and lilies. There was an office, a laundry, dressing rooms with showers, a dispensary for horse medicines, and a kitchen for preparing the horses' hot bran mashes.

Black grooms in starched khaki trousers bathed horses in tiled wash stalls plumbed with hot running water. The tack room was paneled in cherrywood and furnished with leather armchairs and brass lamps. Its walls were covered with framed show photographs of horses in flight and ribbons and silver accumulated from years of showing. English-made saddles rested on custom-made wall racks and filled the room with the aroma of glycerin-soaped leather. Each horse had its own bridle and halter with the horse's name engraved in brass, its own winter felt blanket and summer cotton sheet tailored in Liz's stable colors with the horse's name embroidered on the hip.

On the way home, Cappy didn't mention the horse he had looked at, and Jane didn't ask. Jane gushed about what she had seen. Cappy discounted it, saying Liz would give her eyeteeth to have Fitz.

Pop dreaded his career coming to a close sitting at a colonel's desk in Washington. Ever since he was a cadet, nearly thirty years prior, he believed he would be a general. Now he had the credentials for promotion to brigadier (one star) general, but the war was over, and downsizing killed possibilities for advancement. He would finish his career as a staff officer for the chief of engineers, a three-star general. "Peeing on the highest fire" was how he described his job. The tasks could range from negotiating labor disputes slowing the Corps of Engineers in building flood control levees to tracking down construction budget overruns to helping congressmen push bills that would bring big civil works projects to their districts. It was a letdown from commanding 3,000 men in combat across France and then serving as the XV Corps Engineer during the Battle of the Bulge. With no hope of promotion, his drinking picked up.

Then he suffered a heart attack fighting a fire at Mauka Farm that burned down the kitchen appended to the side of the house. The army retired him with full disability and a small box of nitroglycerine syrettes. He kept them in his shirt pocket should chest pains return.

Unable to accept a sedentary life, he would start drinking by himself in the early afternoon, and by suppertime he was probing for a fight. Mother was his usual target, but one night it was Jane's turn. With time to ruminate over his own career disappointments, he resented Jane's success in the jumper division, where less than 10 percent of the entrants were women.

"What about the professional men trying to put food on their tables?" he asked her. "It's not a sport for them, Jane. It's a living."

Her face turned red. The rare gal in the jumping classes usually rode her own horse and would never consider selling it. Women were hardly a threat to the professional's livelihood from horse sales. But there was no arguing with him when he was drinking. She sat mute.

"What you're doing attracts spectators hoping to see blood, women's blood," Pop said. "It's morbid. Wouldn't consider letting a man ride Fitz, would you?"

"Even if a man could ride him, the answer is *no*," she shot back hotly. Jane understood the whiskey was talking for him, but she was infuriated by the two-fisted betrayal. He knew what she had endured in reforming Fitz and becoming a top athlete herself. She had done it largely for Pop's praise.

"Back in Hawaii I was worried about him killing you!" Pop's voice rose in anger at her insubordinate tone. He slammed his glass on the table, sloshing whiskey on the tablecloth. "Right now, I'm worried it's *you* whose going to kill the both of you. He'll do whatever you ask him, and he's a Thoroughbred, so he'll die trying, even if he *knows* it can't be done!"

Jane and Mother stared at their plates. Pop finished what was left of his drink in one long drawn-out sip. Ice cubes rattled as he righted his glass. He stood, scraping his chair on the wood floor, and the sound startled Jane. Her twitch caught his eye. He paused to stare at her, turned his head in disapproval, and left them for a refill and a cigarette in the privacy of his study.

In the morning, Pop's pride in his daughter would resume, and he would not remember his attack at the dinner table.

Taking Cappy's advice, a month following Madison Square Garden, Jane entered Fitz in the hunter division as well as the jumper division at the Capital Area Horse Show. Jane had been foxhunting Fitz regularly since 1942. It was highly unusual that a top open jumper could also be used as a field hunter. Hunting required a calm temperament, rare in jumpers. As a show hunter, Fitz would be judged on manners and jumping style. He was skinny and had a long, thin neck and a slightly roman nose, which would hurt him in the conformation classes. Jane entered him in the working hunter classes to narrow the field. Conformation horses were too valuable to hunt and were thus excluded from the working hunter classes and their championship points. Conversely, she would forfeit the conformation hunter classes and their points.

The Capital Area Horse Show was held indoors at the Fort Myer riding hall. Stately government quarters for the nation's highest-ranked generals stood nearby on top of the hill overlooking the Arlington National Cemetery and the Potomac River. Fort Myer had a large stable furnishing cavalry for parades, duty and recreational mounts for army officers stationed in Washington, and the horse-drawn caisson used for state funerals. President Teddy Roosevelt promoted then Captain "Blackjack" Pershing four pay grades, directly to brigadier general, on the basis of his confidence in the young officer developed during their rides together from Fort Myer.

The show was the last one of the year and prominent for the region. The box seats were occupied by senators, cabinet members, congressmen, and Pentagon brass. Horses came from as far away as New England. Cappy and Alex Aitkins were entered.

The Chronicle of the Horse described Jane's risk in its article on the show: "He was ending a season that would have meant shaky underpinnings for most horses—campaigning almost every Sunday, hunting, hacking and then the long, wearying trip to New York for the National Horse Show. . . . While Fitz was jumping in every open class, Jane had to keep the old horse prepped for the working hunter division, in which she had entered him. Friends spoke to her rather severely about this, pointing out that Fitz's dual role might tire him out so completely that he couldn't win the jumper crown."

Proving his versatility, Fitz won the ladies' working hunter class and the $1,000 Working Hunter Stake from among twenty-six entrants. Jane accepted the blue ribbon from General Jonathan M. Wainwright, the World War II Medal of Honor hero of the Battle of Corregidor and the Bataan Death March. Fitz missed the reserve working hunter championship by one point but amassed enough points to finish ahead of the recent reserve working hunter champion at the National Horse Show at Madison Square Garden.

In the jumper division, Jane considered the in-and-out class the toughest. Five jumps were staggered between sixteen and twenty-four feet apart, ranging in height to from three to five feet. With fences packed so tightly together, any error made in one jump would be compounded for the next. The erratic technique of the hotheaded jumpers would not work on this course. Fitz's stride would have to be rated not just for the fence dead ahead but also in anticipation of the fences beyond, and five leaps in such rapid succession would require efficiency to conserve strength.

Fitz's small size and agility were a distinct advantage here, and he went through the course with delicate momentum and bounce. A tie resulted for first place among Fitz, Parole, and Chamorro, both trained and ridden by Cappy. Two jump-offs were required to settle it. Sixteen feet is precious little room between fences, and as the jumps were raised, the interval between them effectively diminished, allowing no space for corrections. With the bars at six feet, the outcome was finally decided at 1:00 A.M. Fitz won. Jane considered this class the most physically difficult accomplishment of Fitz's entire career.

The confidence necessary for this extreme performance came from having acquitted themselves at the National Horse Show. Subsequent goading from Cappy had focused Jane precisely on what could be improved, and studying under him had renewed Jane's self-discipline. She actively sought the great horseman's caustic scrutiny and condescending explanations to understand how faults developed and why a specific correction might work. Her relentless questioning invited his irritation, but this persistence inadvertently bred her confidence with the top horsemen she would compete against.

As they left the ring with their ribbons from the in-and-out class, Cappy offered his hand to Jane in congratulation. She grabbed it eagerly. The student's gratitude was reciprocated by the teacher's pride. Jane felt his respect, and at that instant she knew Fitz had made his mark. But fate didn't stop there.

The three-day knock-down-and-out competition was spellbinding. Each evening of the show, a knock-down-and-out class was held. Prizes were awarded for each class and for the cumulative outcome of the three classes. On the first night, twenty horses out of thirty-one were eliminated at the first fence, a double pole, four feet high. A surprise was in store from Anne Morningstar from Connecticut, only seventeen years old and riding three entries, one of which was Pabst Brew, a stocky gray mare and former livery horse rented out for two dollars an hour. Competing against Cappy on Chamorro, Irish Lad with Alex Aitkins up, and Fitz, young Anne and Pabst Brew enchanted the audience with their rocking hobby-horse style, jumping slowly and brilliantly. At one point, Anne was close to taking a fence in the wrong order, which would have disqualified her. Yells from the audience sent her back to the right jump.

Pabst Brew, Chamorro, Irish Lad, and Fitz tied for first. The bars were raised, and Fitz and Irish Lad were eliminated in the first jump-off. Cappy and Anne went at it through two jump-offs. With the poles raised to five feet six inches, Chamorro went out on the second jump. When Anne cleared the second jump, a roar of applause shook the rafters of the riding hall.

Then, in the open jumper class, Fitz won, and Pabst Brew was third. Cappy did not place.

Forty-two horses entered the Olympia class. Waiting for her turn, Jane felt assurance that provoked twinges of superstition about jinxing herself from overconfidence. She had not schooled Fitz for this type of jumping, but both of them had been raised on training doctrine evolved over three decades of army participation in the Olympics. Jane remembered when she was fourteen and Colonel Chamberlin answered her letter, Sergeant Mope barking at her in the ring, the fluid beauty in Colonel Van Deusen's jumping and his optimistic dissent leading to Fitz's purchase. If she and Fitz could earn a ride in the Olympics, it would be a fine tribute to them.

On the Olympia course, Jane felt anxious pride. Anne rode her mother's Play Girl to second, and Fitz was again third. In Jane's mind, third was a bronze medal, and a berth on the future civilian Olympic team was possible. It was just a matter of time before the gender rule would change.

In the last of the three-day knock-down-and-out classes, Pabst Brew placed second. The points accumulated for the Jumper Championship were now so close between Pabst Brew and Fitz that the outcome would be decided by the final feature of the show, the $1,000 jumper stake class. Irish Lad barely edged out Chamorro for the prize. Fitz was fourth. Pabst Brew's shoulder was sore, and the mare came in sixth.

When the results were totaled, the Jumper Championship went to Fitz with seventeen points and the Reserve Jumper Championship to Pabst Brew with fourteen points. Cappy and Alex were far behind, but Cappy did win a $500 bet with Alex. It was incredible that Fitz and Pabst Brew had just beaten Cappy on Chamorro, the jumper champion of the National Horse Show.

The Chronicle of the Horse recognized Fitz's utility in its article on the show: "There are few horses out today who could do it—but Jane Pohl's easy-striding airy-jumping Fitzrada proved himself to be among the best of them as he won not only the jumper championship of the National Capital Horse Show at Ft. Myer, but also major honors among working hunters. . . . No horsemen would have denied Fitzrada's ability—but at Ft. Myer, many became convinced that he is one of the finest fencers showing today."

Jane and Anne became acquainted and continued the friendship at successive shows. Although Anne was a teenager, she and Jane shared the same enthusiastic appreciation for competing with the best horsemen in the country.

The press was delighted that male supremacy in the jumper trade was under siege. The *Washington Times-Herald* sports page headlined Jane's victory: "Jane Pohl, 21, . . . showed the way to both amateur and professional riders when she won the jumper championship. Ann Morningstar, 17, . . . was reserve. The young girls made a show of the two top men riders." The accompanying photo was of Anne and Pabst Brew. It was captioned "Girl Who Left Male Riders with Red Faces."

As Jane pasted Fitz's clippings in her scrapbook at the end of 1946, she reflected. If delayed gratification is a hallmark of athletes, nothing in Jane's life had inspired her to be so patient as her relationship with Fitz.

Now, during the intense pressure of horse shows, Fitz had the ability to sense Jane's intent and overrule her doubts. She felt gratitude for the old horse's trust.

∪

Late in life, Cappy Smith befriended actor Robert Duvall and Tully Rector, a show horse importer. They witnessed Cappy jump what was probably his last fence. Cappy was over eighty years old, and it was right around the year 2000. Duvall's young wife had a horse habit, and Cappy was whetting the actor's appetite for a sale. Cappy warmed up his horse in the ring and ordered his man to set the bar at five feet. Tully and Duvall raised their eyebrows at the big number. Cappy cantered to the fence, and the horse slammed on the brakes. Cappy fell hard. His friends were sure he'd hurt himself and were relieved to see him stir.

"Damn it!" Cappy shouted as he quickly got up using one hand. "That was my fault, not the horse's."

His friends saw his little finger jutting out at a sickening angle, broken at the knuckle and swelling. They were stunned as Cappy turned his back on them to catch and remount the horse.

"We've got to stop him," Duvall whispered to Tully. "At his age, he can't take another fall like that. He'll kill himself."

"Cappy," Duvall called, "it's OK. We don't need to see any more."

Cappy wheeled on them, mad as a doused cat.

"I'm not doing this for you!" Cappy snapped. "I'm doing it for *me*."

In the ensuing silence, he cleared five feet with a foot to spare.

11

HORSE SENSE DESERTS JANE

Jane had dated infrequently in college. In her most serious relationship, she had dated a bombardier while he was stationed with his flight crew near Vassar. He gave her a pair of his silver wings, and she wore them to signify the relationship was exclusive. He owned a baby-blue Harley and let her drive it once in New York City with him on the back. It got away from her, and they ran up on the sidewalk, scattering pedestrians. When she finally got it stopped, they quickly switched places and escaped. She enjoyed those escapades more than supper and a movie. But she drank sparingly and avoided impropriety. Even the appearance of sleeping with a boy by staying out all night was damaging to a girl's reputation. Brides were expected to arrive at the altar as virgins. The relationship ended when he shipped overseas.

By 1947, three years after graduation, the majority of Jane's former Vassar classmates were starting families of their own. Jennet was engaged to a West Point cadet, Harry Spillers, whom Pop embraced as a lost son. Jane was a bit envious. Richard would soon meet the daughter of an army officer, Anne McMorrow, and within six weeks marry her at Fort Bliss, Texas. Although the war had altered the norm by accepting women into the workforce, at the war's conclusion they were expected to give up their jobs to men and resume roles as wives, mothers, secretaries, and teachers. An unmarried woman approaching thirty was considered a spinster. If she had career aspirations, frigidity or lesbianism was suspected.

Jane would not have minded falling in love, but the prospect of giving up horses for cooking and laundry did not appeal. Celebrity status was a glamorous change from her awkward life in high school. On the horse show circuit, she was vastly outnumbered by attractive men who respected her ability as an athlete, accepted her as an equal, yet held the door for her. They were colleagues, and she did not want to complicate her life on the circuit by romance with a competitor.

In the summer of 1947, Jane was introduced to David Rust by his sister, Mary, whom Jane knew through the local foxhunt. At twenty-three, Dave was the same age as Jane. Folks called him "a long drink of water" because of his lanky height, but there was liquid in his lithe gestures. His father invested in real estate, foxhunted, and bred racehorses with a passion for bargain bloodlines. The old man's farm, Gobbler's Knob, was about five miles from Mauka. Dave lived in an a apartment over the garage next to the house he grew up in and worked for his father, tending the horses and other farm chores.

Jane immediately liked his easy, self-deprecating style. He had large ears, thick brown hair, and a persistent wry smile, as if something were amusing him and he was on the verge of sharing it. Dave had the southern way of opening conversations with concerned inquiries about Jane's family and interests, then patiently letting the topic wander. He kept two coonhounds and hunted raccoons at night with local farmers, standing beside a campfire, drinking moonshine, and listening to their hounds run. Yet he was proud to trace his family line to Peter Rust, whose land was registered in the county's first deed book, dated 1705. In the surrounding counties, he knew the locations of former homes of ancestors who had made their marks in the history: George Washington's adjutant, several judges, a commander of Confederate cavalry, and Teddy Roosevelt's physician from San Juan Hill through his presidency.

Jane's first date with Dave was a happy evening in the clubhouse overlooking the Charles Town track, eating supper and placing two-dollar wagers on the races under the lights. They stayed through the last race and left at eleven. On the way to take Jane home, he turned the car into his father's driveway.

"Where are we going?" she asked, surprised and wary.

"Got to pick something up at my place," he said casually. She suspected otherwise but did not question him further.

He parked the car next to his parents' big stone house, opened Jane's door for her, held her arm in a gentlemanly way, and ushered her to his apartment over the garage. He went straight to the bar and pulled out two glasses and a bottle of bourbon. Photographs of racehorses hung on the wall. Bridles and old copies of *Blood Horse* magazine sat in piles on the floor and in worn chairs. Her eyes got big seeing how much Virginia Gentleman bourbon he poured into each glass. He handed one to Jane.

"I'm sorry," he said, noting the expression on Jane's face. "Would you like something else?"

"That's awful strong for me," she said.

He topped off the glass with water and handed it back to her. "Better?" he asked.

She nodded. *I don't have to drink it all*, she told herself.

Jane examined a framed war photo on the wall. In it, a teenage Princess Elizabeth officially thanked an American aircrew, including Dave, while the airmen stood at attention beneath the nose of their B-17 bomber, one crew among many lined up for the ceremony. Dave explained he had enlisted for the war, and in a rare flash of military intelligence, the army made him a blacksmith and sent him to the Remount Depot at Front Royal. He could have spent World War II thirty-five miles from home. However, he wanted to fight and volunteered for the Army Air Corps. Tail gunners were desperately needed in England, so they shipped him across the Atlantic by boat and trained him on the ground.

The first time he ever flew in a plane was for a mission over Germany. The rear end of the B-17 fishtailed through the air, making him violently sick. He spent all twenty-five missions vomiting out the bomb bay doors. Dave said his value as a tail gunner was well known in the squadron, and after the predawn mission briefing in the Quonset hut, the pilots would have a fistfight. The loser had to take Dave.

"That's the crew whose pilot lost the morning fistfight," he said to Jane, pointing at his face among the boys in their sheepskin bomber jackets basking in Princess Elizabeth's gratitude. In the picture, Dave looked skinny and vulnerable, but there was no mistaking his easy smile.

He said the best part of his tour was off-duty time at Aintree. A family that trained racehorses took him in and gave him a room in their house next to the Grand National race course, the world's most famous horse race over fences. He helped the family with their horses and rode some of the fences on the course. He was awed by one famous fence, Becher's Brook, a jump in a turn, notorious for the spills it caused throughout the Grand National's hundred-year history. Dave decided he would become a racehorse trainer after the war.

Before Jane knew it, her glass of bourbon was empty.

Jane felt important with Dave. With strangers, he was delightfully charming, maybe too much so. Inwardly, he was shy, but when he talked to her, she believed nobody else existed. She felt like he needed a friend, and he'd trust her with his secrets.

Dave's insecurity struck a chord in Jane. His good humor served to buoy him above his problems, but insecurity made him human, even endearing. After several more dates, each of them passing through his apartment on the way back to Mauka, she was in his arms and then in his bed. In the morning, her head hurt, and she regretted it, but as with Fitz those many years ago, she felt that whatever had hurt Dave, she could accept, she could love him, and he'd be better for it. What she didn't notice in him was the same despair that haunted Pop.

$$\cup$$

"I hear you're dating Dave Rust," Steve Canty, the blacksmith, said bending over Fitz's hoof. Every six weeks, Fitz's hooves grew out enough to need paring and new shoes. Steve pulled the old shoe off and rasped the horny tissue flat with long strokes.

"You know him?" Jane asked.

"Sometimes we go out and get 'pifficated,' as he calls it." Steve shook his head putting the leg down. "It's his old man you gotta watch out for."

"What do you mean?" Jane asked.

Steve said old Mr. Rust had a string of second-rate broodmares. The old man was friends with Mr. Phipps over in Middleburg. He bred the mares to Phipps's good stallions and shipped the yearlings to the annual sale at Saratoga, New York. Until then, the yearlings were turned out to pasture since foaling, and he never laid a hand on them. Some years ago, Mr. Rust called Steve to trim their hooves before shipment to Saratoga. The yearlings were wild. To trim their hooves, Steve had to halter break them and teach them to stand in cross ties without going berserk. A job that should have taken a day took a week. The following year when Steve did the job again, he gave the old man a huge bill.

"The old man," Steve continued, "was outraged and said to me, 'Last year you charged a fair price for hoof trimming.' I answered, 'That's for breaking your damned yearlings for you.' He paid up, but never called me again. Finds a new blacksmith every year and agrees on the price ahead of time."

Jane laughed, and Steve rose to the bait with another story. As a kid, Dave and the old man walked into Edwards drugstore in Leesburg. Dave asked his father for a milkshake from the soda fountain.

"Mr. Rust pulled a nickel from his pocket," Steve said, "and held it in front of Dave's nose. 'Now you can take this nickel and spend it on a milkshake,' he told Dave, 'or you can go down the street to Peoples Bank and put it in a savings account. Two years from now it'll be worth six cents and ten years from now it'll be worth twelve cents . . . ,' and so on."

Jane smiled, imagining Dave saying, "Okay, Father, forget the milkshake," as the nickel's value approached fantastic sums in a future too distant for a boy to imagine.

"Why's he drink so much?" she asked Steve, trying to sound unconcerned.

"Father hates him," Steve said. "Mother spoils him to make up for it."

Steve said Dave's father never forgave him for not going to college after the war. Mr. Rust thought the world of his other boy, even though that one disappeared for weeks at a time, drunk, coming home once with a new Cadillac. Couldn't recall where he bought it or how. The old man had to find out and return it, hoping to get his money back. Another time, contract papers showed up at the house demanding payment for a whole shipload of grain in New Orleans. The wandering son vaguely recollected a poker game.

As soon as Dave returned from overseas and was discharged, he took one of his father's horses across the river to Charles Town's tracks and started training it. A problem over Dave's trainer's license kept him from running his first race. Dave lost his temper and tried to provoke a fistfight with the track steward.

"Swore he wouldn't come back," Steve said, "even if they begged him, not that they would. Too bad. He's a damned good horseman. Knows how to train, and he can sit a horse."

Dave went back to work on the family farm. Old man Rust made a point of paying Dave less than his lowest-paid farmhand and bragged about not "spoiling" his son. Steve thought the real reason was because the old man was such a tightwad. Steve wished Dave would leave the farm and start a life of his own. Even if Mr. Rust felt any respect for his son, he'd never show it.

"Maybe Dave thinks you'll see something in him to be proud of," Steve said, winking at Jane. She blushed.

Dave didn't introduce Jane to the old man, and as far as she could tell, father and son avoided each other. Jane wondered if Dave wasn't afraid of him. The only stories he told concerning his father were about Dave's trips as an adolescent, traveling by himself in a boxcar to Saratoga with his father's yearlings, thrilled with the responsibility. For the trips, Dave took two days of sandwiches in a paper bag packed by his mother, and he drank from the horses' water barrel. On the first trip he didn't sleep. Clinging to the inside ladder with his head poked out the trapdoor in the boxcar roof, he was mesmerized by the cities and scenery flying past him. He felt so proud leading the yearlings off the rail siding at Saratoga, their coats shiny from his grooming on the trip, their legs in thick sheet-cotton, all safe and sound. As far as Jane knew, this was the only time Dave felt like he had pleased his father.

On dates, she enjoyed herself until it was time to go home, when on a pretext he'd insist on taking her by his place.

"C'mon," he'd say to her in his apartment, "let me freshen your drink and show you a book I found on steeplechase racing."

"It's late," she said. "I'm riding Fitz early tomorrow, before it gets hot."

He'd charm her into looking at the book and proceed to get sloshed without her. Once, at three in the morning, after a month of dating, her patience wore through.

"Dave, take me home, now!" she insisted.

"Oh Baby," he lolled, "I'm too pifficated to drive. Stay the night with ole Davy. I'll get you home in the morning."

"Absolutely not!" She flung his arm from around her shoulder and jumped up from the couch.

He sat up straight. He'd never seen her lose her temper before.

"We're not married," she was almost screaming, "There's no way I'll spend the night here. Now get up, right now!"

"Oh c'mon. We'll get married in the morning."

She grabbed his wrist and pulled him hard down the stairs to his car. She threw open the passenger door, pushed him in, and slammed it shut. By the time she got in the driver's seat, he was giggling and fumbling to remove the keys from the ignition where he had left them. She pushed him away, and he slouched up against his door.

"You should act like a lady," he said, waving his finger lazily.

"I am," she seethed.

She left him asleep in his car, parked in her driveway. The car was gone when she woke up at six to make coffee, smoke a cigarette, and get Fitz ready. She wondered if Mother and Pop heard him leave and figured he'd been passed out in the driveway. They had not said anything to her about the late hours she kept with Dave. Even though Jane was an adult, she was still living under her father's roof and knew Pop could not approve. Pop would surely confront her at supper one night when he didn't have anything else to harp on.

When Jane left the barn on Fitz at eight, Dave was waiting for her on one of his father's horses. He had gone home, tacked up a horse, and ridden five miles back to Mauka. She noticed he'd shaved and changed clothes.

"I'm sorry," he offered.

"You should be," she said tersely.

They rode together through the lush Virginia countryside, smelling the honeysuckle. He was contrite, and it seemed heartfelt. He picked raspberries from a bush he could reach from his saddle and offered them to Jane.

Damn it, she said to herself. *I've forgiven him.* "Dave, how did you drive home this morning? How did you get on a horse and hack up here? You should be in a coma right now."

"Couldn't stand having you mad at me."

She liked the sound of it but frowned at him.

"Well," he reconsidered, "That, and I've had practice."

The word got Jane's attention. Pop had adopted alcohol as a practice. She had a vision of her father at the supper table with Mother in his crosshairs. There was also a moral consideration. Being alone with Dave in his apartment was improper by the standards of her upbringing as an officer's daughter and a Catholic. She felt the guilt of sin and regretted her newfound sophistication as a headliner on the show circuit.

"I don't want to go out with you anymore."

"Why?" He was struck.

"We always wind up at your place. I don't like the drinking. I'm tired of it."

"If that's what you want," he said sympathetically, "I won't bring you over to my place. Take you home whenever you want."

"You've promised me that before, and every time I wind up kidnapped."

"It's just that I know you'll have a good time." He smiled at her with all his charm.

"You can come over here and ride with me, but I'm not going out with you. Not unless it's a double date and I get dropped off first."

"Fine," he said. His tone was cold. "You'll be sorry when ole Davey baby's gone." He turned his horse for home, and she felt he was right.

12

IN THE SPOTLIGHT

In his first four shows of the 1947 circuit, starting in Maryland and ending on Long Island, Fitz did not place well in the open jumping classes. Jane said with a shrug, "Sometimes it's luck," but Fitz was spending many hours on the road, which is hard on an old horse. However, the shows at Devon and Piping Rock were right below the Garden in prestige, so losing was no disgrace.

Then, showing near home, Fitz won five Jumper Championships. Among them was McLean, his second win of this show's championship in as many years, and Mt. Vernon, where he took the triple bar class, jumping a spectacular nine-foot spread with the top bar at five feet. At Middleburg, Fitz was reserve champion jumper to Ringmaster, a top horse with a nasty habit of ducking under single-pole jumps that were set high. The horse lowered his head and took the blow on its mane, leaving the rider to deal with the pole then flying up into his face. But Ringmaster surprised 3,500 spectators to clear the single bar and every other obstacle in the $500 jumper stake class. Fitz placed second to him in this class and another, and won the triple bar class, but it wasn't enough.

Exploring Fitz's Olympic possibilities, Jane entered Fitz in the Maryland Hunter Show's Modified Three-Day Olympic event. The stadium jumping course had twice the number of jumps Fitz was used to in the show ring. On the cross-country course, Fitz finished too early and was penalized for his fast pace. However, his combined score was enough for reserve champion of the Modified Three-Day event, and

Jane was convinced of Fitz's Olympic potential. Continuing to build a résumé as U.S. Equestrian Team hopefuls, Jane entered Fitz in Warrenton's modified Olympic stadium jumping class, where he tied for first place. Instead of a jump-off, the riders elected a coin toss to settle the tie, saving their horses for later classes. Jane lost, and her friends chided her for turning down the jump-off. The Jumper Championship was a near thing, but Fitz ultimately won it by one point.

U

By 1947, Marie and George Greenhalgh, of the Libby-Owens Glass fortune, had established one of the top show hunter stables in the country at their Springsbury Farm in Berryville, Virginia. Marie Greenhalgh, known as "Mama" G, had imported a mare named Portrush from Ireland and bred from the mare a dynasty of top show hunters, including the famous and gorgeous Portmaker, which she sold to and showed for Dr. Alvin I. Kay. Portmaker was the conformation hunter champion of America at the 1946 Garden and had been cleaning up on a heavy 1947 schedule by the end of the summer circuit, including winning the Hunter Championship at the prestigious Devon Horse Show.

In her sixties, Mrs. Greenhalgh hunted regularly and was a popular commentator on live television broadcasts of the National Horse Show. To get to the commentator's "crow's nest" just under the roof of the Garden, she gathered her long evening gown in one hand and climbed the rungs of the ladder with the other hand, undaunted by the height. Mrs. Greenhalgh was a witty and vivacious commentator. As a campaigner on the circuit, she knew all the horses, owners, and riders under her perch. On and off camera, when one of her horses entered the ring, she tensed and jumped every jump, letting out a whoop of joy if her horse had a good round. Back in Leesburg, the hometown crowd of horse-crazy young girls, fellow foxhunters, and folks who had lent support assembled in the few houses that had television sets to watch Jane's rides in black and white, called by Mama G.

Mrs. Greenhalgh saw that Jane's riding was smooth and trusting, and her horse responded in kind. In the fall of 1947, Mrs. Greenhalgh introduced herself to Jane, complimented her on her riding style, and suggested that Jane would make a wonderful match with Springsbury's horses.

Jane recognized this as the highest compliment that could be paid to her and Fitz. However, Jane had not considered riding for others. Responsibility for Portmaker's record would carry considerable pressure, in and out of the media, and Jane balked at the conflict of interest it might present. She told Marie she wanted to keep showing Fitz in both the jumper and the hunter divisions. She'd be showing Fitz against Marie's hunters.

"Of course," Mama G said. "You're free to bring him along to the shows in our van."

Jane accepted. The assistance afforded by Springsbury in transportation alone was significant. It would extend the number of shows available to Fitz and seemed well worth the extra work in riding Springsbury's horses. Besides, campaigning Portmaker and other top Greenhalgh hunters would be a thrill. As an amateur, Jane would be compensated only for travel expenses.

By this time, there were two other horses at Mauka. What had started as a companion horse for Fitz turned into a hunter prospect or two under Jane's training and intended for sale. When one sold, Jane found another to work with. Marie Greenhalgh purchased one of these, named Four Get, as a personal hunter.

One day in October 1947, climbing the ladder to the hayloft at Mauka to throw down a bale, Jane felt suddenly exhausted. She wondered if she was coming down with a bug. With three horses at her barn and working three of Springsbury's horses, there was no time to be sick, and she swept it from her consciousness. When Jane came to the house for lunch, Mother was already eating and reading the newspaper. She had laid a place at the table for Jane with what they always had for lunch: lettuce, cling peaches, and cottage cheese.

Jane took a bite and made a sour face. "Ugh. This cottage cheese is spoiled."

"No it's not," Mother replied. "I bought it today. Here, taste mine."

Jane sampled some of Mother's. "Yup, it's sour."

Mother looked a her suspiciously.

Jane overslept several times, unusual for her, but she blamed it on the heavy schedule at Springsbury and Mauka. Preparations at home were extensive: sewing suede patches to the inside of her breeches for better grip on the saddle, repairing tack, replacing tires on her trailer, and greasing its axle. There was often less than a week at home between shows. It would take a day just to clean the tack and launder the clothing, horse sheets, and shipping bandages. Jane's breeches and coats would have to be dry-cleaned. The day prior to shipping, she'd have to pack it all up. Jane was too busy to pay attention to her monthly cycles. From being lean and leading a strenuous athletic life, the cycles had always been irregular. Besides, she considered "female problems," as she called them, revolting.

When it dawned on Jane that she might be pregnant, the consequences were too drastic to deal with, and she delayed. Marriage to a man she knew was not right for her or ready for a family was a bleak prospect.

For Catholics, self-inflicted miscarriage or abortion was a mortal sin, guaranteeing an afterlife in agony. Pregnancy out of wedlock was a scandal avoided by a six-month absence to an out-of-state home for unwed mothers. There, the term of "pregnancy" was completed in secrecy, followed by adoption. The family generally covered it up as an extended visit in caring for a distant bedridden aunt. Jane feared Pop's scorn most.

Chores and riding became excuses to put off dealing with what loomed. Since childhood, riding had been a balm for Jane's troubles and an escape. *If I can still feel this good on a horse,* she reassured herself, *I can't be all bad.* Jane kept her secret and continued to avoid Dave. A part of her felt it was none of his business. The predicament was her fault, and she'd deal with it by herself, although she didn't yet know how.

Jane was conflicted over the physical and moral risks to the fetus from riding. Despite her Catholic upbringing, Jane hoped for an end to the pregnancy such that no one would ever know. She rationalized that the sin hinged on intent. She would not seek an abortion but was not averse to miscarriage. Intent was a gray area best not dwelled on.

Doctors' advice to pregnant women of the era was to continue their normal activities but not to attempt anything strenuous. In the horse community, many women continued to ride into their third trimester, although on quiet horses and at a walk. Jane had heard the wives' tale about bouncing on a horse's back to induce miscarriage and knew it to be drivel. Falling was another matter, and show jumping invited crippling falls. However, Jane believed the chance of injury was slim. She'd been hurt only once—the fall from Fitz on the Hale Kula parade ground—and that accident had been foreseeable.

Jane had made a commitment to Marie to show Springsbury's horses and to herself to campaign Fitz. If Fitz kept up his record, he could win the Virginia Horse Show Association's jumper of the year. Quitting now would invite scandal, as Jane could not think of a plausible alternative excuse to offer Marie or the press. There was only a month left to the end of the season; she'd stick it out.

Disaster struck at the Pennsylvania National Horse Show, held at the Farm Show Arena in Harrisburg. With Jane up, Portmaker won the lady's hunter class and took fourth in the Corinthian class, putting him solidly in the running for the Conformation Hunter Championship and its huge Pennsylvania Steel Challenge Trophy. However, he would have to continue to accumulate points to stay at the head of the pack. In the next class, the ladies' green hunters, Jane rode two horses for Springsbury Farm, one of which was Duke of Orange.

Mama G had recently purchased Duke of Orange, a good-looking gelding, as a show hunter prospect. The few other times Jane had ridden Duke, he seemed like an honest horse, and Jane had no reason to expect what came next.

Riding into a fake stone wall, Duke stood back, took off early, and landed on it. They both went down hard. The jump was demolished.

Jane fell flat on her back, the wind knocked out of her. Duke lay next to Jane on his side and raised his head to look over his shoulder at her. Jane was motionless, sucking for air in feeble wheezes. The 1,200-pound Duke then slowly rolled onto her, his hip over her chest. Pinned under him, Jane felt her ribs cracking. Seconds dragged on. The pain was excruciating, and she could not inhale. Jane believed that Duke actually intended to suffocate her. *Oh my God*, she thought, *this is the end.*

Mama G jumped over the rail from her box, falling several feet to the ring and splitting her Elsa Schiaparelli dress. Mama G and the ring-master grabbed Duke's hind legs and rolled his hindquarters off Jane. The ambulance rushed into the ring, and its crew carefully lifted Jane to a stretcher and loaded her into the ambulance. As Jane was taken from the ring, the bandleader, with a macabre sense of showman's humor, struck up the "Funeral March."

The doctor told her that the X-rays showed two cracked ribs. He taped her torso, put her arm in a sling, and told her not to ride for six weeks, emphasizing that another fall before the ribs healed could break one of them and puncture her lung. She did not tell the doctor that she might be three-months pregnant. Duke had missed her abdomen, but Jane shuddered in imagining what could have happened if the point of his hip had rolled into her one foot lower.

The horse show announcer called the hospital for a report. "We've just received word," the loudspeakers boomed in the stands, "Miss Pohl sustained two broken ribs in her fall in the ladies' green hunter class. She's going to be all right." The spectators applauded with relief.

The next morning, Jane found Mr. Greenhalgh in the show ground stables. She had spent the night thinking about the accident. In her years of riding, she had known a few horses who were malicious, but none of them were as premeditated as Duke in waiting for the right moment. He had taken her totally by surprise.

"I want to ride Portmaker today in his classes," Jane announced.

"Are you nuts?" George Greenhalgh asked. "Your arm's in a sling. You can hardly breathe, let alone move."

"Port's in line to win the Hunter Championship," she argued, "but he won't if he forfeits any of his classes. Besides, I don't want to dwell on what happened with Duke." Jumping was her life. She needed to replace doubt and fear with success.

Mr. Greenhalgh eventually threw his hands up.

Jane had herself taped like a mummy. Because of the pain, she rode Port with one arm. They won the ladies' hunter class, earning enough points to win the Conformation Hunter Championship and the Pennsylvania Steel Challenge Trophy.

"How did you do it?" New York horse show reporter Lester Rice asked her after the class. "Jumping with one arm, broken ribs, the pain?"

"He carried me around beautifully," she answered in clipped breaths. "I just sat on his back and hung on. He seemed to know I winced with pain every jump he took because friends watching told me he never traveled smoother."

From an uncredited newspaper clipping that Jane pasted in her scrapbook, "Jane had been dogged by bad luck since Harrisburg where Mrs. Greenhalgh's Duke of Orange fell in a green class and lay on her for what seemed like hours. Jane's polite, 'Please get up, Dukie,' is a phrase which will go down in show history."

Just three weeks after the accident, Jane rode in the 1947 National Horse Show at Madison Square Garden. Springsbury brought a van load of horses, Fitz among them.

Although still riding with taped ribs, Jane could inflate her lungs to almost full capacity without pain and had nearly complete use of her arm. She had kept the pregnancy secret, and the baby was not yet an athletic hindrance. Months earlier, she had entered Fitz in the National and committed to ride Mama G's horses in the hunter division. Having won on Port the day after the accident, the ribs would not be a plausible excuse for quitting. She was committed to building on her psychological recovery from the accident. The National was the last show of the season. After it was done, she told herself she would face the coming changes to her life.

Fifty-five horses entered the morning elimination for the open jumper class. She and Fitz qualified with a clean round. Then in the evening class at the next-to-the-last fence of the course, Fitzrada hit the crossed poles and nearly fell. Jane lost her stirrups, was thrown up on his neck, and suddenly had a choice to make. She could play it safe with her ribs and her baby by sliding off Fitz's neck to the soft tanbark before the last jump. But if she bailed out, they would be disqualified for not finishing the course.

Jane was certain to suffer a much harder fall by hanging on and jumping without stirrups. She briefly feared for her baby, but she had come this far and decided to try to make it over the last fence, the hog's back. The jump consisted of three poles with the near and far ones set at three feet six inches and the center pole set at four feet six inches. Out of position, wallowing far up on his neck as he set to jump, she grabbed Fitz's ears for handholds. The lurch of his jump lifted her, and by the time his front feet touched the ground, she was suspended above him without her stirrups and headed for the arena floor. Of those seconds, Jane later remembered being thankful that she was not entangled with Fitz and that there were no scattered poles waiting on the ground. The tanbark floor looked soft and deep, but she wondered if it was enough for the baby. Twisting in midair to protect her bad ribs, she fell in a heap. The jump crew helped her slowly to her feet and walked her from the ring. Inspecting herself, the injuries seemed to be limited to bruising on the shoulder and hip opposite the cracked ribs. She was relieved there was no abdominal pain.

The rules specified that the horse had to finish the course with its rider. It was not obvious whether Fitz had finished the course with Jane, but it was in Jane's favor that she fell on the far side of the last fence. The judges deliberated. There were cheers from the audience when they announced that Jane and Fitz had completed the course. But they had amassed ten and a half faults, far out of the ribbons. Fitz continued to go badly until the last day of the show.

The 1947 National is best remembered for the Conformation Hunter Championship. Portmaker, the defending champion, with Jane up, and Substitution, with Ellie Wood Keith up, battled to the last class. Toward the end of the week, Portmaker had sixteen and a half championship points to Substitution's fourteen. Lester Rice, reporter, approached Jane.

"You're doing a grand job," he said. "Portmaker's certain for the championship."

"Don't say that," Jane replied superstitiously. "You'll jinx him."

At the entry gate, Prompt Payment, the stablemate of Substitution, lashed out with a kick. Jane felt Port flinch and leaned to see a minor cut and no blood. Although he never put in a lame step, Portmaker knocked down many bars. Near the end of the show, Substitution pulled ahead by just two and a half points. The championship would be decided by the outcome of the $2,000 hunter stake the on final evening of the National Horse Show.

"Portmaker's the best mannered and most honest horse I've ever ridden," Lester Rice quoted Jane in his article for the New York papers. "By honest I mean he's always given everything he has in every class. Extremely well trained, he's the perfect ladies hunter because he's not in the least temperamental." It was a rare public display of confidence for Jane, but she was grateful to Port for renewing her confidence after the fall with Duke a month ago.

However, Portmaker's foreleg bruise filled with fluid. Before the hunter stake, Port flinched when the bruise was touched, and he was lame. Although scratched from the class, Portmaker had enough points for reserve champion.

The National was a long week for Jane. She was swept up in the excitement of riding for Springsbury and being recognized as one the top riders in the country. Jane now felt so comfortable in this community that she attempted a practical joke. "Honey" Craven was an affable man who had been the ringmaster at the National for almost twenty years. Each evening he walked to the center of the arena in the red coat and black silk top hat of an old English mail coach guard, raised his fifty-two-inch brass coach horn to his lips, and blew the call to start the venue. Jane remembered Jennet stuffing the reveille cannon at Schofield Barracks with toilet paper. When the MPs fired the cannon in the morning, the parade ground looked like the floor of a cotton mill. To Jennet's amusement, the MPs spent the day picking up nickel-sized fluff. Jane grinned at the thought of Honey, standing tall in his scarlet coat and black silk hat, slowly raising his gleaming brass horn to his lips for dramatic effect, puffing his cheeks to blow the call for the next class, and ejecting flimsy shards of toilet paper. But as the week wore on, anxiety over her pregnancy was hard to keep at bay, and she was tiring. She rode five horses for a total of over twenty classes, four times the workload of the previous year when she was a nobody.

On the last day, Fitz was entered in the $250 knock-down-and-out, a course that was one of the wickedest of the show and the same one used for the international military jumping class. Eight jumps from four feet three inches to five feet high were set with three reverses of direction. Among the fifty entries for the morning qualification were officers of the Army Horse Show Team. There were only three women, one of whom was the future Mrs. Robert Kennedy, Ethel Skakel.

Six horses went clean in the first round of the evening class, requiring a jump-off. Jane and Ethel Beck on Black Watch were the only women. At the end of the jump-off, first place was not resolved, and the jumps were raised to five feet six inches. Fitz again went through the entire course clean, and so did Black Watch—until the fifth jump in the last round, where Black Watch knocked down a rail. Jane considered this win to be one of the most significant of Fitz's entire career.

Ethel Beck also wore glasses, prompting *New York World Telegram* reporter George Coleman to write the following in his article "Surprises Abound in 1947 National": "Two equestriennes, Jane Pohl and Ethel Beck, both looking more like librarians, battled the top horsemen in the country to finish one-two respectively in the knock-down-and-out jumping."

Jane was invited by fellow competitors to a Broadway play that started shortly after the class ended. She anxiously covered her exposed bruises with makeup and rushed to change into a dress. Tomorrow she would pack for the trip back to Virginia. The thought seized her that this might be her last National. The baby was coming.

In the taxi and during the first act, she imagined herself as an old woman with fading memories of what it felt like to be a part of this, to soar over fences in front of 15,000 people on the best horse that ever lived. "You only get one good horse in a lifetime," Cappy used to say. She was startled by the audience's laughter and realized she was missing the play.

During intermission, Jane sipped a cocktail, smoked, and laughed at stories of shared humiliation and practical jokes on the show circuit, such as the recent stuffing of Honey Craven's horn. But somebody had tipped off Honey, so the National was spared. Nobody admitted to being the rat, but there was finger-pointing and feigned ignorance surrounding Jane in the lobby.

When the audience was settled for the next act, the house lights dimmed. A lone spotlight found center stage. Then the stage manager stepped through the curtain into the spot. He wore a tuxedo with a black cummerbund. The light bleached his starched shirtfront. He smiled, waiting for absolute silence.

"Ladies and Gentlemen," he announced with a magnanimous spread of his arm toward the balcony, "Tonight we are honored to have in our audience," he paused, "the winner of the difficult knock-down-and-out class at the National Horse Show—Miss Jane Pohl. The class was decided earlier tonight in a spectacular jump-off."

The spot moved from center stage to Jane's seat. Jane froze in panic. The crowd applauded, and some women stood to honor her. Jane's buddies pushed her to her feet, where she smiled meekly before sitting down quickly.

Something about it seemed final to her, like the end of a journey. Later in life, when younger horse people asked about her career, she'd say, "I used to ride in the 1940s," and offered nothing further.

For Fitz it had been a banner year. Since his first show in Hawaii six years ago, Jane had been ironing Fitz's ribbons after each show and storing them carefully in old suitcases she kept under her bed. Once a year she renewed the mothballs in the suitcases. Pop found a used mahogany display box, fixed it up, and gave it to her. It had a hinged glass front and was so big that two people were needed to lift it. Jane strung wires inside the box so that eight rows of ribbons could be hung behind the glass. It quickly filled to capacity. To make room, Jane removed all but the blue ribbons and the tricolor (championship) ribbons. Based on his ribbons in 1947, Fitz was named the Virginia Horse Show Association's champion jumper of the year. Considering the consistency required to win it and the jumping talent in Virginia, it could be argued that Fitz was the best jumper in America. However, Jane was about to face a challenge demanding more patience and self-sacrifice than taming a rogue horse.

13

SHOTGUN WEDDING

Within a week of returning home from Madison Square Garden, Jane sat at the kitchen table, smoking a cigarette and staring blankly at the ashtray in front of her. Mother poured a jigger of Coca-Cola syrup from a half-gallon jug and dumped it into a glass of ice. She carefully squirted seltzer water into the glass until it was full and stirred the fizzing mixture with an ice-tea spoon.

"Would you like a Coke?" she asked.

"I'm pregnant," Jane replied.

"Oh, Jane," was all Mother said. She placed a sympathetic hand on her daughter's shoulder. In the silence, Jane grabbed Mother's hand and started crying. There was little relief in sharing the secret. The baby would be here in less than six months. She didn't know where she would live or how she would raise a child alone.

"We'll have to tell your father," Mother said with a sigh.

"I'll tell him," Jane said, pulling an old tissue from her pocket. It came out in a frayed ball. She dabbed her cheeks and blew her nose.

"You want me there?" Mother patted Jane's shoulder.

"No, that's okay," Jane replied. "I better get him early in the day before he gets started drinking. This isn't gonna make him any happier."

The night passed slowly with Jane anticipating her father's wrath. After breakfast the next morning, Jane found Papa reading the paper in his study. She closed the door behind her.

"Papa, I don't know how to say this, so I'll just say it: I'm pregnant."

"Who?" His response was immediate, and his voice was hard. "Dave Rust?"

Jane nodded.

"Does he know?" Pop clenched a fist.

"No, and I don't want him to," Jane said. "It was a mistake. I'll take care of it."

"How? If you get an abortion, you're a murderer in the eyes of the Church. My eyes, too."

Jane stared at the floor, and he didn't wait for her reply.

"Adoption?" His rage was building. "No! You'll make this right."

Pop went to the hall for his coat, and she followed him.

"Papa, please don't go over there."

"What you want has got no sway here," he said. "You gave that up when you had *relations* with him."

Two hours later, Jane was lying on her bed, fully clothed, when she heard his tires crunching down the driveway's gravel. A rosary, an empty glass of water, and an ashtray full of cigarette butts kept her company. She chided herself for turning to God only when she was in need. Pop's tread sounded weary coming up the kitchen steps. The screen door twanged open and shut with a slam.

"Jane! Mother! Come here," he ordered. He gestured for them to sit at the dining room table. He remained standing and stared at Jane. "I spoke with Dave's father." There was no emotion in Pop's voice. "You'll marry his son at the justice of the peace's house on Tuesday. You'll need a blood test and your birth certificate."

"But Papa," Jane protested.

He held up his palm for quiet.

"You *will* marry him on Tuesday. His father said he'll keep him on as a farmhand, till he can find a job. Although Mr. Rust acted like his son wasn't willing or able to find better work. Said you two could stay over the garage, and he wouldn't charge rent."

Jane was twenty-three years old and living under her father's roof. Filial and Catholic duty had been ingrained from childhood. She remembered a plea from the Cadet Prayer: "Give me the strength to choose the harder right over the easier wrong." Jane nodded in acceptance of his order.

"You're marrying into a tough outfit," Pop grunted, "but that's the way it is. There will be no announcements."

U

On the morning of her wedding, Jane fed Fitz and lingered in his stall.

"I'm going to be late," she told him, "for my . . . what would you call it? It's not a wedding. I'm going to be late for my 'appointment' with the justice of the peace."

Upstairs in her room, she put on a Sunday suit and pair of black shoes. Jane drove herself to town, dawdling along the dirt roads like a lost tourist. She tried to savor the country views and not to think about a bleak future.

Hope I don't run into John Royston on his mail route, Jane prayed. *He'll want to stop and talk.*

Dave was standing beside his car in front of the justice's house when she pulled up. He wore a brown suit and a carefree smile and held a small bouquet of rosebuds for her. Jane felt awkward but was buoyed by Dave's comfortable style. They had known each other less than seven months.

As they walked into the justice's parlor, his wife sat ready in a starched dark blue dress with her fingers poised on the keyboard of an upright piano. She bobbed her head and began playing the wedding march. The ceremony concluded with Jane signing her name to the certificate. She and Dave pecked on the lips. The justice of the peace and his wife watched with sentiment as the new couple walked to their separate cars.

"Shall we go home?" Dave asked with a kind smile.

She followed him to the apartment over his father's garage. He had cleared the books and tack from the chairs, but much remained on the floor. A bottle of champagne and two glasses waited on the card table used for dining. He served her, held up his glass to eye level, and puffed out his chest.

"To us," he said cheerfully.

"To us," she replied. It occurred to her these were the first words she had spoken to him all day. Her vow to love, honor, cherish, and obey until death's parting had been addressed to the justice.

Dave offered to refill her glass.

"No," she said. "I'm going home to change clothes. Then we're going to clean this place up."

When she got back, the bottle was empty, and Dave was gone. Four hours later he pulled his car up to piles of loosely sorted debris in front of his father's garage.

"Hey, Baby!" he called, jogging up the stairs cheerfully, "Why didn't you wait? I would've helped you."

"I did wait," she said tersely.

"Hey, you're the one that didn't want to celebrate," he defended. "Couple of the boys came by to congratulate us. Hauled me off for a few drinks. Nothing I could do."

Jane was holding a stack of magazines with both arms.

"Here, let me take those," he said. "Have to feed Father's horses. Come right back to help. Okay?"

She handed him the stack and followed him down the stairs with another.

The next morning she left him sleeping and searched the kitchen. There was nothing but a loaf of bread in the refrigerator. She served him black coffee, toast, and oatmeal for breakfast. He smiled at the two place settings.

"I'm gonna like being married," he said, stretching happily. "Normally, I have my breakfast at the house with my mother. She makes me a sack lunch, and I eat with the farmhands. But now," he grinned, "I'll come home and eat with my *wife*." Jane did the breakfast dishes and went to Mauka to feed the horses.

After the accident at Harrisburg, Jane had told Marie she wouldn't ride Duke again because he'd know she was afraid of him and take advantage of it. But a man from Chicago inquired about buying Duke, and Mrs. Greenhalgh begged Jane to show the horse to him. Jane reluctantly agreed on the condition that the fences were small and she wouldn't let him out of a trot. During his warm-up just before the arrival of the buyer, Duke set up for the same stunt he had pulled at Harrisburg. Jane pulled him up hard as soon as he started to collect himself for his early leap, aborting the jump. During the demonstration for the buyer, he started to do it again. Jane snatched him and kicked him hard. He hesitated but put in the extra stride and cleared the little fence. Jane was glad to see him loaded for shipment to Chicago. For Christmas, the Greenhalghs sent Jane a present. Marie's note thanked Jane for her wins with Springsbury's horses. Jane unwrapped a heavy gold bracelet.

In the weeks after the wedding, Jane heard relief in Pop's voice, no doubt from the change in her title to *Mrs*. Jane took this as an apology for the cold way it had happened, but Pop never asked about Dave, and Jane didn't volunteer any information, knowing it would be rubbing salt into a wound. However, she told Mother about Dave's progress with his father's horses and farm chores. The news was initially spoken with the optimistic pride of a newlywed. Mother gave Jane cardboard boxes of spare linen and cookery.

Dave ate Jane's elementary dishes heartily. Seated on the other side of the card table from him, she broached their future.

"The baby'll be here by summer," she said. "Have you thought about a job?"

"Got a job," Dave said between bites. "Got a place to stay."

"It's too small for three," Jane said, more as a suggestion than a demand.

"This is my home." He waved his napkin toward the big stone house he grew up in. "I don't want to move."

The time Jane and Dave spent together dwindled. Increasingly, his supper sat cold on the table late at night as he crept uneasily by it, shoes in hand. He had the hiccups and giggled at trying to keep them quiet. Exhausted from her day, Jane did not wake.

Jane found relief from the impasse in her chores at Mauka. At the barn, she could forget the present in one-sided conversation with Fitz about their past, when things were simple. Jane remembered the same anxiety on the voyage to Hawaii nine years ago, when she dreaded the future. But then, that future had delivered Fitz to her, and she hoped for a similar deliverance in maternity. Richard's wife, Anne, was expecting their first child. Jane rode Fitz casually around the pasture, envisioning a fulfilling role as a mother helping her child to a bright life surrounded with animals and cousins. Her eye traced the Blue Ridge down the cut of Snicker's Gap. Turkey buzzards idled over the Valley of Virginia below her. She felt fit and, in a way, honored to introduce a baby to such a beautiful place. The wind suggested spring and brought the rising shrill of the noon siren from the Purcellville fire station, ten miles up the valley. Jane checked her watch, estimating how many more hours she could delay returning to Dave's place. Dave warmly accepted his friends' congratulations on impending fatherhood but continued to dismiss Jane's misgivings about their housing and finances.

As Jane's belly got bigger, she used the stone wall buttressing the earthen ramp to the barn for mounting and dismounting. She would walk up the wall's incline, leading Fitz on the flat below the ramp. When the saddle was well below her and Fitz was dead still, she'd push her knee across the cantle and find her seat and stirrups. Riding was her sanity, and the old horse seemed aware of her condition, moving with deliberate care. Still, she did not push her luck by jumping, and over the next months, she restricted herself to walking. Working in the barn, Jane felt no strain in mucking stalls, climbing the ladder to the loft, and throwing down thirty-pound bales of hay.

Jennet dropped out of college and came to Mauka, waiting for her future husband to graduate from West Point in June. They planned a ceremony in the Catholic church in Leesburg with a reception at Mauka. Jane would be a maid of honor. With men of their own, neither sister laid a primary claim on Pop's affection, and sibling rivalry relaxed. Both sisters' impending events were a source of family pride, although Jane felt regret that her shotgun marriage precluded a church wedding and that Pop shared pistols and cameras with Jennet's cadet but avoided Dave.

Jane wanted to keep Fitz in work so that he could return to the show ring as soon as she recovered from childbirth. Olympic tryouts for civilians would likely be held with little advance notice. If Fitz went soft at his age, it might take six weeks to get him back in shape. Jane was confident her body would need less time. But without help, his work could not begin until she was healed, and they might be out for ten weeks after the baby was born.

In Jane's opinion, Jennet was the best candidate for Fitz's conditioning. From Fitz's army experiences, Jane did not want to risk a setback by asking a man, although Dave was qualified. Jennet was living at Mauka, affording barn time for Fitz and Jennet to get to know each other, and giving Jane absolute control over the training. A more experienced rider might resent Jane's micromanagement. Jennet had jumped low fences in the junior hunter classes at Schofield Barracks but had not ridden much in the seven years since. Nonetheless, she was fit, full of nervous energy waiting for her wedding, and taking on household projects at Mauka as if they were dares.

Uncharacteristically, Jennet hesitated when Jane asked her to ride Fitz. Jennet remembered helping Jane undress on returning from the hospital after the incident on the Hale Kula parade ground. The front of Jane's blouse was entirely soaked in clotting blood. Jane's face was unrecognizable from the swelling of the broken nose and two black eyes.

"Is he still . . . ?" Jennet asked, referring to Fitz's disposition.

"He's fine, so long as you don't get in any fights with him," Jane replied. "Guide with your legs and let him do the rest. If he says no, you've got to respect him."

They started with flat work, an hour a day, walking up and down the steep pasture for conditioning and trotting for balance. Jane corrected Jennet's posture and leg position, insisting that Jennet visualize and maintain Fitz precisely in a straight line or an equal-radius turn. There was a gleam in the old horse's eyes. He carried his head high and pricked his ears forward with interest. He knew the drills and cooperated willingly, glad to be working again. Jennet acted like she was riding a barrel of nitroglycerine, so she welcomed Jane's instruction, and there was no need to tell her to be gentle with her legs and hands. In fact, Jane had to push Jennet to use her legs firmly and early, as Jane did, in holding Fitz to a route. At supper, the family happily discussed progress and commiserated with Jennet over her sore muscles, not yet used to riding. It was the rare time the sisters would collaborate as a team without jealousy.

Steve Canty, the blacksmith, came to Mauka at the end of April to shoe Fitz. Jane was due in a week, maybe two, and held Fitz on a shank for Steve. Jennet was in town shopping for the wedding.

"Smuggling a melon under your shirt?" Steve teased. "Why don't you go lie down?"

Jane took the ribbing as a challenge and decided to show him—and herself—that she was stronger than ever from carrying her baby and working in the barn, relaying buckets of water and bales of hay, sometimes with one in each hand. When Steve was packing up to go home, he turned away from her while folding up his leather apron. Jane took a deep breath, squatted to cradle his eighty-pound anvil in her arms, lifted it smoothly from its portable stand, and hobbled toward his truck. When he discovered her, she was a step away from her goal, the truck's tailgate.

"What the *hell* do you think you're doing?" he yelled.

As she hoisted the anvil to the tailgate with a grunt, her water broke. She felt a rush of warm fluid running down her legs. The rest of her went cold with fear that she'd hurt her baby. A puddle spread from her feet, and she was horrified at how big it was.

"Don't you move!" Steve screamed. He dropped his apron and ran to find Mother.

Jane propped herself against the truck, waiting to be taken to the hospital. Her knees started shaking from anxiety. She didn't know how long the baby could survive without a placenta but was certain it couldn't be long. Looking down at the puddle, she cursed herself for being so stupid. *No pain and no blood*, she said to reassure herself. *That's a good sign, I think.*

Without complications, she gave birth to a son the next day, May 1, and named him Richard, after her brother.

Pop filmed Jane's return from the hospital. In Mauka's yard, she held her sleeping son in her arms and beamed broadly. In the ensuing weeks, the three women switched off washing baby bottles, mixing formula, feeding, and changing. Pop monopolized his grandson, bouncing the baby on his knee, embellishing eyewitness accounts of Army football games past, and selling the infant on West Point.

"Got a stout midriff," Pop said holding the baby up, cloth diapers sagging. He appraised his wiggling offspring at arms length as if the child were a fine painting. "You gonna wrestle for the Golden Knights of the Hudson like your old grandpa? Let's see, you'd be in the class of 1970." Pop's drinking slowed when the baby was available for him to court. Jane felt that Pop was making up for lost time, having put his career ahead of his own children when they were little and regretting it in retirement.

The front yard was the only area on the mountainside farm flat enough to set up jumps. Pop cut the yard with a reel mower. Its temperamental engine made a racket that rattled loose windows in their old house. The family's two young Dalmatian dogs, Sweetie and Snitch, chased the mower tirelessly up and down the lawn, barking and baiting it as if it were a groundhog, their favorite quarry.

With Fitz's shipping bandages drying among cotton diapers on the clothesline behind them, the two sisters set up Richard's playpen in the shade. Jane sat in a folding chair, and for an hour, twice a day, Jennet schooled Fitz over small jumps. Jane's instruction stressed steady and smooth. In the course of two weeks, Jennet was comfortably jumping Fitz three feet. Jane asked Jennet if she would ride Fitz in the Loudoun Hunt Horse Show, little more than a week away. Without hesitation, Jennet said yes. The show was held at Ross Lipscomb's lavish Thoroughbred breeding farm, Raspberry Plain, near Leesburg. Mr. Lipscomb erected a beautiful ring and an outside course for the show.

At the "In" gate for the knock-down-and-out class, Jane reached up to pat Fitz on the neck and then Jennet on the knee. It was good to see the old horse fit and ready to go into the ring. Jennet was fidgeting.

"Just have a good time," Jane advised her, "and let him do his job."

Jane watched from the rail. She anticipated the jumps and rode in pantomime with her sister, squeezing her legs, clenching her fingers. Fitz won the knock-down-and-out class, beating Greenhalgh's Flying

Dutchman, who was second. Then Fitz was second in the warm-up jumping class and fourth in the Jumper Sweepstake behind Flying Dutchman. But the feature class of the show was the Master's Challenge Bowl, open to hunters from Loudoun Hunt who had won a blue ribbon at the current Loudoun Horse Show. Fitz won it, and Jennet could not believe her luck. But Jane was overjoyed for a deeper reason. The entry of horse and rider is only as good as the weakest link. But if the rider stays on course, more than half the outcome is dependent on the horse. The win proved to Jane that Fitz was willing to trust others and not take advantage of a less experienced rider. She was gratified that his rogue temper was healed and that, physically, he was back to his previous form. It only remained for Jane to get in shape, and they both could return to the ring.

In the days just before Jennet's wedding, Jane fitted the bridesmaids into their dresses while they stood in turn on a box beside the sewing machine in her old bedroom. Jane was the tallest of them. Anticipating Pop's scorn, Dave did not come to the wedding. Six lieutenants, dressed in new tan uniforms, formed an arch of sabers over the church steps as Jennet and her husband, also in tan, descended. As is the custom at military weddings, the cutting edges faced skyward to protect the new couple from harm, and the last saber bearer whopped Jennet on the butt with the flat of his saber. "Welcome to the Air Corps, Mrs. Spillers," he said, and bystanders clapped.

The reception was at Mauka. Thirteen-year-old Gail Graham, the daughter of a horse-dealer neighbor and friend, babysat Richard in her Sunday dress, too shy to mingle with the guests drinking and laughing in groups on the flagstone patio. Jane was struck by the flower arrangements in the church and at Mauka. It was a stark contrast to her own ceremony, where her bouquet from Dave was the sole decoration. Jane posed for pictures with Jennet's wedding party. There were no photos from Jane's ceremony and no arch of sabers as she had fantasized as a little girl, planning her own wedding. At Jennet's reception, there was exuberance, family, and friends. But Jane was not overtly given to regret. She had a beautiful healthy baby son. She would play the hand that was dealt without rancor.

Shielding their giddy faces from a shower of rice, Jennet and Harry departed for a honeymoon in Mexico and then reported to their first duty station, San Antonio, for Harry's flight training. Jane was sad to see her go.

In June, five weeks after giving birth, Jane was back in the saddle. In July, she returned to the circuit with a large load, showing Fitz and five of Springsbury's horses in both the hunter and the jumper division. Mother or Gail Graham took care of Richard while Jane traveled to the shows, which usually amounted to a few overnights every two weeks.

Fitz went to the National at Madison Square Garden with Springsbury's horses. Although Jane was a seasoned and respected veteran, she and Fitz were not favorites to win the jumper classes. Fitz was now eighteen, twice the age of most of his competitors, and until recently in the season, he had not done well.

In the open jumping class, Fitz refused the Liverpool (a low wooden barrier in front of a high brush fence) twice. A third refusal would eliminate him. Cappy, having finished his round in the same class, stood by the gate observing Jane and saw the problem. As a pretext to talk to Jane, he quickly asked the ringmaster if he could enter the ring to fix Jane's stirrup. The ringmaster did not question Cappy, announced a delay for tack safety, and motioned Cappy through the gate. Jane was puzzled at the interruption. Cappy walked straight to her with a determined swagger. In silence, he abruptly removed her boot from the stirrup and adjusted her stirrup leather's length from one hole to another and then back again. The audience was silent, watching to discover what the problem was. Jane looked down at him waiting for an explanation. Cappy kept his eyes focused on his hands.

"You're throwing him away at the fence," he said softly, so as not to be overheard. "Keep contact on his mouth and drive him to it with your legs." Cappy abruptly turned and walked back to the gate. Jane circled to approach the fence at a trot and pushed Fitz to a canter. Heeding Cappy's advice, she kept her legs into him and held a feel of his mouth in the reins. Fitz sailed over the fence with a foot to spare, but his previous refusals placed him out of the ribbons.

After the touch-and-out class, Jane returned Fitz to his stall in the basement of the Garden, threading him through aisles clogged with owners, riders, and grooms braiding manes and tails, feeding, and mucking. Jane put Fitz in his stall, stripped him of his tack, and put a sheet on him to keep him from cooling too quickly. She removed the cardboard entry number tied around her waist and her derby, jacket, and hairnet. Out of the hot clothing, she rolled up the sleeves on her blouse and set to work. Returning from the spigot with a bucket full of water for Fitz, she minced her way back through the jam. A nondescript middle-aged gentleman in a tweed jacket stepped toward her with a sketch pad under his arm.

"I've been admiring your horse," the stranger said without introducing himself. "Would you mind if I sketched him?"

Jane hung the bucket in Fitz's stall, removed the sheet from his back, led him out, and backed him a step or two to get his hooves in the classic profile pose (legs on the side closest to the artist further apart than those behind). The man sketched in pencil, glancing frequently from Fitz to his pad. After a minute, the man held up his half-finished sketch for Jane to see. She immediately recognized the economy of line and elegant style of the artist. In addition to authoring and illustrating numerous children's horse books, his work was prominent in advertisements for Brooks Brothers clothes, wall calendars, note cards, and stationery. He'd never owned or ridden a horse, but no photograph could equal his dead-on disclosure of horses' personalities through their eyes, ears, and body language.

"You're Paul Brown!" she gushed in amazement. "I've collected your drawings and books since I was a little girl."

Years later, the sketches arrived in the mail. They were exquisite. With them was a note requesting some photos of Fitz that Paul might use to paint watercolors. He wrote, "After the holidays I felt like a tired horse which is pulled up in the stretch and then finds he has to get going. So—instead of turning to things I wasn't anxious to start on I turned to pleasant things—memories of you and Fitz and tried my poor hand at the impressions I've always wanted to do of two great competitors." Paul said he intended to write a book about Fitz, but he died before Jane saw any drafts, so she never knew if he started it.

By the beginning of 1948, the dismantling of the U.S. horse cavalry and horse artillery was in progress. Thirty-thousand horses and mules wearing the U.S. brand had been put up for sale. Most went to productive use. Those too old or injured went to rendering plants. No organization was forthcoming in sponsoring a team for the 1948 Olympics in London, so General Eisenhower convinced President Truman to keep the Army Equestrian Team through the 1948 Olympics so that the United States could be represented.

The demise was bittersweet for Jane. The army stables she and Fitz knew were being converted into warehouses and motor pools. Fort Robinson would be closed. The military horsemen she had idolized and learned from were reassigned to other duties. However, Jane was relieved that tryouts for a civilian team would be put off until well after she had recovered from childbirth.

The last Army Olympic Team, comprised largely of veterans from previous Olympics, won team gold and individual silver in the Three-Day event and team silver in dressage. Army teams over the course of seven Olympiads from 1912 to 1948 earned eleven medals, and two were team gold. Today, the last remaining vestige of the army's horses consists of the dozen at Fort Myer used to pull the caisson for state funerals.

14

THE WAY OUT

Folks on the street plying Dave for news about Jane and Fitz in 1949 often knew more than he did just from the papers. "I have to work for a living," he'd say, explaining his absence from the shows. At night, he paused with fascination to watch the alien baby wiggling in the crib. He was proud to have met his duty to his ancestors in continuing the family name, but he felt ill prepared to shoulder his millstone.

Dave couldn't find the initiative to break free of his father's farm to start a life with his new family. His mother blamed Jane for the paralysis that sapped her son, although for the old woman it was a blessing. She dreaded the life that awaited her in an empty nest with her cold husband. Dave felt the implied obligation. He was her youngest child and the last living at home.

In the mornings, Jane descended the garage apartment's outdoor staircase to the car with her baby in one arm and a bag full of diapers and bottles in the other. Jane imagined the old woman staring at her from the big house, seated formally alone at the kitchen table with a cup of tepid tea and the ticktock echoing from the tall ancestral clock in her parlor.

Jane gave up trying to coerce Dave into moving out and getting a better job, but she knew their marriage depended on it. His casual dismissal of her concerns made her angry. If he was drinking and she pushed him hard, he'd lose his temper. She preferred distance to confrontation, unconsciously accepting the stalemate. He got the message and spent his spare time with his friends.

Jane was essentially living at Mauka, all but sleeping there. As for Dave's ability to assert himself as husband and head of household, Gail Graham, who babysat Richard, would say years later that *Jane was too strong for him.* Jane's strength was demonstrative on the show circuit, but at home it was passively resistant in avoiding Dave, and both undermined his self-esteem. Dave wanted a doting wife in his mother's mold, but Jane felt revulsion and pity for his mother and her role. Meanwhile, the old woman gratefully coddled her son. Dave's father viewed the situation as a triangle of weaklings.

For eight years Jane had been hunting Fitz, believing it was a good diversion from the tension of shows. Hunting offered to horses what they liked to do—run over open country in a herd. Fitz was at home in the hunting field, unusual for a show jumper, many of whom were volatile to the point of being uncontrollable. Most owners would not risk valuable show horses to injury by galloping them over unprepared ground with hidden dangers, such as groundhog holes, hornet's nests, and coils of scrap barbed wire. But Jane had confidence in Fitz's horse sense, and retreating from a failing marriage, she found liberation in the thrill of the chase and the serene beauty of the countryside.

One morning in the early spring, Jane hacked Fitz through the woods and down the mountain from Mauka to the Glebe Plantation for a meet with Loudoun Hunt. A subtle green tinge to the dormant gray forests across the valley showed that the trees were thinking about budding. Jane was cold but hoped for good hunting where the exertion would generate warmth. The ground was moist, the sky was overcast, and there was no wind, ideal conditions for holding a scent. The hounds seemed to know and were eager. In the spring when foxes are breeding, dog (male) foxes roam far looking for a mate. Everyone was hopeful for a long run in pursuing one back to his home territory. By midmorning the hounds struck a fresh scent on the southern end of the Glebe. The fox ran consistently south without a check to catch his breath, indicating he was a stranger to this country and eager to return to land he knew and could use to advantage. As twilight descended, the fox found a den and went to ground near Aldie (nine miles distant as the crow flies and probably more than twice that distance riding to hounds). Never before or since has Loudoun Hunt had such a run. The hounds clamored at the hole to dig him out. The staff called the hounds off, sparing him in hopes he would lead them again on another day. It was near midnight when those few who had not tired and pulled out earlier returned to the Glebe. Even horses in the best condition were spent.

Jane thanked Hunton Atwell, the master, for a grand day and said good-bye to the remaining saddle-weary hunters loading their horses by headlights. It was so late that Jane thought it would be an imposition to ask for a lift in someone else's van and decided to ride Fitz back home. She had a choice: four miles up the mountain on the route they had come or twelve miles if she stuck to the roads. In the interest of saving time, Jane opted for the shorter route, uphill through two big pastures and then on a trail through the woods to reach the road that ran along the mountain's spine to Mauka. The sky was still overcast, and no moon or stars could be seen. Despite the poor visibility, she was confident in Fitz's inborn sense of direction, especially when heading home.

In the Glebe's pasture, she unknowingly walked straight into the open end of a cow barn that was built on a bank. The barn floor was earthen and sloped upward with the hill to meet the ceiling on the uphill end. The height from floor to ceiling decreased with every step forward.

Jane hit her head on a ceiling joist. Thinking she was outdoors, she assumed that it was a tree limb, so she bent forward over Fitz's withers and urged him to continue. In the next stride, her shoulders were pushed into Fitz's neck by the ceiling. She still could not figure out what had happened, but backward was the only alternative. In backing Fitz out of the barn, she recognized where she was. The odds of threading such an unforeseen needle were incredibly remote. She shuddered at what might have happened if he had reared or wheeled in that trap or if they had been trotting instead of walking.

Moving up the mountain in the pitch black, Fitz came to an abrupt halt and would not move forward. Jane sensed from him that something was wrong and leaned forward in the saddle to run her hand down his chest. She touched the top strand of a barbed-wire fence. He stood immobile with his chest pressed into the fence, waiting for her direction. Jane prayed that he had not put a hoof through, as it would be impossible to see how to extricate a leg from tangled wire in the dark. She backed him without incident and turned parallel with the fence to find a gate so that they could climb higher on the mountain.

It was an arduous, nerve-racking climb. Sometimes Fitz scrambled on slick rocks he could not see and tripped over fallen trees, but Jane stayed centered on him and he found his feet. They were often hit in the chest, legs, and face by branches. If the limb was high enough for him to pass under, it caught her in the chest, almost sweeping her off his back. He sensed this when it happened and stood still while she recovered and asked him to back up. He was bone weary from the long hunt and should have been short tempered. Yet he kept his head, a seasoned veteran compared to the wild animal she hunted at Vassar eight years ago. His patience and understanding of calamity reminded Jane of how he had surprised her in the quicksand at Fort Bragg, and she was reassured.

They arrived home just before dawn, exhausted. Under the bare lightbulb in the barn's aisle, he stood untied, head bowed, and eyelids drooping and did not flinch at the stings as she dabbed his cuts with wads of sheet cotton dipped in gentian violet antiseptic. Snippets of the day replayed in Jane's head: galloping headlong down pastures musty with last year's decaying grass and the promise of new growth, steam shooting from horses' nostrils, splashing through creeks in single file with skim ice clinging to the shaded shore, and riders' reddened faces intent on the ground ahead. The memories brought Jane a feeling of euphoria that she hoped would linger to distract her from the disappointments of marriage.

Entering a dozen shows during 1949, Fitz and Jane won eight tricolored ribbons (championships or reserve championships), equally divided between the hunter and jumper divisions. She was also Springsbury's lady jockey for twelve tricolored ribbons in the hunter divisions.

On the circuit, some owners asked her to ride just one horse in one class. The only experience she might have had with the horse would be the warm-up immediately preceding the class. As an amateur, Jane was free to ride for whomever she wished. She considered it an honor to be asked and often accepted in the spirit of sportsmanship to help a good horse build a record, out of curiosity about the ability of these other horses, and for the fun of it. With these "pickup" rides, she sometimes rode for multiple owners in the same class and sometimes against Fitz. This led to her riding famous jumpers owned by legends in the horse community, such as Paul Fout's buckskin mare Golden Chance.

At the Loudoun Hunt Horse Show, Fitz won $74 in prize money, enough for several months of oats, but the thrill was in taking the Master's Challenge Bowl for the second year in a row; the last time was with Jennet up. General George C. Marshall of World War II fame, author of the Marshall Plan, and the current secretary of state, presented the bowl to Jane.

After the local newspaper coverage of the win, Pop wrote to the editor of Leesburg's *Loudoun Times-Mirror*, "[I want] to express our thanks for the complimentary articles you have written on 'Fitzrada' and for the kind words he has received from his many friends in Loudoun. . . . Behind that story on the front page of your paper last week there were eight years of Jane's sweat, a few tears, and even a little blood. . . . When Jane first took 'Fitzrada' to Madison Square Garden three years ago, she painted 'LEESBURG, Va.' on her tack box in big white letters, and the box has gone to a lot of shows since then. 'Fitzrada' belongs to Leesburg and Loudoun."

A string of bad luck ensued. At Altoona, Pennsylvania, Fitz lost the Jumper Championship by one hind tick, costing half a fault. But he won the Working Hunter Championship over Betty Bosley's Count Stefan. Altoona's spectators were astounded to see Fitz entered in both divisions, let alone placing. The rivalry with Count Stefan would continue at the Garden that year, playing out with a human twist. At Berryville, because of a miscount of championship points, Fitz tied for reserve jumper champion with Circus Rose (who would win the 1950 Jumper Championship at the Garden and go on to win a bronze medal at the 1952 Olympics under the name Miss Budweiser) and lost the coin toss. At Middleburg, Jane lost two coin tosses yet had enough points to tie for the Jumper Championship, which was settled by another coin toss, and Fitz lost.

In August at the Ohio State Fair, Fitz's luck changed, and he won every class he entered except one, where he was second. Then at Bellwood, Pennsylvania, the knock-down-and-out class was finally decided after four jump-offs to five feet six inches where Fitz was second to Black Watch, who, like Fitz, had been recognized by the press as having potential for the first civilian U.S. Olympic team.

Jane was in her element on the circuit, happily distracted from a fading marriage. At the conclusion of Bellwood show, Jane's seamstress skills were responsible for a joke. As a pickup ride, Jane rode Paul Fout's famous jumper, Golden Chance. The last class was the *bareback* working hunter class over the long course outside the ring, simulating the terrain and jumps of foxhunting. Jane rode in her Corinthian coat and silk hat, wearing loafers instead of boots for better grip without a saddle. Golden Chance was also informally dressed. From an uncredited clipping in Jane's scrapbook: "The crowd was hysterical as [the mare] plopped out over the hedge jump onto the outside course clad in pajamas and a nightcap. She must have been tired too because she had a black circle around each eye." Fifty-six years later, in researching this book, the author sent Paul a copy of the article and a photo of his horse in costume. Paul wrote in response, "Golden Chance was my first good horse. . . . What fun we had back then."

At Madison Square Garden, Jane entered nineteen-year-old Fitz in six hunter classes and one open jumping class. Substitution, ridden by Ellie Wood Keith, and Betty Bosley's Count Stefan, the Pennsylvania working hunter champ, were going like well-oiled machines. Despite a first- and two second-place ribbons, Fitzrada was far behind them both in points, but luck intervened. The last class, the $1,000 Working Hunter Stake, would decide the Working Hunter Championship of America between Count Stefan and Substitution. But Betty overslept and arrived at the Garden to discover that her horse was still at the Squadron A Armory stabled with the overflow. She watched from the sidelines as Fitz took second place to Substitution, giving Fitz enough points for reserve working hunter champion of America. Had Betty not forfeited her possible points, Count Stefan probably would have beaten Fitz for reserve.

By the end of 1949, women had earned their place in U.S. show rings. From Jeanne Hoffman's article for the *Sunday American*, "Girls Risk Limbs for Show Honors": "New York, Nov. 26 [1949]: The National Horse Show at Madison Square Garden proves for all time that jokes about women as 'back seat drivers' belong to the Gay Nineties. . . . Women such as Liz Whitney of society fame, Caral Gimble, wife of baseball's Hank Greenberg, Ellie Wood Keith, Jane Pohl Rust, and Ethel Beck are probably more famous in their field than the male riders. . . . Generally considered America's greatest rider is small, youngish looking Southern belle named Jane Pohl Rust of Leesburg, Va., who looks about fourteen, is twenty-four, and for the past five years has made her reputation mainly with one mount, the temperamental Fitzrada."

Jane regarded herself as a competitor, not a prototype feminist or a barrier breaker. The gentlemanly respect male riders extended to her as an equal was proof to her that gender had no bearing in the ring.

With less than three years remaining to prepare for the Olympics, objection to the ban on women gathered steam. From Jane's perspective, the rule was unfortunate but not the injustice suggested by the press. Tom O'Reilly's wrote in his syndicated Sunday supplement article dated October 30, 1949, "Sidesaddles Will Never Come Back": "The National Horse Show, . . . is the only sporting event which finds the girls showing considerable superiority over the men . . . Consider a 19-year-old thoroughbred named Fitzrada and a plucky girl named Jane Pohl. Their story is the answer to Olympic officials who feel that only men—and preferably Army officers—should ride in their wonderful games." Jane was not comfortable being the poster child for this cause and refused to comment. She appreciated being treated like a lady and playing by the rules. When the women's rights movement surfaced in the 1960s, Jane spurned it over bra burning. She felt differently about racial and religious discrimination.

U

For Jane and Dave, a pattern of mutual avoidance set like a stain in 1949. Dave came home late, usually pifficated and after he knew Jane was asleep. She faced the fact that Dave was an alcoholic and envisioned a future worse than what she had known with her father. Jane started staying overnight at Mauka, and her two-year marriage died a muffled death. Divorce papers changed hands with child support set at $100 per month. Dave never missed a payment, but it was not enough. As a single mother raising a son and effectively barred by gender from earning a living on the circuit as a professional, Jane was lucky to find a job with flexible hours drafting construction drawings for a Middleburg architect.

15

FROM THE GARDEN
TO THE PASTURE

Foxhunting required stamina, and in 1950 Fitz would turn twenty. But because they both enjoyed it so much, Jane decided to cut back not on the frequency but rather on the exertion and risk of injury. She opted to hang back a mile or more from the hounds, reducing the mileage Fitz traveled by straightening the meanders of the fox's path as it tried to escape the pack. Listening patiently to the hounds crying in the distance, Jane and Fitz could choose a more direct and leisurely path through the day, with time for opening and closing gates to avoid bigger jumps.

Centered more on observing than participating, the practice was known as *hilltopping*. It required expert knowledge of the location of fence lines, creek crossings, and trails through the woods. Mistakes led to getting boxed into corners and having to backtrack or getting lost. But Jane and Fitz had four years of coursing over this territory. If she lost her way, she'd hold a heading until they reached a known road. As he tired, Fitz gravitated toward home or the horse trailer with increasing facility. Jane used the tendency as a compass to navigate back through unfamiliar woods. She remembered Sergeant Mope telling her that on forced marches when horses were spent, they'd perk up when you told them they didn't have far to go, and it worked with Fitz.

Despite lacking the thrill of pursuit at the heels of the pack, hill-topping revealed wonderful insights not available to those up with the action. Jane was astounded at foxes' understanding of the chase as a challenge of wits and their delight in making fools out of the hounds. While hanging back on a dirt road one morning, she listened to hounds giving cry on the overgrown bank bordering Goose Creek's flood plain. The trees were bare of leaves, lending a gray hue to the hills. The hounds were turning toward her, and she might have to move out of the way. It would be embarrassing if the fox used her and Fitz somehow to lose the pack. Jane heard more hounds joining in. Fitz took the opportunity to scratch an itch under his bridle's cheek strap. He extended a foreleg and pitched his head forward to rub on it. Jane moved in the saddle to accommodate the drop of his shoulder. He worked his head full length from ear to muzzle against his bony knee. Jane followed his strong strokes with her hands, keeping elastic tension in the reins.

Suddenly, a red fox ran out of the woods right in front of them. Fitz pulled his head up and trained his ears on the creature, watching for a threatening move. Jane reassured him with a gentle stroke on his shoulder. She was close enough to see the fox's gossamer black whiskers and didn't want Fitz to spoil the moment. The fox glanced at them, unconcerned, and padded toward the one-lane steel-truss bridge. Jumping onto the bridge's pedestrian handrail, sure of his balance, he trotted to the center, then crouched and leaped into the stream. It was a drop of maybe eighteen feet. His dive was that of a racing swimmer in full extension, and his body remained horizontal as he splashed into the water on his belly. He had aimed wisely and landed where the current was strongest.

As he paddled downstream with his nose above the water and his red brush floating behind, the hounds started pouring out of the woods onto the road, their noses working his scent in a din of exuberance. The scent was so fresh that the hounds were certain that even if he ran as fast as he could, they would have him in a minute. They galloped to the bridge, raised their noses at the railing, and followed it. A logjam of hounds accumulated at the point where the fox had jumped, boiling over each other, yelping in anger at having no further scent to follow. Fights erupted.

The huntsman arrived in his scarlet coat to direct his hounds. A sour expression clouded his sweat-streaked face. Jane knew he had to call his hounds from the railing and cast them down the bank of the stream. They might refuse to leave such strong odors for blank ground. But the huntsman's bigger problem was in guessing from which shore the fox would debark to seek cover. His horse chomped the bit and shuffled, anxious to continue. Jane smiled for the fox.

Jane felt blessed to have been let in on the chase from the fox's perspective, and viewings of foxes became her favorite tales. In later life, her fascination with foxes strengthened and combined with her pack-rat instinct to clog her house with all manner of fox images and figurines, most of them bought in gift shops but some crafted by her from plaster of Paris or papier-mâché and painstakingly painted or glazed by her own hand. Her foxes' conformation was primitive, eyes and teeth eluded her, but she diligently bent whiskers and paws, canted ears, and lolled red felt tongues to suggest a predicament, a mood, or a motive. It seemed to her that foxes considered hounds, at worst, an annoyance. Rarely were Loudoun Hunt's hounds able to catch and kill a healthy fox. It was during rabies epidemics—for which the hounds were vaccinated—that the most foxes were accounted for.

Hilltopping also entertained Jane with human foibles. Once she and Fitz chanced on several men from the hunt field gathered around a haystack. Each was on his knees, digging in the base of the stack with one hand, holding his horse with the other. These men always hunted aggressively, riding full tilt, as close to the heat as they could get. She asked them what they were doing, thinking that they had seen a fox burrow into the hay and were willing to risk bitten fingers to flush him out.

From beneath the stack, one of them pulled a mason jar of what looked like water and replaced it with a dollar bill from his pocket. He unscrewed the lid and passed it to his eager friends. Looking up at Jane, he held a finger to his lips. She then understood this to be a retail moonshine stand—probably Thompson Bailey's—operating on the honor system.

Foxhunters had a code about such things. In the hunt field, the ties that bound were shared humiliation. Eventually every foxhunter uprooted his face from the suction of ankle-deep mud to see his horse disappearing over the hill at a gallop, shedding broken tack in its wake. The calamity was embellished in each retelling. The humor came at the victim's expense, but it was empathetic. A saying went, "Nothing happens in foxhunting that doesn't involve hard liquor and other people's spouses." Jane drew the line short of both, but she kept secrets. The men's wives might not be amused by their riding to fences while drunk. Nor would Thompson, if the revenue officer found his store.

In 1950, Jane cut Fitz's show schedule in half from the previous year and entered him almost exclusively in the hunter division, where the fences where lower. Their season started early in the spring with hunter trials. Fitz and Runanplay, owned and ridden by Mary Godfrey, wife of radio and television personality Arthur Godfrey, were nominated to represent Loudoun Hunt in the Field Hunter Championship Trials of Virginia, held in freezing cold and on snow-covered ground at Millwood. The trials were run over a three-mile course of natural hunting country at moderate pace under conditions simulating a regular hunt. Two judges voted Fitz first, and two judges voted against him, saying he was "too thin."

Two days later at the Middleburg Hunter Trials, 2,000 spectators came despite a driving cold March wind. From a local newspaper's article, "Fitzrada Takes Middleburg Bowl": "Rolling once more along the glory road so long familiar to him . . . the old campaigner was picked as being the best, safest, and most brilliant horse on which to ride to hounds."

Meanwhile, Joseph O'Connell, a Boston stockbroker, had hired young Mr. Shirley Payne, a show jockey for the Greenhalghs, to establish O'Connell's Green Dunes Farm as the top hunter stable in the country. There was just one restriction, and it wasn't money: O'Connell wanted only chestnuts with white stockings and blazed faces. Shirley lost no time in purchasing four of them, one of which was My Bill, former three-year-old hunter champion of Virginia under Cappy.

Shirley hired Cappy to augment him with the riding but needed a female jockey for the ladies' classes. Cappy recommended Jane. "Men are born to compete, and women are born to cooperate," Cappy may have told Shirley. "Jane's unique. She gets to horses through cooperation and asks for their all. That spirit works, even on the tough and lazy ones." Jane readily accepted Shirley's invitation. It was a chance to hone her skills riding with Cappy on the best show hunters money could buy.

Jane's first ride for Green Dunes was at the 1950 Philadelphia National Horse Show, which coincided with the Loudoun Hunt Horse Show in Fitz's hometown. Fitz had two legs on the Master's Bowl, and a third win would retire it. Mr. O'Connell agreed to fly Jane back and forth so that she could compete in both shows. From the local newspaper's article, "Pohl Horse Wins Challenge Bowl for Third Time": "Thanks to a brilliant performance by the beloved old performer, Fitzrada, . . . Loudoun Hunt is going to have to purchase another trophy for its Master's Challenge Class. The aged brown gelding, . . . ridden by Mrs. Jane Pohl Rust, one of the Nation's best known horsewomen, took the blue in the class for the third consecutive time." The big silver bowl was retired to the mantle at Mauka. Fitz was the first horse to do it.

With Jane sharing the riding in seven shows from the Midwest to the East Coast, Green Dunes won ten Hunter Championships, including the Green Hunter Championship of America at the Garden. Based on points, O'Connell's Rainslicker and My Bill tied for second place on the 1950 American Horse Show Association Conformation Hunter List.

Jane brought Fitz to Madison Square Garden in 1950. She entered him in five working hunter classes and one jumping class, the pen. At the National, the pen was one of the most severe. Fitz had entered it in each of his four previous years at the Garden, qualified for it only once, and then did not finish in the ribbons.

The pen class required jumping in and out of a simulated hog pen six times from different directions. The rectangular pen was made of heavy post-and-rail fence panels. In one corner was a white garden gate, only four feet across. An additional two fences were outside the pen: a chicken coop and a pole jump. At the pole jump, the rider was required to stop and lower the top bar while still mounted, then back up and jump the lowered fence.

Unlike the other jumper classes, the pen was timed, and way of going was considered along with performance and promptness. The course was grueling because a U-turn and an S-turn were required inside the pen, the dimensions of which were only thirty-six by forty-eight feet, precious little room to make corrections. For the horse, it was an unforgiving test of the ability to judge distances, brake quickly, twist like a polo pony to carve tight turns, and then instantly build impulsion sufficient to jump four feet. From the rider, it required clairvoyant intuition.

Jane's strategy was to save time by keeping the turns tight to reduce the distance covered. This meant that Fitz would have to keep his speed down, but too slow would rob him of impulsion. Jane would set the pace, think three jumps ahead, leave the intervening problems for Fitz to sort out, and compensate for his choices with adjustments in the path taken.

In the morning qualification round, Fitz ticked a fence with a hind hoof. But it was the cleanest and quickest round of any entrant in the qualification, and the judges used it as the standard for manners and time in whittling the field of forty-six down to twelve. Jane was the only woman among the survivors.

In the final, Fitz and Jane jumped smoothly into the pen for the S-turn and out over the gate, turned left over the chicken coop, then through a U-turn carrying enough steam to jump four feet back into the pen. Here, Fitz had a front tick. Then, jumping out of the pen with a right turn to a dead stop immediately after landing, Fitz had to stand still with his neck over the outside jump's bar while Jane lowered it with one hand. It bounced on the ground with a resounding boom, but Fitz did not spook. Hastily jumping it from a standstill and cantering through another U-turn, two jumps remained, the roughest: a four-foot panel into the pen, followed by a wicked reverse inside the pen with only its short dimension available, then out over the four-foot panel to sprint across the finish line.

Fitz finished the final with just the front tick, which, totaled with the morning's hind tick, good time and manners, was enough to win this extreme contest. One article was headlined "Fitzrada, at 20, Is Still a Top Flight Jumper."

A fledgling U.S. Jumping Team was touring the 1950 fall show circuit seeking donations to compete in Europe. Since women were jumping in Great Britain where FEI rules were not recognized, the U.S. team included two women. In an upset at the National, the U.S. Jumping Team won the International Perpetual Challenge Trophy, competing against Canada, Chile, England, Ireland, and Mexico. Jane felt patriotic pride and a little envy since she considered herself at least as good as the best woman on the team.

The team captain was Arthur McCashin. Before the war, he had been an accomplished international show jumper and steeplechase jockey. After Fitz's win of the pen class, McCashin approached Jane with a cocky swagger and an earnest expression, indicating to Jane that he had something on his mind. He introduced himself, congratulated Jane, and complimented Fitz while suggesting the pen course required skills valued in international stadium jumping. It dawned on Jane that he was about to offer her an invitation to join the team, and her smile broadened. She had brief visions of jumping against the best in Europe at the White City and Royal Dublin Society horse shows. McCashin quickly got to his point in asking her to lend Fitz to the team. His wording indicated that the team was interested only in the horse.

Jane's answer would reflect on her patriotic duty to support the new U.S. civilian jumping team, whose survival hinged on donations. She resented this leverage and felt a flush of outrage. Jane had rescued Fitz and spent five years reforming him. She suspected that McCashin wanted Fitz to help his second woman rider look good. *Damned if I'm going to let her get the credit*, she thought to herself. Jane looked McCashin in the eye. The smile had left her face.

"I'm retiring Fitz after the show," she told him. Jane had been contemplating Fitz's retirement for some time, but now it was done. Her response to the team captain's request was a public announcement. Saying it out loud brought Jane's heart to her throat.

Fitz finished the 1950 National fourth in Working Hunter Championship points, competing against familiar friends: Substitution, Black Watch, and Golden Chance. It was Fitz's last trip from Mauka farm.

In his final year on the circuit, Fitz won four tricolor ribbons, one of them in the jumper division. "I wanted Fitz remembered at the top, not as a has-been," she later explained her answer to McCashin's request. "Besides, it was more honorable than just saying 'No.'"

After the National Horse Show in November 1950, Jane turned Fitz out to pasture at Mauka—no more showing and no more hunting. He had more than earned complete retirement. With a late start in life, Fitz won twenty-three Jumping Championships and was reserve jumper champion seven times. Based on points, Fitz was Virginia Horse Shows Association Jumper of the Year in 1947 and remained in the top ten for the next two years. He was the first horse trained and ridden by a woman to such success in the jumper division. At Madison Square Garden, he placed in the ribbons four out of five years.

Particularly remarkable, he simultaneously served as field hunter, riding to hounds every year from 1941 through 1950. On the circuit, he won three Working Hunter Championships and was reserve working hunter champion four times, one of them at the Garden.

During Fitz's retirement, Jane put her son, nieces, and nephews on him and led the old horse around the barnyard while Pop filmed. The footage shows Fitz with as many as five kids on his bare back. The urchins are worried, Jane is smiling proudly, and Fitz's expression is resigned, asking, "What did I do to deserve this?"

Among those old enough today to have followed Fitz's career, he remains etched in their memory as one of the top show jumpers of their era, coming from a bad beginning over a hard path and finding the best of equine and human traits: the will to try, or, as they call it, *heart*. In a recent interview, Bill Miller, who entered these shows with his wife riding their only horse, remembered with a wistful smile, "I got a kick seeing Fitzrada cantering in front of the grandstand at Warrenton after a blue ribbon was pinned on him. He held his head high and cocked toward the stands as if to say, 'Hey everybody, look at me.'"

Part III

16

SOWING SEEDS

Starting in 1948, Jane helped with pony shows around Leesburg. The shows were for children, organized by parents, and held at a volunteer's farm or on a grammar school athletic field. For Jane, they brought back happy memories from her childhood. In the small county, Jane knew many of the parents, who often asked her to judge the classes.

Few kids had any formal riding lessons. After school, they tacked up ponies in their backyards and rode unsupervised through the countryside, teaching themselves and their ponies how to jump from books and the occasional unsolicited adult critique, but mostly by trial and error. The kids were well aware of Jane's stature, and many were timid about having her judge them. Jane put them at ease with a pat on their pony's neck, a compliment, and an inquiry into the pony's past to coax out the child's pride and find common ground. After the class, she sought them out to give encouraging advice.

In the hunt field, a handful of pigtailed girls rode with Jane, pumping her for stories about showing on the circuit. Among the girls were Adele Hawthorne, age twelve, and the three Graham sisters: Gail, thirteen; Nancy, twelve; and Barbara, eleven. "Too young to drive, we used to bum rides to see Jane and Fitz jump against the professional men in the bigger shows close to home," Adele recalled in a recent interview. "I guess you could say we were her fan club. We'd sprawl over the show ring rail and say to each other, 'Hey, if she can do it, we can do it!'"

Just like Jane, these girls cared for their ponies without help. Brought up to work hard and shoulder responsibility on the family farm, they were dedicated understudies. "Televisions were new, and we didn't have one," Barbara Graham said of those days. "So, we went to a neighbor's house to see Jane jump in Madison Square Garden. I was so nervous for her, I cried through every one of her rides. I was eleven or twelve, and all I wanted to do was ride like Jane."

Gail Graham had a broad grin and fluffy golden brown hair. She liked Richard and babysat for him, sometimes taking the toddler home with her when Jane was gone overnight to shows. Jane helped Gail with her pony, Calico Cat, offering free advice, and was as insistent as the cavalry sergeants had been. The sisters shared Calico Cat in the pony classes at the local shows and often won.

Fitz was going so placidly at the 1949 Loudoun Hunt Horse Show that at the last minute Jane invited Gail, then fifteen, to ride him in the junior hunter class. Gail had never ridden Fitz. But having observed Jane with Fitz and learned from her with Calico Cat, Gail was confident and accepted eagerly. Pop mentioned the ride in a letter to the editor of Leesburg's *Loudoun Times-Mirror*: "It was nice to have him win the Master's Bowl . . . , but it was more thrilling for me to see young Gail Graham get up on 'Fitz' for the first time and ride to win the Junior Hunter class on the old open jumper."

Adele Hawthorne on her large pony, Black Sparkle, qualified for the master's challenge class at the Loudoun Hunt Horse Show in 1950, competing against Fitz and Jane. Adele was fourteen. The fences were three foot six to three foot nine over the outside course, a little forbidding for Adele. It was her first time competing against adults, and she was intimidated by the experience of the other entrants. Jane had not coached her previously, but Adele recalled, "Jane rode up to me before the class, saw my concern, and said, 'Every rider and every horse here make mistakes. Those making the fewest mistakes will win.'" Adele and Black Sparkle placed second to Jane and Fitz.

After retiring the Master's Challenge Bowl at the 1950 Loudoun Hunt Horse Show, Fitz was in contention to win the Jumper Championship with one class to go when Jane had to catch the plane to make a class at the Philadelphia National, where she was riding for Green Dunes Farm. She asked her friend, Bobby Burke, if he would ride Fitz the rest of the way. Bobby had served in the horse cavalry during the war. In 1950, he was beginning his career as a professional horseman. He had never ridden Fitz, but Jane admired his relaxed style with high-strung horses.

"The only advice she gave me was, 'Have fun,'" Bobby said of the Loudoun show in a recent interview. "I was not aware of Fitzrada's reputation as a man-killer. Before the class, I rode him easily once around the practice ring of jumps and said, 'That'll do.'"

Bobby and Fitz handily won the Jumper Championship. "Just starting my career, it was quite a feather in my cap," he said of that championship win on Fitz. Bobby was the only man ever to ride Fitz after the horse left the army in 1941. Bobby's career spanned the next fifty years, and he has been inducted into three show hunter and jumper halls of fame. He is still training. Horses ridden by him are known to retain a light "feel" for days afterward.

Adele Hawthorne and Nancy and Barbara Graham went to Madison Square Garden in 1951 for the National's junior classes. Gail stayed home to work the farm. Sam Graham hauled his daughters' ponies in his canvas-topped truck, and Adele hitched a ride for Black Sparkle in a van of show horses from Middleburg. The girls were in their mid-teens. It was their first trip to the Garden and an extravagance for their families. Barbara said, "I was late for my first class, because I found out I could earn three dollars a horse for braiding manes and tails, and we needed the money."

Because of the tight schedule at the National, juniors were not offered the opportunity to walk their courses to study them. Jane made time from riding for Green Dunes to stand with the girls and watch the other entrants precede them through the courses. She coached only by asking them to look closely, identify the mistakes the judges would note, and speculate on the causes. If the girls floundered, she'd give a hint.

"I was petrified," Adele recalled. "It was such a long way from home. Jane saw me crumbling and said, 'There's nobody here that has any better chance than you do. Folks back home will be looking in the paper for our names. We may not win any ribbons, but by God, neither of us will be on the DNF [did not finish] list!'"

Adele had registered to enter the junior Corinthian class without knowing she would need a shad-belly coat and silk top hat. Such items were beyond her family's budget. Jane looked at her in her hunt coat and cap before the class and said, "You're not going in there looking like that." Jane hastily fitted her coat to Adele by taking in seams with safety pins while Adele stuffed the silk top hat's band with tissues. "I had a mentor who took the clothes off her back and put them on me," recalled Adele.

None of the girls won any ribbons at their first National Horse Show. But now approaching their seventies, Barbara and Nancy Graham maintain successful professional careers with horses. Nancy gives lessons and breeds, trains, and sells hunters, keeping fifty or more on her farm near Mt. Gilead. She and her daughter do the riding. Barbara was a race jockey and holds one of the early racehorse trainer's licenses issued to a woman. She has sixty horses and a staff at the Middleburg training track, breaking yearlings and training racehorses. Despite numerous broken bones from falls over the years, she still rides multiple horses every day. Of the three sisters, Gail considers herself the only smart one, having escaped the labor and injuries inherent in working with horses. Adele hunted up until a few years ago, still keeps a horse or two, and rides.

Carolyn Rogers came to Leesburg in 1947 as a new bride from North Carolina, where she had showed her father's gaited saddle horses, one of which she brought with her. Carolyn said in a recent interview, "People in Virginia looked at my horse like it was a skunk. If I wanted to ride here, I'd have to learn how to jump. That's how Jane and I got together." Jane helped Carolyn with Halo Miss, a hunter that Carolyn showed successfully. Twenty years later, Carolyn was the fourth woman to be issued a racehorse trainer's license.

After Fitz retired in 1950, Jane helped Tom Taylor train his horses. Tom was a Quaker farmer who lived down the mountain and loved foxhunting. He bred and trained rock-steady hunters and had four kids who did most of the riding and stable work. Other kids hacked their ponies to Tom's ring and rode through courses they constructed themselves. On a dare, Tom's daughters bounced around a course of low jumps riding double and bareback, the rider yelling at the passenger to stop laughing. Occasionally, a kid raced down the hill to Tom's house to get help for a runaway horse or an injury.

Tom had a gift for conjuring contraptions that bristled with twanging springs and scissoring arms to automatically close his farm gates after they were pushed open. Tom's pony shows tested the nerves of the steadiest mounts. His schooling ring had a chicken-coop jump with a giant bloodshot eyeball painted on it. Jane suggested eyelashes.

When the Pony Club, an organization for kids, took root in Leesburg, much of it centered around Tom's farm. Jane understood its value in fostering horsemanship in the next generation and volunteered to serve as a coach and the local club's secretary.

In the sweltering summer afternoons, she stood in the center of Tom Taylor's outdoor riding ring, wearing a light cotton sundress. She hid from the sun under a wide-brimmed straw hat with fake flowers sprouting from its band. Her red water jug sweated beside her feet. A half dozen kids rode around the outside the ring in a single file. Pivoting to keep them in view, she made baby steps in her white Keds.

"Now trot," she'd say. "Heels down. Head up. Relax your elbows, pull your shoulders back. *Make* those damned ponies trot."

With British roots, the Pony Club awarded skill ratings by formal testing. In addition to hunting and jumping, tests included stable management, veterinary care, and, more important for future U.S. Olympic teams, dressage. In each skill level, local clubs competed in regional rallies to go to the national rally. Teams of three riders and stable manager were judged in modified Olympic events, horsemanship knowledge, and maintenance, which included the stables, equipment, and horses.

Tom Taylor's son, Henry, tested and rode for his Pony Club "A" level rating with Jane's help. The A level represented the highest rank of horsemanship, and he was one of the very first in the United States to try for it. Years later, she was as proud when he won a Pulitzer Prize for his poetry. She especially liked his poem "Riding Lesson":

I learned two things from an early riding teacher.
He held a nervous filly in one hand and gestured with the other, saying,
    "Listen,
Keep one leg on one side, the other leg on the other side, and your
    mind in the middle."

17

AN EMPTY STALL

One morning at Mauka Farm in early September 1952, Jane went to the pasture to get Fitz, put him in his stall during the heat of the day, and feed him. He was not at the gate with the gray mare and the pony as was usual at feeding time. With his lead shank slung over her shoulder, Jane walked uphill through the pasture to find him. He was standing on three legs with his head hung low and did not turn to her when she called. She walked closer, and a prickly sense of dread came over her. He was shiny with sweat and shivering, slightly weaving his shoulders back and forth, taking short breaths. She broke into a run and, drawing closer, saw that his left hind leg was horribly swollen at the hock. Touching the hock gently, she knew immediately it was broken and guessed he'd been kicked by the mare or the pony, grazing nearby in Mauka's only pasture.

Jane ran to the phone in the house. Her mind raced. She couldn't remember the vet's phone number. Fumbling for the right page in the phone book, she dropped it and cursed. Her fingers shook when she dialed, and she forced herself to concentrate. Listening to the phone ring on the other end, she wasn't sure she'd dialed the right number and checked the page again. The phone kept ringing, and she was convinced she'd misdialed.

"It's Fitz," she said in a sob when he picked up. "Come quick. His hock is broken."

Mother and Pop overheard the conversation from their bedroom. Pop shuffled down the stairs lifting a trouser suspender over his shoulder, while Jane hunched over the phone listening to the vet. Pop touched her on the arm on the way out the door to hitch the trailer and pull it to Fitz. Mother went to the clothesline to get Fitz's leg bandages and started rolling them so they would be ready if needed. Jane ran back up through the pasture with a bucket half full of water and a sponge. Rinsing Fitz's sweating flanks, she talked to him.

"It's not so bad," Jane told him, knowing the tone in her voice said otherwise. "A few months and you'll be okay." She ran out of things to say and started the litany over to keep herself from sinking. She kept looking at her watch. Pop waited with her in silent empathy.

The vet injected Fitz to dull his pain so they could move him. Dragging the damaged leg, Fitz lurched in small, deliberate steps up the ramp into the trailer. Pop drove the trailer into the barn, and Jane urged Fitz gently to his stall. They fitted the veterinarian's canvas sling under his belly and chest, hooked block and tackle to a rafter, and heaved on the rope until the sling lifted Fitz's weight off his legs. A horse can lie on its side for only five hours before suffocating from the weight of its own body. To a lesser degree, the sling has the same effect in squeezing ribs. Eventually, Fitz wouldn't have enough strength to inflate his lungs against the pressure of the sling. He would have to be lowered to carry his own weight several times a day. The bone would not knit if the break was moved, so Fitz had to remain still, especially when the sling was lowered. Fitz was twenty-two. Jane knew that few younger horses recovered from this break. Except for racehorses with breeding value, most folks wouldn't even try.

Jane reset her alarm clock every four hours and went out to the barn to relax the sling so that Fitz could inflate his lungs to full capacity. She'd untie the overhead rope from its cleat on the wall and lower him slowly to support his own weight. If he moved or flinched, she'd take in rope to support him.

By the end of the first week, he'd lost a lot of weight. One night, Jane tried to adjust the sling because the rear strap under Fitz's belly was pinching into his flesh. She had to tug on the free end of the strap to release the buckle and misjudged the weight it carried. The strap shot from her hand and through the buckle with a loud click. The back of the sling fell open, and Fitz started sliding out. He made a stab with his hind legs to try and save himself and recoiled from the pain in the broken leg. His hindquarters crashed to the floor with his front legs still suspended in the sling. The angle of his bad hock was obtusely wrong. At the sight of it, Jane felt herself start to throw up.

There was no way to get him up. It would take the vet an hour to get there. The sling was cutting into his forelegs and chest, so she lowered him the rest of the way. His breathing was labored, and he broke into a sweat and ground his teeth in pain. Jane ran to the medicine cabinet, pushing bottles, gauze, and balm aside to find a pint glass bottle with a frosted neck and a conical glass stopper, like those in laboratories. It had a paper label stuck to it in Pop's handwriting: "Chloroform." They used it to put nests of hayloft mice to sleep. She snatched a roll of sheet cotton and tore off a foot-long length and ran back to Fitz sobbing. Avoiding looking at his broken leg, she draped the sheet cotton over Fitz's muzzle and tugged unsuccessfully on the bottle's stopper.

Jane pulled out her shirttail, wrapped it around the stopper's key handle, and twisted it so hard she grunted. The stopper refused to move, and Jane started to panic. Then she remembered what Pop did when glass stoppers refused to move, ran into the aisle away from the straw in Fitz's stall, and pulled a box of matches from her pocket. She held the flame to the bottle's neck. After three matches, she tried the stopper, and it broke free.

She adjusted the cotton to evenly cover Fitz's muzzle. He did not resist his trusted friend. She poured a steady trickle of chloroform onto it and waited, poured again, and waited. Eventually, Fitz blinked and started to relax. A while later he was asleep. Again, she poured and waited. When his breathing slowed to a whisper, she lay down in the straw, rested her cheek on his neck, and hugged him.

"It's okay to let go. We did it all, didn't we? Thank you, Fitz," she told him softly. He drifted deeper into sleep. His breathing ebbed, and she knew he was gone. Over the next hour, she felt the cold creep into his body.

When finally she pushed herself up from his side and wandered out of the barn, dawn was suggesting itself from a dingy orange glow beneath the eastern horizon. Jane saw the light in the kitchen go on. Mother or Pop was starting a pot of coffee. She couldn't tell them just yet and stood in the barnyard, stunned and sick at heart.

Pop and Rojah Chin chose a spot for Fitz's grave beside his favorite apple tree. It had a commanding view of the Valley of Virginia where he hunted and of the Blue Ridge Mountains beyond. Jane lay down on her bed and put pillows over her ears so she couldn't hear the digging, which lasted into the afternoon. She hoped the hole was big enough for Fitz to lay his neck out straight but couldn't bear to go see. She realized Pop would do it right regardless of the extra effort. Fatigue had put her to sleep before Rojah's team of two mules dragged Fitz's body to the grave. By twilight, the men had walked the mules over Fitz many times to pack the soil and returned to their houses to mourn in silence with a drink.

Since college, Jane's church attendance had dwindled to once a month, confessions twice a year. Guilt ridden about having attempted to adjust the sling by herself, Jane went to confession the next day and took Holy Communion at Mass with Pop on Sunday to pray for Fitz's delivery to a comfortable afterlife. The only person Jane ever told about the sling was her second husband. Pop and Mother guessed but never asked. The family's story was that the vet put Fitz to sleep.

The *Loudoun Times Herald* printed the rare obituary for an animal. It was headlined "Fitzrada Dies in Retirement": "Fitzrada, the little Thoroughbred jumper and hunter that has been well known in Northern Virginia for the last six years, is dead at the age of 22. He died on September 11 and was buried on his favorite spot in the pasture that he has roamed since his retirement two years ago. . . . The story of Fitzrada is the story of a horse which made a girl and a girl who made a horse. Jane Pohl made headlines as a horsewoman because of the great heart of the old Army horse, and Fitz would have died an unloved Army nag had it not been for Jane."

Pop was inspired to write a poem, "Fitzrada, Foaled—April 15, 1930, Died—September 11, 1952." He had not tried his hand at poetry since the war, when he was in Africa and acknowledged his loneliness by writing about the land's sad barren beauty and the poverty of its peoples.

> Now only a mound of green Virginia hill
> To mark your grave;
> An empty stall, and the voice of little Butch [Pop's nickname for
>   Richard],
> Asking, "Where's Fitz?"
> And the dimmed eyes of those who loved you.

> No more the bugle and the cavalry spur
> Of your fractious days;
> Nor the gentle hand of Jane, and her voice
> Saying, "Whoa, son."
> Nor, of recent years, the happy laughter of children,
> Glad and proud to ride Old Fitz.
> No more the deep-throated roar of the Garden Crowd
> When your great heart drove your slender legs
> To win among the best.

> Only an empty stall
> Some silver, and bits of colored cloth remain behind.

In Fitz's ribbon display box, each of eight rows held an average of fourteen ribbons, all of them blue or tricolor championship ribbons. His lesser ribbons filled two suitcases in the attic. Despite the difficulty of moving the ponderous ribbon box, it would hang beside Jane's bed in every house where she lived.

18

THE INVESTIGATION

In Fitz's retirement, Jane's résumé had taken a huge boost. Sharing the riding with Shirley Payne in 1951, Green Dunes won 149 ribbons, fifty-four of them blue, in ten shows. My Bill was American Horse Show Association (AHSA) Conformation Hunter Champion of the Year with an astounding 1,400 points, twice as many as the second horse on the list. Pop had bought a gray mare that had similar conformation to Fitz. Jane named the mare Grayrada and started showing her with the intention of entering U.S. Equestrian Team (USET) tryouts held after the 1952 Olympics. (Flying Dutchman, a horse Jane had ridden on the circuit for Mrs. Greenhalgh with mediocre results, carried Marjorie Haines to seventeenth place in dressage. Marjorie was the first woman to ride for the United States in the Olympics.)

Not two weeks after Fitz's death in 1952, a letter arrived for Jane from Andrew Montgomery, board member of the AHSA and secretary and treasurer of the USET. The AHSA governed U.S. horse shows. Jane knew Drew. He lived nearby and was a judge at shows she had entered. Jane opened the envelope, thinking it held clarifying details of the upcoming USET tryouts.

The letter read, "Your amateur status was placed in question at the recent Warrenton Horse Show, along with a number of others." Jane was shocked, thought it was a mistake, and checked for the correct spelling of her name and address on the page. She suddenly realized what was at stake. Women weren't issued professional licenses. If she lost amateur standing, her show career was over. Drew had been appointed head of an AHSA committee to investigate. He requested a statement from her as to whether she was a professional and added that if she claimed to be an amateur, it would be necessary for her to appear before the committee. He handwrote a postscript, "I could not be more grieved about anything than to read . . . of the death of the Dear Horse. . . . I know what a friend you have lost, and I am sending you my sympathy."

A surge of unfounded guilt swept through Jane's stomach. An officer's kid who got caught cheating at school would consider staging his own kidnapping to delay the public shame. She had been raised "not to lie, cheat, or steal; nor tolerate those who do." The vow came from the Cadet Honor Code and had been ingrained in her as strongly as in her officer brother, father, and uncles. But then guilt was followed by outraged pride. She had made her name as an amateur mucking her own stalls and cleaning her own tack, unlike the moneyed riders competing as amateurs.

Jane had never heard of anyone's amateur status being challenged. She wondered who the "number of others" were and guessed they were women who were winning too often for the likes of the accuser. Jane contemplated the gray areas between professionals and amateurs. Amateurs universally accepted the monetary purses offered in the classes they won on their own horses. But nobody, not even the professionals, won enough to make a living on purses. Amateurs were typically wealthy or had day jobs, and horses were a hobby. Professionals were paid by owners to train horses and ride them in shows, but the bulk of their income came from selling horses. Amateurs bought and sold horses too, and as far as Jane knew, there were no restrictions on it. The biggest difference between amateurs and professionals was how they identified themselves to the public. Professionals were businesses, advertising themselves as such by reputation, word of mouth, and occasionally in print: horses were for rent or sale, riding lessons, boarding, horse training, and showing.

Jane sat down to type a letter of rebuttal. But without knowing the source or justification of the accusation, it was pointless. She called Bill Perry, a friend, member of the AHSA's board of directors, and vice president and board member of the USET. Bill could not disclose any details but encouraged her to see it though and discussed the process. Five days later a handwritten letter arrived from Drew:

Dear Jane,

Bill Perry tells me . . . you feel you can qualify as an amateur and want to go into the [USET] Tryouts at Warrenton. . . .

You must be the judge of your amateur standing yourself but would have to justify it before the Committee of Challenges. It's simple: An amateur is one who rides for the love of the sport not in any way lucrative—He must not profit from the practice of the sport. You must not have drawn your means of existence from the sport—Bought, sold, rented, schooled, worked or caused to be worked, horses with a lucrative end in view—But you can accept your expenses as long as they are reasonable—And I *think* you can accept reasonable presents . . .

So let me have your age & weight & I'll enter you [for the USET tryouts]—And then I'll know that we have at least one respectable (in that respect Only!!) representative.

Sincerely,

Drew

The night before she was to appear before the Committee of Challenges, Jane couldn't sleep. She imagined herself sweating at a spot-lighted table with a microphone on it. She kept rehearsing her replies to imagined questions, honing each sentence to make it clearer, counting arguments on her fingers to make sure she didn't forget any: she never took any payment for teaching kids and never received any money beyond reimbursement for travel expenses.

The next morning, Jane put on the suit she usually wore to church and debated whether to wear a gold bracelet she had received as a present from the Greenhalghs but decided against it as brash. It upset her to be afraid to wear it. Mother was waiting breakfast for her in the kitchen when she came downstairs carrying her shoes, purse, gloves, and hat.

Jane finished only half her eggs and scooted her chair back to rise.

"You'll be an hour early if you leave now," Mother said.

Jane slumped back into the kitchen chair. Mother shook a Camel halfway out of the pack, offered it to Jane, and took one for herself.

"Chin up. This will go better than you think," Mother said.

Jane took a big drag and exhaled a cloud of smoke in a sigh.

As chairman of this AHSA Committee of Challenges, Drew Montgomery was seated between two other men, conferring collectively over papers when Jane entered the room. They stood. Drew smiled, welcomed her warmly, and introduced her to the other two men. They were AHSA stewards, who adjudicated disputes at horse shows. She recognized them from the circuit but had not met them because she had never filed a protest. Drew held her chair, seating her at the oak table opposite their three chairs. A pitcher of water and four heavy glasses sat on a tray near Drew. She wondered how long this was going to take.

Drew stated the purpose of the committee: to determine her status in response to an anonymous complaint. Jane presumed the AHSA would not have accepted it unless it was signed but suspected the committee decided to preserve peace by guarding the accuser's identity. Jane felt it was unjust to question her integrity without naming the source, but she kept quiet.

The questions began on expense reimbursements and presents from the Greenhalghs and the O'Connells. It was expected that her plane tickets and hotel rooms were provided and that she charged her meals and dry cleaning to the room. Per the custom of the era, as a woman, she would not have seen the bills. From their faces, the men seemed satisfied that no money passed through Jane's hands. On their request, she described the jewelry pieces she had been given as presents. Although made of gold, Jane did not think them exorbitant or numerous. The committee did not ask her to estimate their value, which Jane took as a good sign. However, it would have been crass of them to ask and politically unwise to impugn owners who were pillars of the horse community.

The committee moved on to ask her about giving riding lessons and training horses owned by others. Jane stated that she had helped the Graham girls and others with their horses but denied she had been paid for it.

These questions were a warm-up for the area where Jane expected to be vulnerable. The horse community was small. The committee knew her personal situation and could draw conclusions. As a single mother working a part-time job as an architect's draftsman, money was tight, but she still was able to ride for Mr. O'Connell. They asked her how many horses she had sold, and she replied that Pop owned all the horses. Their faces showed they were not satisfied. Jane felt a twinge in answering affirmatively that she had trained these horses and that their value increased as a result.

Her mind raced to figure out the implications. She lived at Mauka. Maybe they considered the training as rent to Pop. It would be outrageous for them to challenge the right of a father to provide free shelter to his child, but as an adult with a college education, she was no longer a dependent.

The sale of Four Get to Mrs. Greenhalgh was thorny because Jane was riding for Mrs. Greenhalgh at the time. They asked her the amount the horse had sold for.

"You'll have to ask my father or Mrs. Greenhalgh," she replied.

Although she knew the answer, prices were private information. Silence ensued. She pressed her lips together and tried not to blink, thinking they would not press further, especially considering Mrs. Greenhalgh's prominence.

The quiet was broken by a question Jane had not anticipated. Mrs. Greenhalgh had taken Fitz on the circuit in her van. Jane denied knowing how much that was worth, but from the question, she understood they considered it to have value. The amount of gas money saved was not as important to Jane as avoiding the fatiguing hours behind the wheel pulling the trailer, especially on the eve of a show. Nonetheless, it was a financial expense that could be tallied, another nail in the coffin. Her palms went wet. The interview concluded on that note.

Jane's neck was stiff from concentrating. She stood and asked how long it would take for them to decide, adding that she was entered to ride at the Pennsylvania National next month and Madison Square Garden the month after. Both of them were AHSA-sanctioned shows. Without amateur status, she couldn't ride. Owners she was supposed to ride for would have to be notified so that they could find another rider. Drew promised a decision in a few days.

On the way home, she thought of things she wished she'd said. She regretted being humble, especially her apologetic tone asking them how long it would take. It was frustrating consolation, but they could not say she acted like a typical female and got "hysterical" in front of them.

Jane closed the car door wearily in the driveway and climbed the stairs to the kitchen. The spring on the screen door twanged and slammed it behind her. She bent over to take off her shoes and rub her pinched toes. Mother was washing carrots in the kitchen sink and asked her if she found out who filed the complaint.

"Probably somebody who doesn't want me riding against them on the circuit," Jane said. "But it's worse if this about a berth on the USET."

"Why?" Mother raised her eyebrows.

"Because the USET represents America," Jane replied. "Like the army, it should stand for fair play."

Mother countered that there were politics in the army and no reason there shouldn't be politics in the AHSA. Jane said she didn't want this to be about women. She'd earned the right to be at the top, fair and square, no ladies' tees.

"If the men want to win, they should get better," Jane said.

A few days after the hearing, a letter arrived from Drew saying her status was still being investigated but adding, "There should be little risk in your entering the amateur classes at Harrisburg and the National." Jane was slightly consoled that the investigation must be going in her favor. But if she won ribbons at those shows and subsequently lost amateur status, the points won would be forfeited and awarded to others. The papers would have a field day. Jane despaired. The longer the accusation was left undecided, the more it festered.

Mother had a standing arrangement with Edward's Drugstore in Leesburg to hold a copy of the Sunday edition of the *New York Times* for her. Jane went to pick it up on Monday when Edward's opened. She parked the car at the curb and left the keys in it, as was the custom if it had to be moved for a delivery truck. A few heads sipping coffee at the soda fountain turned and nodded. Two men rose and approached her to offer their condolences on Fitz's death. She was paranoid about the investigation and tried to leave quickly. Gossip was grist at the soda fountain.

Jane had been schooling Grayrada for the upcoming USET regional tryouts at Warrenton. The mare was not a standout, but she was fit and as ready as she ever would be. Jane thought their chances were fair or better.

However, the investigation consumed her thoughts. *I've been part of this gypsy band of owners and riders on the circuit for six years, and I still can't think of a single person who has the knife out for me.*

Slowly, it dawned on Jane how this would permanently hurt her chances for the USET. The team's riders were ambassadors of sorts, representing the United States on the international stage. They had to project the all-American image of impeccable character. Newspaper articles of USET riders "under investigation" would hinder fund-raising. Even if exonerated, the stain of accusation would follow her for the rest of her life. She convinced herself that even if she was clearly the best rider, there was no way the USET could select her. The day before the tryouts, she cleaned her tack and packed it for the short trip to Warrenton. But the next day, Jane stayed home, alternating between shame and fuming at the injustice. The memory of Arthur McCashin soliciting her to donate Fitz to the team hardened into acrimony. Years later she hotly explained her absence from the tryouts as follows: "I wouldn't give the USET the satisfaction of rejecting me."

For what remained of the 1952 show season, Jane rode at Harrisburg and Madison Square Garden with the committee's decision still pending. Prior to the investigation, she had accepted invitations to ride for other owners in these shows. When the investigation was announced, she offered the owners the chance to back out. The owners stuck by her, and she was grateful for their loyalty. They risked forfeiting championship points if the committee subsequently pulled her amateur status. At the Garden, she rode War Genius, owned by Lyman Wakefield, to win Middle Heavyweight Green Hunter Championship of America.

Two months after the investigation, Jane received a letter from Adrian Van Sinderen, president of the AHSA, advising her that she was rated as an amateur for horse show purposes. She put the letter in her file folder of horse show papers. But she would never need to show the letter to an official. With Fitz gone and having been stung by the investigation, Jane's heart wasn't in it anymore. "I couldn't go back on the circuit, where I'd been so happy," she later explained. "I'd be looking over my shoulder, wondering if somebody was building a case against me." With a son to raise, she opted for a clean break from showing. Jane was twenty-eight.

In 1953, FEI rules were changed to allow "Horsewomen" to compete in stadium jumping. About this time, the last of the two women who were on the original U.S. Jumping Team left to raise her family. No woman tried out for the team until 1958, when Kathy Kusner was picked up as an alternate. Kusner made the first string in 1961 and represented the United States in international jumping on the European circuit. In the 1964 Tokyo Olympic Games, Kusner, Mary Mairs, and two men represented the United States in Olympic jumping. The team finished sixth.

True to her West Point heritage to the end, Jane was extremely conscious of her conduct and never took a dime that didn't belong to her. She railed against favoritism that successfully compromised fair play. But in 1999 at age seventy-five, Jane confessed what she claimed was her only unethical act in showing. In a hack class, she had intentionally clucked when riding beside racehorse trainer Ridgely White's wife from Middleburg. As a result, Mrs. White's horse broke into a faster gait, costing her a ribbon.

Her confession came as a shock, and when asked why she did it, she squirmed. "Fitz deserved to win," she said.

One of the highest compliments to Jane's riding came from Vladimir Littauer, a former Russian cavalry officer who founded a riding academy in New York in the 1930s. He succeeded Harry Chamberlin as the preeminent expert in forward-seat riding and authored a popular book for training working hunters and show horses. Littauer believed in four fundamentals: unity of horse and rider, security of the rider on the horse, nonabuse, and efficient use of the aids.

Having seen Jane ride at Madison Square Garden over the years, he wrote to her in 1953, "Admiring your riding very much, I have wanted for a long time to meet you and now I have a favor to ask [that] offers an occasion to do so." He stated in his letter that they thought alike about riding and requested photos of her jumping to illustrate an article he was writing for *The Canadian Horse*. She sent him two, and he replied, "I like the way the horses go and I like the way you ride. And I am very happy to have my article in Canada illustrated by a well-known American rider." They never did meet.

19

LAST CLASS

Pop had always wanted to live by the sea, so in late 1953, Mother and Pop sold Mauka Farm and bought a house in Watch Hill, Rhode Island. Jane wanted to stay in Virginia, but income was a problem.

Earning a living with horses by buying cheap and selling dear was not possible. With professional status effectively denied to women, she could only show as an amateur. If she earned her living from horses, she was no longer an amateur. She couldn't ask a decent price for show horses that didn't win ribbons—a Catch-22. Jane had no chance for a job teaching riding at a girls' boarding school. A divorcee with a kid was an improper role model for future debutantes. Jane would have had a better chance applying for work as a widow. Working as an architect's draftsman was meager pay, but she was glad to have any job. Richard was in kindergarten. Jane rented a room in Middleburg above the hardware store on the same block of Washington Street as the Red Fox Tavern and within walking distance of her job. Three other folks lived on the floor, some down on their luck, and all shared the same bathroom.

On the weekends, Jane brought Richard to Tom Taylor's farm to play with Tom's children. She started working a hunter of his named Old Fashioned and showed the horse locally. Old Fashioned was a game jumper, and Tom thought the horse would do well racing over fences.

Jane agreed to ride Old Fashioned in the Ladies' Race at the Blue Ridge Hunt point-to-point race meet. Although she was experienced at jumping in the hunt field, it would be her first race. The race was several miles long on a turf course with four-foot fences. The jockeys rode with short stirrups to give them a greater range of motion over the horse. With less leg on the horse's flanks Jane's position was precarious.

Middleburg's Gerald Webb suffered a racing accident that Jane had heard about and never forgot. Webb had a gray horse that could have won most of its races, but since Webb rode with his feet so far back, the stirrup leathers tended to work their way off the bars of the saddle. With no stirrups, he had to pull up and watch the rest of the field stream by him. He remedied the problem by wiring the bars' safety catches closed.

In a subsequent race, he fell, and his foot got caught in the stirrup. Webb hung underneath his horse's belly, his foot tethered above him. With his shoulders and head dragging between the horse's hind legs, the gray panicked. When the horse was finally caught, Webb was dead.

Thereafter, Jane religiously checked saddles to ensure that the bars were open.

The night before the Jane's race, Tom's wife, Mary, who was afraid of horses, dreamed that Jane fell. The next day, Mary, normally conspicuous at Tom's van, was absent.

During the race, Jane found that galloping among other horses vying for position was frightening. She finished well back in the pack and remarked to Tom, "The pace was more brisk than what I'm used to."

A few weeks later, Mary handed Jane pictures from the races. Jane leafed through them and stopped at one of Mary, who looked pained. Mary told her about the dream.

"Had I known," Jane said, "I probably wouldn't have ridden."

"I knew how you felt about jinxes," Mary said, "so I stayed out of your sight." Jane never rode in another race.

Financially strapped in the summer of 1954, Jane followed her parents to Rhode Island to live with them. The nearby town of Westerly was mainly Italian Catholic, and marriage was a sacrament. No employer would consider a divorcee for face-to-face contact with customers.

Driving through town, Jane saw picketers carrying "On Strike" signs in front of the phone company and thought the company might be desperate to keep the switchboards running. Since operators were anonymous to the phoning public, her past might not matter.

Jane parked the car up the street, stubbed out a cigarette, and put her lipstick on using the rearview mirror. She pulled a scarf out of her pocketbook, tied it over her head, and wished she had dark glasses. Jane threaded her way through the picket line to the front steps, careful not to bump any of them. Across the street, a policeman observed impassively.

Inside, Jane joined a line of customers waiting to apply for phone service or pay bills. When she finally got to the cashier's window, she found herself facing a pale withered man with a dark green visor on his bald head.

"I'd like to apply for a job as an operator," she whispered.

His face showed irritation. He slowly reached for a form stacked in a cubbyhole.

"Scabs have to park on the street," he said, as he pushed the form and a booklet of rules under the bars.

After a week's training in Providence, Jane returned to Westerly to start work. She sat on a stool in front of a switchboard, wearing a headset, connecting calls by plugging retracting wire cords into holes on the switchboard. Several dozen operators did the same, arranged in rows. Most of the operators were just out of high school and looking for a husband.

The supervisor was an older woman supporting her family of five and a husband who'd lost a leg in the marble quarries. The supervisor walked the rows of operators, holding the lead from her headset in her hand, able to plug into any operator's switchboard. She roamed the floor to keep the operators from reading magazines, gossiping among themselves, or eavesdropping on customers. When the supervisor wasn't in sight, the young operators gossiped and giggled like schoolchildren. Jane kept to herself. She didn't want to hasten the discovery that she was a single mother.

Mother and Pop booked an ocean voyage from New York to Puerto Rico. It was to be a second honeymoon of sorts and an escape from the bleak Rhode Island winter in March 1956. At supper on the third day at sea, Pop looked pale. He excused himself from the table to lie down. Mother went on deck to see the twilight glistening on the water. When she returned to the their cabin, Pop was lying in his pajamas. She placed her hand on his shoulder to comfort him and knew at once he was dead. The ship's surgeon wrote "heart attack" on the death certificate. It was his third.

For the twelve hours preceding the funeral at West Point, a snowstorm ravaged the East Coast. Jane drove at a crawl through the deep snow, alone with her son, Richard. Finally arriving after eight hours on the road, Jane found Mother in the academy's Thayer Hotel. Mother told her Jennet wasn't coming, explaining she was pregnant and afraid of being stranded by the snow in an airport.

"I don't care," Jane snapped. Tears welled in her eyes. "She was his favorite. She could have at least made an effort."

Jane stared blankly out the hotel window toward the West Point stables. Through the gusts of snow, the abandoned stables faded and reappeared as a mirage. She tried to recall being lifted by Mother to sit on a horse there for the first time, nearly thirty years prior. Papa had filmed her joy. The only animal residing here now was the mule, Hannibal, mascot for football games. Jane felt old, depleted by loss.

In the summer of 1956, Jane was thirty-two when she was reintroduced to Geoff, a childhood friend she had known from family vacations to the Watch Hill beach. He came from the prominent Catholic family that owned the mill in Westerly. Geoff left a life of yachts, squash courts, and Golden Gloves boxing to enlist in the marines and serve in the Pacific during World War II. He was cocky, dark, and a few years younger than Jane and had never been married. He had graduated from

Harvard after the war and was eager to be a young lion in Boston's corporate jungle. He deluged Jane with roses, intent on marrying. She was flattered but wary of her judgment after being swept off her feet by Dave. Mother didn't like Geoff. While she thought Dave had not meant any harm, she felt this one's smug arrogance veiled a mean streak. But after months of his persistence, Jane accepted his proposal.

On a cold morning in the late fall of 1957, they were married in the Catholic chapel at West Point. The chapel and its granite steps were exactly as she remembered, nestled among the brick officers' quarters down the hill from the football stadium. Just before the rehearsal began, she lit a candle for Pop. The next day, Jane wore beige, the proper color for second-time brides. Walking down the aisle with her uncle Buck giving her away, the familiarity of the softly lit chapel and its smell of incense comforted her. Hearing their vows reverberate off the white plaster walls, she felt redeemed to have a church wedding. The spiritual emotion was what she recollected from her First Holy Communion, kneeling before the same altar.

Geoff was adamant in maintaining his fitness and had asked Jane to stop smoking. She delayed until her wedding day. Rank edginess from nicotine withdrawal set in on the honeymoon. A week later, they moved into a one-bedroom attic apartment on Boston's fashionable Mt. Vernon Street. Richard, then in the third grade, slept on a foldout couch. There was no elevator, and carrying groceries up five floors required a rest, balancing the bags on a landing rail. The apartment overlooked a soot-stained brick alley, iron fire escapes, and clotheslines. The steam radiators clanked but were no match for winter's chill under the thin roof. In summer, table fans hummed on the windowsill through the sticky nights.

When a contemporary was promoted ahead of Geoff, he fumed for days and talked about picking a fist fight with the rival. There was a possibility he might. Geoff had been expelled from his club (fraternity) at Harvard for breaking his roommate's jaw in a flash of anger.

Geoff demeaned Jane's cooking, the way she packed suitcases in his car, and her prior successes on the show circuit. Two blocks away was Boston Common, a park. Jane would sneak over there to smoke cigarettes when acrimony was thick. She tucked a damp washcloth and a bottle of perfume in her purse to scrub the oily odor from her fingers and lips.

Geoff wanted children, but Jane felt there was no money and no room for another child. But his temper intimidated her, so she did not voice her objection a second time. When he found a diaphragm in her dresser drawer, there was hell to pay. Thereafter, she resisted his advances with a host of pretenses, and he told her she was frigid.

After work, Geoff fastidiously hung up his Brooks Brothers suit and emerged from the bedroom in white boxer shorts and black socks with garters, often carrying two pairs of boxing gloves from his Golden Gloves days. Seeing the gloves, Richard would stand up from doing his homework, take off his shirt, and help Geoff move furniture to make a ring in the tiny apartment. Geoff critiqued Richard through a regimen of jabs, guards, and one-two kill punches, and then they squared off to spar.

"There's a boy your age in Russia, waiting to meet you," Geoff teased sternly. "His name is Ivan. Right now, he's cleaning his bayonet, thinking how he's gonna run it through your throat." Richard circled Geoff, tentatively looking for an opening, and Geoff easily blocked his punches. "Come on, *hit* me, ya little girl."

Determination alone couldn't get Richard through to land a punch. He tired from punching uphill into Geoff's midriff, and when he dropped his guard, Geoff tagged him. The boy saw stars and lost his balance. Recovering from the shock, he burst into tears and locked himself in the bathroom. Geoff leaned on the other side of the door.

"You can bet Ivan wouldn't cry," he said. Later exercises in preparation for Ivan included weights, bayonet drills with brooms, and cold baths to inure the boy against fear of pain.

One weekend Jane took Richard to visit friends, leaving Geoff to fend for himself. Returning on Sunday night, lugging suitcases up the stairs, she was winded when she swung open the apartment door. From behind a newspaper, Geoff asked what was for supper.

"I don't know," she said. "It's late. I hadn't thought about it."

"*It's* not late. *You're* late," he said, folding the paper down to glare.

Jane abandoned the suitcases on the doormat and marched to the kitchen. She pulled a can of soup from the cupboard and opened the drawer for a saucepan. It was empty. All her pots, a wedding present, were gone. He'd ditched them out of spite. She confronted Geoff. He ordered her to bed, intent on submission.

After Jane and Geoff feigned celebrating their second wedding anniversary, she secretly rented a big sedan and parked it a block away. The next morning, Geoff ate his breakfast, put his coat on, straightened his tie in the mirror, and left. Jane listened to his footsteps fading down the stairs. She turned to Richard, loading his book bag for school.

"You're not going to school today," she said. They packed the car, terrified that he would return for something he might have forgotten and catch them. The car overflowed with clothes, books, pictures, wedding presents from her side of the aisle, a footstool, houseplants, and a floor lamp. She left his possessions and, as a statement, the remaining cookware. They fled to Rhode Island, where Mother was packing to move back to Leesburg. Both women were looking forward to a life free from a domineering husband.

The phone rang persistently. Geoff was outraged, then conciliatory. When Jane refused him, he was furious, and she hung up on him. Minutes later, he would try again. They took the phone off the hook, and Jane hired a lawyer to do her talking.

On the civil side, Jane's lawyer told her she had to pick grounds for divorce. He suggested "cruel and abusive treatment," and Jane reluctantly agreed. She was thirty-four years old and offended at the implication that she was a helpless female victim. Jane petitioned the Church for annulment of her marriage. In reciting her rehearsed list of civil abuses to the priest, the complaints seemed weak to her. Starting with Dave, she knew she'd committed many sins, which in aggregate were worthy of excommunication. Probably the gravest sin was refusal to bear Geoff's children.

"Reconcile before Geoff changes his mind," was all her priest said. A lonely pang shot through her. Since childhood, she had embraced Catholicism and relied on its offer of refuge and transcendental acceptance. When she recognized the Church's abandonment of her as a betrayal, anger replaced her guilt and fear.

Months later, a letter arrived with the bishop's seal on the envelope. She threw it in the trash, unopened, certain that it ordered her excommunication. The crucifix in her bedroom came down but lay on a shelf covered by paperbacks she read to fall asleep, mostly spy thrillers. When she moved houses, the crucifix could be found similarly concealed. Jane never set foot in another Catholic church, except during her brother's West Point funeral.

"Man is the only animal vain enough to conceive of an afterlife," she'd say of organized religion.

From the ages of thirty-five to thirty-eight, Jane took a job as a secretary at Rivers Country Day School near Boston. The pay was slim, but as an employee, tuition was relaxed for her son, and they both had the same vacations. Jane rented a room in houses owned and occupied by widows or spinsters.

Meanwhile, Mother bought a lot, not far from Mauka Farm, and built a house of her own design. She hired Dave Rust's new wife, Joanne, one of the few architects in the area, to draw the plans. They became friends and did not talk about Dave. Jane and Richard spent the summers with Mother, riding Tom's horses with him and his children. Richard lobbied to stay in Virginia, which was, for him, idyllic compared to the suburbs of Boston. In 1962, they moved in with Mother.

Jane took a job as a sixth-grade teacher at Leesburg Elementary, and Richard started at the local high school. The school board had no objection to her past. Because many of the teachers were only high school graduates, Jane's education was valued. Besides, her personal situation was no longer unusual. In Jane's first year of teaching, there were two pregnancies in her homeroom. Students who flunked the same grade consecutively were given a social promotion after the third failure. Those who progressed only by social promotions reached the sixth grade praying for their sixteenth birthday, the legal age for quitting school. School was agony for them. When puberty came along, it was the only thing that held their interest. Disruptions were constant. Jane asked to be dropped back two grades, saying, "I want them *before* sex rears its ugly head."

Even without puberty, fourth graders were a handful. Jane advocated the invention of breakfast cereals that sapped energy from kids and decided that the best way to manage them at recess was mandatory slow-pitch softball. She brought a bat and a ball to school and before the first game naively agreed to the boys' demand for teams by gender. Then, realizing the inequity, she appointed herself as pitcher for the girls' team. The boys smirked. None knew of her jumping career because she thought that the feminist movement in the 1960s was trashy and did not want to be revered as a pioneer. Jane proved to be a lousy pitcher, and the boys guffawed at the girls' errors. At bat, wearing a plaid skirt, white blouse, and flats, Jane waited for the right pitch through a storm of heckling. She silenced them by ripping a line drive, scattering the infield for a triple.

"Your gray-haired old-lady school teacher isn't so feeble," she yelled from third base.

News spread through the school, and kids envisioned humiliating their teachers on the field. The rivalry escalated to a faculty-versus-student softball game at the end of the year where the teachers clobbered the students. Teachers needled the kids through the succeeding school year, culminating in a rematch. The score was again so lopsided that the principal yielded to parental rumblings and ordered mixed teams for next year's game. Jane said the decision was spineless.

Whenever the principal referred to teaching as a "profession," Jane braced for another after-school duty or an attempt to discourage them from unionizing. She resisted joining the union and referred to her job as a public babysitting service, counting the days to her retirement. A fellow teacher egged her on with letters to her from a fictitious parent: "We cannot be interrupted from watching our soap operas to come pick up a marginally sick child. Our schedules are very demanding with pedicures, shopping, and hair appointments. Therefore, before calling us, please obtain a note from each little darling's pediatrician verifying that he or she is indeed sick." Having started late, Jane was in her sixties before her pension was viable, and she retired in 1986 with twenty-five years service.

"I don't want teaching anywhere in my epitaph," Jane often said. Walter Devine, one of her former fourth-grade students, would disagree. He was afflicted with palsy and recovering from an operation to help him walk. At recess, instead of having him stand immobile beside her on the playground, she gave him a super-ball from her locked drawer of confiscated items. Contrary to rules, he was free to bounce it in the classroom alone, where he could use the desks and chairs to support himself in chasing it. He said in a 2006 interview, "Now, I'm a teacher, and I understand how rare kindness is in the classroom."

In Leesburg, Mother turned her attentions to painting, amateur theater, and study of the occult. She visited abandoned haunted houses for contact with the spirits trapped there, sometimes successfully, according to her. Jane scoffed at the possibility. Mother's motive was more curiosity than salvation. In her eighties, she painted a landscape of the afterlife, dominated by abstract tornadoes in soft spring hues. Looking at the painting, Jane asked her if she was afraid to die.

"I consider death as the next great adventure," Mother replied.

Jennet inherited Mother's fascination with the occult. During one of Jennet's seances in Texas, Pop spoke to her through a medium. Mother and Jane were amused by his message.

"Don't waste any more money on votive candles in church," he told Jennet. "There's no such thing as purgatory."

Despite Jane's skepticism, the night her brother died in Vietnam, she was awakened by his voice calling her name and knew immediately what it meant. The next day, Mother was officially notified that he had been killed in a helicopter crash. A week later, a letter came to Jane from him, postmarked days before the crash. For the rest of her life, she kept it in the top drawer of her dresser, unopened.

Richard was buried several graves down from Pop at the West Point cemetery in July 1968. Jane's son had just entered West Point and was in the phase of training known as "Beast Barracks," a shock-treatment introduction to the military for new cadets. While Jane was at Vassar in 1943, her brother had entered West Point. His first letter to her said, "Beast Barracks is meant to weed out the men from the boys. The men have gone home and us boys are still here." At the funeral, she watched her son, dressed in new cadet uniform, help bear her brother's casket down the stairs from the Catholic chapel.

Ancestors of Jane's had fought in every American war, including the Revolution, and none had been harmed. Vietnam claimed her brother, Uncle Buck's son-in-law, and Jennet's brother-in-law. Yet Jane never reversed her position that Vietnam was a just cause and did not dwell on the possibility of losing her son, who also chose the army for a career. Jane's pride for her brother was as strong as her grief.

In 1963, Jane bought an unbroken filly named Metacles because the horse looked so much like Fitz in conformation and color. Jane's intent was recreation and hunting. Spiral notebooks of Cappy's advice came off the shelf for consultation in making the young horse. Metacles progressed nicely, and Jane enrolled with the mare in combined training clinics, schooling over obstacles found in the Three-Day event. She bred Metacles and named the filly Divarty's Eagle in memory of her brother, serving in the 101st Airborne Division, nicknamed the "Screaming Eagles," when he was killed. Metacles foundered from the strain of delivery and had to be destroyed. Jane bottle-fed the filly, who, within a year, developed a twisted intestine and also had to be destroyed.

Thereafter, Jane gave up owning horses and helped Anita White with hers. Anita was master of foxhounds for Loudoun Hunt and needed two horses ready to go at all times. Jane worked to make them safe, willing hunters. In the midst of an acrimonious divorce, Adele Hawthorne moved her horse into Anita's barn and spent afternoons on long rides with Jane. It was good therapy for Adele, but Jane's position wasn't often empathetic. Jane advocated dignity at all costs and had no sympathy for women who portrayed themselves as victims. In a 2006 interview, Adele said, "Jane was my best friend during that time, but you didn't ask her a question unless you wanted an answer."

Jane maintained a few cats. But for companionship, Jane adopted dogs from the animal shelter. She owned only one at a time and insisted on mongrels. The one she loved the best was Sindy, probably because she and Sindy grew old together. Sindy came from the shelter when she was a pup, part Springer Spaniel and part Border Collie. Sindy knew the meaning of over one hundred of Jane's words, including the names of the cats and each of the four exterior doors from the house. Jane kept a list of them on the kitchen table and added a new one each time Sindy demonstrated its meaning. When Jane exercised Anita's horses through the countryside, Sindy trotted nearby, parting a meandering path through the tall grass with her nose elevated to keep the seeds out. Jane would whistle when the dog darted off or fell behind to investigate a scent. On hot days, Jane stopped at creeks to water her horse. In the stream's deep holes, Sindy paddled in serpentines, her tail floating in the wake, lapping water at the same time.

At age forty-eight, Jane sat on a borrowed horse, waiting to enter the show ring at the Washington National Horse Show. It had been twenty years since she entered a class A competition, and she regretted letting herself to get talked into it by Elizabeth Rogers, a younger woman who hunted with Jane and knew of her show record. Representing Loudoun Hunt, she and two other women entered the hunt team class against twenty other teams from across the country. The hunt teams were to jump six jumps in tandem and finish over the seventh riding three abreast. Spacing, style, and pace were judged, along with jumping faults. Jane had schooled with her teammates for three weeks, but in the arena's floodlights, the shiny multicolored jumps looked huge to her.

Just before the class, the band belted out a jaunty tune. Jane was grateful that the mare stood through it on three legs, ears at half-mast, unperturbed. Stirrup irons clicking together, the three women re-hashed strategy as they moved forward a length at a time in the long line. Reports filtered back about riders being dumped ignominiously at the last fence. No team had been able to jump the last fence abreast. When they were second from the front, conversation died. Jane's old shad-belly coat, silk top hat, and canary breeches were tight. She later wrote of her thoughts before the entry gate: "My former show companions had the good sense to quit this business. I am a stranger in a world which once was my life. . . . I miss the familiar voices wishing me luck. . . . [It] brings back memories of my own beloved Fitz, Portmaker, My Bill."

From the forced crowding and long wait, one horse snapped at another. Jane massaged the mare's withers with her fingers, and the horse relaxed. She hoped, just as in the old days, her butterflies would disappear beyond the gate.

Entering the ring, Jane welcomed the comparative tranquillity and focused. The horses picked up the spacing as planned, with Jane in the middle. Jane heard the rhythmic thud of cantering and pebbles thrown by hooves, splattering the ring's plywood walls. *The feel of the mare's body as she leaves the ground, never altering her stride, the flip of her hindquarters as she clears the fence, and the landing, galloping on, send a thrill up my spine . . . the little mare is as honest and willing as any champion I have ever ridden.* On the next-to-last fence, the horse ahead dropped its hocks and hit the rail. Miraculously, it stayed up, but Jane knew that the error would keep them out of the ribbons. She put it out of her mind and set for the task no team had yet accomplished.

Head-to-head, her team circled for the last fence. A roar built from the crowd. There was no hesitation, and all three left the ground as one. The audience whistled and screamed as the horses landed and pulled away together. Applause continued after they left the ring. Knowing that the task was done, the horses pulled the reins through their riders' fingers to relax. The three women were grinning at each other, breathless from the thrill of the last fence. It was Jane's last class.

When Jane was in her late thirties, she had taken up skiing with her young son. Despite studying ski magazines diligently, she never advanced beyond intermediate. Her son made the West Point ski team as a Nordic, and she drove six hours to many of his National Collegiate Athletic Association meets in New England. When he was a lieutenant at Fort Carson, Colorado, she visited and skied at Telluride, where panoramas of massive bedded uplifts and erosions overwhelmed her geologist's eye. A black diamond run there, named "The Plunge," was a regular for her son and his buddies. The view down the canyon wall onto the tiny rooftops in the mining town below invited vertigo. Before looking over the edge, Jane planted her poles firmly in front to avoid accidental entry. Jumping six foot ten inches on a rogue horse was something she worked up to incrementally and when she was young enough to heal quickly from injury. She asked many questions about the Plunge, weighing the potential for disaster against the adventure. Several times she screwed up her middle-aged courage to try the Plunge but chickened out at the top.

Jane continued to ski into her late sixties, miffed that when she approached the age for senior citizen discounts, they moved the age up. Despite the escalating expense, she returned to Telluride every few years.

"Promise me," she said to her son, "you'll scatter my ashes on the Plunge because that's the only way I'll ever make it down that monster."

Jane's fascination with geology led to prospecting. It started with drooling over display cases in rock shops and progressed to solo summer trips out West picking through tailings at abandoned mines. Her return luggage astounded the airline clerks, but they rarely charged her for the extra weight. At home, peering over her glasses at a lump of garnet between her fingers, she'd recount the story of its discovery, starting with a tip from a gas station attendant, followed by a punishing trip in an airport rental car over deteriorated logging roads.

In Canon City, Colorado, she saw a huge tailing at a working mine. Ignoring the signs against trespassing, she drove to the tailing within view of the office trailer. She intended to ask permission but decided to peek first, and if it didn't look promising, she'd leave. A muddy gray cobble the size of a basketball caught her eye. She chipped a piece off with her geologist's hammer. It was amethyst. She rolled it over and chipped again. Her heart raced in discovering that the crystals went all the way through. Too good to pass up, she hefted the cobble in her arms and staggered toward the trunk of the rental car. The office trailer door slammed open, and a hard-hatted foreman strutted down the steps toward her. She stammered about being a fourth-grade teacher from Virginia, hoping to show the specimen to her students. He allowed the prize and warned her not to come back.

During a summer vacation from teaching, she signed up for a trek across Iceland on Icelandic ponies. The ponies looked so diminutive that she doubted their capacity to make the trip but was soon impressed. They covered thirty miles a day through volcanic landscapes bordered by glaciers, switching to a fresh pony after lunch. Around the campfire at night, the guides taught the lore of Iceland. She made the trek again the next year.

One day, riding alone on one of Anita's horses, she was long overdue back at the barn. Anita went out looking and found her sitting on the ground in the woods, dazed. Although Jane had ridden that path many times, she did not know where she was or how long she'd been there. She did not remember falling. The doctor concluded she'd had a ministroke. It scared her, and although the effects disappeared, she did not go riding alone again.

Shortly after the stroke, Jane became enamored with Don Trayser, an outdoorsman she'd met in 1955 at Watch Hill, Rhode Island. He invited her to Colorado and introduced her to trout fishing. The relationship with Don did not last. Her parting words to him were, "You don't own me." But she was willingly possessed by trout.

After an aorta replacement in her early seventies and an artificial heart valve a few years later, Jane effectively gave up riding, although she wouldn't admit it. Fly-fishing filled the void, and she never looked back. She commuted into Fairfax for night fly-tying classes and accumulated casting videos and books ranging from entomology to piscine vision. Catalogs clogged the mailbox, and she bought multiple versions of every new gadget. Replaced equipment was enthusiastically pushed onto nephews, son, and other potential converts. Harry Middleton's books were Christmas presents to the deserving few. Her note cards were decorated with a print of medieval monks fishing. The picture was titled "Thursday," suggesting Catholic preparation for the following day's supper.

Up to her death, each autumn Jane would splurge on a trip to Wyoming for ten days of guided fishing on the Snake River. The grand scale of western mountains, sky, and wild water soothed her soul. The thrill for her was matching wits with truculent trout, enticing them to strike a bit of unlikely fuzz she had fashioned, and feeling through her own hands the primeval fight in a hooked fish. She let all her fish go. Despite Jane's inexperience, the guides in Jackson Hole called her the "Queen of the Snake" because she routinely caught more than the world-class anglers. It was no accident. On the river, the guides would row their boats to shore for the noon hour and serve lunch to the clients. Fishermen squeezing in a week on the Snake between Scotland and Argentina welcomed the break with wine, sandwiches, and tall stories. With her back turned to them, Jane fished from the bank. When the guide tried to lure her to the folding table and camp chairs, she'd reply, "I saved my retired schoolteacher nickels to come out here to fish, not to eat." At night in the Nordic Inn, she'd go to bed early with aches, heating pad, ice bag, and liniment, intent on being fit when the guide arrived in the morning. During the intervening eleven months in Virginia, local ponds held no interest except to take grandchildren. In the winter, she'd call the guides she'd befriended out West to ask about snow accumulation and speculate on river flows during the week she'd booked in the coming summer.

Mother's mental and physical capacities deteriorated, but Jane respected her wishes to stay at home. Eventually, Mother slept in her clothes, forgot to bathe or take pills, and fought Jane about it. Not strong enough to safely lift Mother in and out of the tub, Jane put her in a nursing home and visited daily.

"You just put me in here so you could get my house," Mother spat. It wounded Jane to the core. She'd kept the house up for Mother for over thirty years.

"That's not my mother talking," Jane told herself.

Mother died in 1989 of pneumonia, just before her eighty-eighth birthday. Because of the shortage of space at the West Point cemetery, she was buried on top of her husband. The irony of Mother finally getting the upper hand was not lost on Jane. Jennet came to the funeral, and a truce between the sisters existed for a day. Jane expected trouble from Jennet over the estate, but Mother's house quietly passed into Jane's hands. The funeral was the last time they spoke.

20

THE NEXT GREAT ADVENTURE

Jane's house stood high on the ridge in thick woods. Decaying leaves clogged the gutters, smothered Mother's old flower beds, and smelled musky. The building contractor had been forbidden by Mother to cut any tree outside the footprint of the foundation. Winter winds arrived at the ridge from the northwest with but brief interruption from the Appalachian Mountains. Trees were valued for windbreak and shade. The house was heated by an oil furnace and two big woodstoves. Oil was expensive, and Jane heated with wood. A dented chain saw with a bag of freshly sharpened chains resided on the concrete inside the garage door, but she sawed only trees that were already dead. When Mormons or Jehovah's Witnesses knocked on the door looking for a convert, Jane continued Mother's custom of cutting their pitch short by announcing she was a druid (tree worshipper).

The woodstoves had been installed in the fireplaces within a few years of moving in, forty years prior. She initially fed the stoves limbs culled from the forest floor, already broken by nature to the right size. I bought the chainsaw at a pawn shop and gave it to her for Christmas. Friends teased her that it was not a suitable gift for a lady, and she said it was the best Christmas present she ever got.

In her late sixties, Jane was diagnosed with cervical cancer. The cancer could have been detected earlier, but she had avoided annual examinations and Pap smears. Like most women of her time, she referred to all things gynecological as "female problems" and considered them to be revolting. Dots were permanently tattooed on her belly for aiming the radiation gun at the tumor. During the treatments, she subscribed to wellness magazines, changed her diet, and visualized gamma rays zapping the cancer cells as in a video game. Twice a day in winter, regardless of mud or snow, she pushed a wheelbarrow of firewood up the steep grade from the stable, using the size of the load to gauge her recovery. It took almost a year to get back in shape. Subsequent checkups were clean, but no one knew the radiation fused an intestine to her aorta, slowly precipitating an aneurism.

Up until her aorta was about to rupture in her early seventies, she had never been in a hospital overnight except to give birth to me. In the six weeks it took to diagnose the aortic aneurism, she wasted away from fever and vomiting. The doctors had doubts about her surviving the operation.

A year after the aorta replacement, an artificial heart valve was recommended. She put it off to gain physical and mental strength and scheduled it so as not to conflict with her annual fishing trip to Jackson Hole. Her St. Jude heart valve was made of metal. Seated in the quiet of her kitchen, its clicking was audible. I teased her about sounding like the crocodile that swallowed Captain Hook's alarm clock.

In April 2001, at age seventy-seven, she pulled a groin muscle. Over the next month, it refused to heal. She eventually hobbled to her chiropractor, who told her one leg was shorter than the other. An X-ray showed that the hip was broken. During the hip replacement, a biopsy found cancer in the bone. It was also in her liver and lungs. The doctors gave her a few months.

The nearby Museum of Hounds and Hunting was holding an exhibit of Paul Brown's art. Prior to discovering she had terminal cancer, Jane had lent to the museum the watercolors and sketches of Fitz that Paul had given her. She was determined to go to the opening, and her doctors consented. The museum asked Jane to write an article. She completed it a few weeks before she died: "Gifts From Paul Brown": "When General Sultan saw the horse delivered to him at Schofield Barracks, Hawaii, he was not a happy man. The year was 1941, Fitzrada was a modest horse, and General Sultan, all 200 pounds of him, had misgivings about the mount he had ordered from the Cavalry Training School at Fort Riley, Kansas." Jane went on to describe her failure to reform Fitz, his scheduled destruction by the army, her browbeating Pop into buying Fitz, and the road to their unlikely successes. "Fitz and I foxhunted for nine seasons together; giving me glorious memories of crisp autumn days and hounds in full cry—and the run from 11 A.M. at Glebe Plantation nonstop to Aldie after dark. We also spent a lot of quiet time hacking around our Virginia countryside and enjoying everything it had to offer us.

"He was the finest horse I ever knew and I'll never forget him or his undaunted spirit. That spirit comes alive in his portraits drawn by Paul Brown. Brown's masterful technique, both in pencil and water color, portray Fitz's personality as well as his physical splendor and extraordinary abilities. I will treasure these forever."

Jane was flattered by the number of people who came to Loudoun Long Term Care to say good-bye to her. "I had no idea I was so well liked," she said.

One of the visitors was Mary Cothran, a friend of thirty years and a nurse.

"Mary, what's it like to die?" Jane asked.

"Well, you're in hospice, and that's good. They'll make sure there's no pain."

"That's not what I mean," Jane said.

"I know you're preparing for a leap, but I don't know what shape you'll be in when you land."

Toward the end, Jane didn't eat more than a spoonful from the trays that were brought to her bed. She weighed ninety pounds. As the morphine dosage increased, her voice got softer, hovering on the verge of sleep. I asked her if she had any sense of anything on the other side, mindful of her position on the subject.

"Funny you should ask," she said, licking her dry lips. "Yesterday, I felt people I knew gathering around me. I couldn't see them, but I could feel 'em. Don't know names." Four days later, she slid into a coma.

The next week, the morning nurse came in and found her sleeping and breathing normally on the floor beside her hospital bed. How she got there was a mystery. The railings were still up on the bedsides. There were no bruises from the fall. The nurse said it was not uncommon. She thought when the spirit left, it the lifted the body.

She died before the sun came up on June 21, 2001. Although her breathing had stopped, I lingered, held her hand, and felt her body warmth ebb before I called the nurse and left to fulfill a promise. The finality of honoring this promise was crushing.

I went to the kennel where Jane's dog, Sindy, was boarded. The dog had been there for more than a month. Over the last twelve years, Jane and Sindy had been separated this long only once, during Jane's aorta replacement. Even at home with Jane in town running errands, Sindy would scratch through a door and run away to find her. Jane boarded Sindy on her fishing trips.

At the kennel, Sindy was delighted to see me and expected Jane to be close behind. Sindy was gray in the muzzle, and her lower eyelids drooped, but her black-and-white coat was shiny and thick. The old dog wiggled, sniffed, and backtracked, energetically searching for Jane.

"Freedom!" Jane used to say, witnessing Sindy's excitement when she got the dog out of the kennel and took her leash off.

I couldn't take Sindy home and have the dog search high and low for Jane, and I couldn't bear to keep my promise just yet. Late into the afternoon, I walked Sindy on a long leash up and down the creek banks and pasture where she had romped and explored with Jane on afternoon rides over Anita's farm. With the wavy feathers of her hair bouncing, Sindy sniffed out her old haunts and trotted in the water of the creek.

As I drove Sindy to the veterinarian's office, she lounged on the backseat, panting. Bill Rokus had been Jane's vet since he first came to

Leesburg, almost thirty years prior. Sindy perked up when I pulled into Rokus's driveway. Even for Jane, it was a tough task to get Sindy from the car into Bill's office, but today she didn't balk.

"Ma died this morning," I announced.

"I heard," Bill said. "She was a great lady." Somebody must have called him, but I couldn't remember talking to anybody since I left her bedside.

"I want you to put Sindy down," I said.

Bill stared at me too long for my liking. "Why are you doing this?" he asked.

"Because Ma asked me to. She thought the dog would search for her, run off, get hit by a car, or starve. She wanted Sindy cremated with her."

"Sounds like Jane," Bill said. His shoulders sagged.

I held Sindy on the stainless-steel table while Bill found a vein in her leg and pushed the plunger home. Sindy dropped. We loaded her limp body into a cardboard box and carried it to the car. Then, I drove to the funeral home, where Jane's body waited. I traveled down the road where I remembered walking on a pony behind Jane on Fitz, almost fifty years ago. The one-lane dirt road was known to us by its county number, 729. Now, washboarded by a legion of sport-utility vehicles commuting from McMansions sprouting on the adjacent farmland, reflective bright-blue street signs proclaim it Shelburne Glebe Road. Tom Taylor's old farm and the Glebe Plantation still remain in pasture, but their days are numbered by escalating land value.

The old memory was vivid, though I must have only been four or five at the time. The three-mile trip from Tom Taylor's back to Mauka was my first ride of any significant duration. She encouraged me to trot, but I was timid. We'd have to hurry to get home to Mauka before dark. Jane was riding Fitz with one hand. In the other, she held a lead shank clipped to the piebald pony named Beauty, trailing behind her. I was too young to do much more than hang on. Jane clucked to Fitz, asking him to move faster. The lead shank went tight, and Beauty reluctantly dragged to a trot. I bounced along with a death grip on Beauty's mane. Jane looked back over her shoulder at me.

"Try posting," she said. "It'll be easier on your rear end."

"I've tried and can't get it," I said.

"Keep trying," she said.

I pushed down on my knees to get off the saddle and then relaxed to fall back. Initially, it exaggerated my banging. Coordinating with Beauty's short stride was frustrating. But somehow I finally found a rhythm, and the ride smoothed. With a little push at the right time, Beauty's stride tossed me slightly off the saddle, where I remained suspended through the next hoofbeat, and gently caught me as he fell back, over and over.

"Look! Ma, I'm posting," I yelled.

"Yup, doesn't it feel good?" she asked.

As I was carrying Sindy's body on the same reach of dirt road, a scrawny red fox jumped out of the hedgerow in front of the car and danced its hindquarters from side to side in a playful lope, like a child skipping, for sixty yards before ducking back into the hedgerow. I had the feeling Jane was behind it.

In the intervening days before her memorial service, I began excavating through seventy-five years of accumulated family debris. Despite two house fires and a moving van fire, the amount that survived was staggering. Military families were so frequently uprooted that they kept and repaired crumbling mementos offering continuity: boxes of seashells found on Hawaiian beaches; a console iron with a four-foot anvil and powered roller for ironing sheets; a miniature outrigger canoe carved in Samoa, the eastern limit of Pop's World War II duties; steamer trunks of dresses and uniforms, including Mother's World War II Red Cross volunteer uniform from Fort Bragg; Jane's tarnished silver trophies, boots, riding clothing, and dusty grocery bags of ribbons; Fitz's mildewed bridles and bits; Mother's paintings and art supplies; Vassar textbooks; Christmas and Halloween decorations; on and on. Relatives kidded me that I was now the curator of the Pohl museum.

A digital wristwatch sat on her dresser, its battery corroded with age. Unable to decipher the instructions, she'd called me at odd hours to defeat or activate its alarm, reset the time and date, and understand its modes. When I went behind the former Iron Curtain for the army,

I gave her a used computer and an e-mail account so we could keep in touch, but she was too timid to venture beyond playing solitaire on the computer. She signed up for an adult education class in home computing at the high school with other novices of her age. When she accomplished a task on the screen, she would scream, "I got it! I got it!" to the irritation of the other students. Many nights I spent on the phone with her going through a litany of keystrokes that she copied longhand for future reference.

Dave Rust's steeplechase racing saddle sat on the basement rack. A friend of his had recently given the saddle to me because my father had won the Virginia Gold Cup twice on it. After leaving his father's farm, Dave lived in many places in the county, earning his living in real estate and helping his friends cut up their family farms into lots. He died of leukemia three years prior to Jane. Fourteen years before he died, Dave's second wife, Joanne, had divorced him for his drinking and moved into a townhouse in Leesburg to raise their two children. She and Jane became friends and joked they would dance together on his grave. But in the end, neither attended Dave's graveside funeral at his ancestral cemetery in Alexandria. He had published a list of people he didn't want there, including his sister, whom he had sued for their mother's inheritance. My half sister and I greeted the few family members that came. For years, Dave had predicted his death as impending, using it as bait for codependency with us. At best, we remembered him for his fun-loving charm. There was no grief in our party. But separately, two young couples came to us, sobbing. We did not know them and thought they were at the wrong funeral. As it turned out, Dave had sold them their houses, introduced them to his friends, and visited often. "He gave us not just a house but a hometown," they said.

Military moves placed no weight restriction on officers' libraries. I found letters all the way back to 1902, two footlockers full of Pop's 16-mm film reels, and book boxes that had not been unpacked since 1941. For the past fifty years, Mother subscribed to monthly science-fiction, mystery, and astrology magazines and stored every copy in the attic. As an engineer, I expressed concern that the ceiling would collapse. But Jane was a worse hoarder than Mother: elaborate miniature dioramas of foxhunts, plastic flowers she'd made, cracked plaster horse statues, abandoned sweaters with rows of stitches on the needles, and nearly a dozen pairs of mud shoes in various colors. After her ministroke, a wellness magazine suggested crossword puzzles to fight senility, so half-completed books of *New York Times* crossword puzzles littered the house with a pencil and a big eraser in each. There were jars of nails, screws, and hinges she had saved, including buckles from pocketbooks and bridles that had disintegrated long ago. She used to defend herself by saying, "You never know when you might need it." She knew where all that stuff was in the house, and I never did figure out her logic for keeping track of it. She used to say to me about the clutter, "I pity you, when I die."

U

Jane's memorial service was held on a humid June day in the tiny historic Episcopal church where Anita's husband, Lige, was the reverend. Jane relied on Lige when stumped by crossword puzzles, forever impressed that he knew the origin of the saying "Tinker to Evers to Chance." Over the years, Jane had infrequently attended the little church at Anita's urging.

Among the fifty attendees were her brother's widow and children; her son and a grandson; fellow teachers; her veterinarian, Bill Rokus; members of the local hunt; neighbors; and farmers. More than a few knew her when she was riding Fitz. Bobby Burke, the Graham sisters, Carolyn Rogers, and many other legends from the horse industry hobbled outside on the grass to greet each other and reminisce about the postwar show circuit. A neighbor, Willi Burkhart, said of the people at the service, "They represented a way of life, the passing of an era." As amateur competitors fifty years ago, they were thrilled to be riding against professional men. Bobby Burke said, "Back then, it was about fun; now it's about money." He told the story of Pappy and Ginny Moss, who lived in Southern Pines, North Carolina, and hunted and showed with Jane and Fitz after the quicksand fiasco at Fort Bragg. Pappy arrived at shows not able to afford entry fees. For six dollars from a hastily assembled audience in the parking lot, he would jump his horse over the hood of a car. It was enough for entry fees, lunch, and gasoline for the trip home.

Ken VanAuken, her brother's roommate from West Point and a lifelong family friend, read the eulogy: "Whatever subject caught her attention, she practiced, experimented, invented. She longed for the clean line, whether it is the flow of a horse, the cast of a rod, or the grammar of our president [George W. Bush]. Fortunately for us, she infected us with her enthusiasm to try. May God love her and welcome her into the kingdom of Heaven, where she will be with her family, friends, animals, and Fitz."

On an overcast day the following February, I skied alone to the edge of the Plunge at Telluride. In my backpack was the black plastic box that held her ashes. I paused on the spot where she had been attracted by the challenge and wrestled with her judgment. Here, she asked me many times about iced moguls, narrow chutes, and other dangers below. Caution prevailed, and she turned away each time, reluctant to leave but temporarily relieved.

Pushing off the edge, I felt like I was trespassing on ground she had somehow claimed by longing. I skied carefully through calf-deep snow into a copse of tall evergreens at the head of the first steep pitch. Kneeling in the privacy of the trees, I released her ashes and thanked her.

The snow melt in the spring of 2002 carried her ashes down the Plunge, through the spectacular geology that lifted her spirits, past the trout she sought to fool, and into the same Pacific she crossed in 1938 on the way to her destiny with Fitz.

EPILOGUE

From my mother, I inherited an addiction for the kinesthetic. In my adult life, I didn't often live where there were horses, but when my life soured from divorce or career failure, I sought them out for the reassurance. Barns are a magnet for me, and that's no wonder. My earliest memories are playing in our barn while my mother mucked out stalls, cleaned tack, fed, doctored, and attended to the countless other tasks of keeping horses.

A favorite pastime of mine was—and still is—leaning on a stall door stretching out my empty hand, palm up, toward the horse inside. I like waiting for curiosity to bring the animal to smell my hand, an offer to meet a stranger and make a friend. A twinge of anticipation comes when something so large turns toward me. I look to the ears for a sign. Some are indifferent, some demand respect, and some shamelessly nuzzle and rub. I don't like those that are hostile when there isn't a peppermint in it for them. Either they're spoiled or having a bad day, and I never know which. It says something nice about horses that almost every one will come to an empty hand.

Jane insisted on good riding habits from my cousins and me, even when we were very young, just as I imagined the cavalry sergeants had demanded of her. When she rode with us, she wore a tattered black-velvet hunting cap and alternated between critique and encouragement.

At the end of her riding lesson, the care of animals came before human needs. She'd show us how to groom and harp on us until it was right. I was five when we left Virginia for Rhode Island and Boston, where we did not ride.

We moved back to Loudoun County in 1962. I was fourteen and envious of the kids in my high school who were raised on farms and had a horse or two. Even during the week, they'd get off the school bus to saddle a horse and ride to congregate at one of their farms, much like kids today hang out at the mall. Clayton Kephart, a carpenter down the mountain from us, kept a pack of hounds and hunted on the Sabbath. The invitation was open, and there was no dress code. The formal fox-hunters considered hunting on Sunday to be a sin against the sport, but Clayton's hunts were well attended by kids in jeans.

When Jane felt I was jumping well enough to get by in the formal hunting field, I was fifteen. We borrowed the proper clothing, and she fitted me using basting stitches and safety pins.

"Your behavior is a reflection on me," was a recurring refrain from her at that irresponsible stage of my life.

"Don't run up forward of the Field Master," she drilled.

"Yes Ma . . ."

"Get off and open gates for others."

"Yes Ma . . ."

"If someone is having trouble with their horse, you stop and help them."

"Ma! Enough."

Jane's interest in hunting was centered mostly on the hounds work-ing the fox and guessing what the fox would do next. The riding was incidental for her. But for me, riding over fences and country speed was everything, and foxhunting was a grand excuse for doing it.

I didn't have a horse, but there was no shortage of other people's horses that needed exercise. A few times Jane's old friend, Adele Haw-thorne, offered to let me hunt her big Thoroughbred ex–race horse, Octagon. She claimed he was a powerful brute and a coward and said she had a better horse to ride. On a cold December day, I helped Adele trailer the two horses to a meet with Loudoun Hunt.

During the hunt, I was far behind the field of riders when the hounds found a scent and took off. The field quickly cantered downhill out of my sight on a logging road that led to a pasture in a floodplain. Incised into the floodplain was a creek with banks rising four feet out of shallow water. When the field arrived at the creek, the hounds had crossed and were disappearing over a hill. All of the riders, including Adele, stopped and looked up and down the creek for a ford so that they could safely trot through the shallow water and avoid negotiating the steep banks. Meanwhile, Octagon and I were roaring down the logging road trying to catch up. By the time we got down on the floodplain, Octagon was galloping too fast for my comfort, and I wasn't strong enough to pull him up. However, the creek didn't look that wide to me. As we got closer, though, it got wider—too wide, maybe ten feet across. I had my doubts and could feel Octagon doing the same. But at our speed, it was too late to stop.

"Oh, gawd!" Adele screamed, seeing what we were going to attempt.

I had a premonition of our arc falling short and Octagon smashing into the lip of the far bank on his belly. *Broken back, maybe. A punctured lung, for sure*, I thought. If, after the impact, he toppled over backward into the creek on top of me, I'd suffer the same injuries. I clenched my jaw. *Better to go down savoring the attempt than dreading the result*, I told myself.

I was electrified, and Octagon was on autopilot. He knew what had to happen, and I had to stay with him. *Don't hinder him*, I cautioned myself. *Keep your balance centered and let him have all his head for the big stretch*.

As soon as he left the ground, I knew we'd clear it, and I let out a "Whoop!" On the other side, we pulled up to a trot. Octagon strutted sideways, knowing he was the "big man on campus."

"There's nothing chicken about this horse," I boasted to Adele when she caught up.

"You're an idiot!" she said. My mother wasn't there, but Adele reported the exploit to her in my presence, and Jane glared at me. Later in private, she let me have it. But I sensed she understood how we got swept over the creek. One of her favorite quotes was from Robert Surtees, a nineteenth-century author: "Ah, Foxhunting, the Sport of Kings. The image of war with none of its guilt and but five and twenty percent of its danger."

Now, I am a retired army colonel with grown children, and I continue to ride occasionally to Loudoun Hunt's hounds over the same ground Jane and Fitz covered. I don't own a horse but rely on the kindness of others, seldom riding the same horse twice. Yet out foxhunting sometimes I still feel that same fool's courage building between us strangers, as powerful as two people falling in love.

Every summer, Jane invited her young grandchildren, grandnieces, and grandnephew to stay in her house and attend a weeklong riding camp for kids at Maintree Farm, near Leesburg, owned by Laurie Shreeve, the widow of Dave's best friend. We'd make the trip from North Carolina in six hours and sleep on bunks in her house. She'd show up at the ring when they were being taught. Even in her seventies, she'd ride with them on the days the class went out for trail rides, wearing her tattered hunting cap and gripping her fly switch.

The counselors were college girls and had been born long after Jane and Fitz were celebrities. They had no idea who she was. In trying to select a suitable mount for Jane, they asked if she had ridden before. Jane replied, "I used to ride a little in the 1940s."

On the trail, she shifted down the line of children offering compliments and advice but was more insistent with family than strangers. At night in her house, she'd serve microwave dinners to her brood and listen to their animated recollections of the day.

"You can't call yourself a good rider until you've fallen off *nine* times," she'd say, when they were dismayed over a spill. They witnessed her fall off—once. When dismounting after a trail ride with them, she got her foot hung in the stirrup. She wasn't hurt.

"Aunt Jane, how many times is that for you?" they asked, looking down at her.

"Hundreds!" she said, smiling wryly through her trifocals from flat on her back.

"Aunt Jane, wait a minute . . . I fell off six times last summer I was here, and four times so far this summer."

"Did I say *nine*? I meant *eleven*," she said.

As these kids approached their teens, fewer returned to horse camp. But three of them—my son Ricky and Jane's brother's granddaughters, Ashley and Trish—stuck with it, their goal to get good enough to go foxhunting. They were in horse camp the summer Jane was dying and visited her in the hospital daily to keep her posted on their camp calamities.

Right after Jane died, all of them were soon to be thirteen, and I told them I'd take them hunting at Thanksgiving. Since the founding of Loudoun Hunt a century ago, the meet was a traditional fixture. Hunting usually ended by noon, allowing plenty of time for a Thanksgiving meal. For the five weeks prior in North Carolina, their conversation centered anxiously on the Thanksgiving hunt.

"Where are we gonna borrow riding clothes?" they asked me. "Hey, Grandma had three hunting caps. They're all beat up, but do you think they'll do?" "Will it be okay to wear a dead person's clothes?"

"Everybody passes riding clothes around," I said. "They're too expensive to throw away."

Inevitably, self-doubt cast its shadow.

"How big are these fences gonna be?" they asked.

Rising silently from the table, I put my hand flat on the kitchen counter, a little higher than three feet, perhaps six inches more than they had jumped in camp. Ricky shrugged his shoulders, feigning nonchalance. Ashley giggled nervously. Trish turned pale. The meet was at Maintree Farm, so we planned to rent horses they knew from camp.

"I want Blinky," Ricky said. "He's not afraid of anything."

"I sure hope I get to ride Kiki," Ashley said.

"I want Samson," Trish said. "He's big."

U

We went to Maintree the day before the meet, got on our horses, and jumped them in the ring until we felt comfortable. However, nobody wanted to raise the jumps to kitchen-counter height, and that uncertainty wore on them through the evening while we went in search of black hunting coats, white turtlenecks, light-colored breeches, and black boots. Ricky was the most confident, Ashley chattered with excitement, and Trish started to back out. I told her I'd send her with the hilltoppers, where she would not have to jump, and she relaxed a bit. After rummaging through closets in three households, we had what I thought would pass. Over the objections of the girls, whenever presented with a choice, I opted for too loose over the too tight. We had Ma's old hunting caps, which in their opinion made us look like veterans from years of hunting. By eleven that night, we had all the gear accounted for.

Thanksgiving morning was damp and cool. The air was still and the sky overcast, good conditions for preserving scent. After a hasty breakfast and pinning them into borrowed clothes, we drove to Maintree to tack up our horses, worried about being late and keeping our riding clothes clean and presentable while we brushed our horses in the muddy barnyard. Horse trailers disgorged immaculate horses already tacked. Riders mounted, greeting each other and making last-minute adjustments. The huntsman released the ten couples of hounds from their little trailer and sounded his horn in pips to pack them tightly around his horse. The hunt was moments away from starting as we scrambled to mount. Trish got on Samson and chewed on her lip. I noticed tears tracking down her cheeks. She begged me to abort.

I estimated her probable disaster-to-adventure ratio. Part of hunting is the certainty that something will go wrong, hilariously or tragically. However, I also wanted her to like hunting and come back to horse camp next summer.

"You remember your great-aunt Jane took your mother hunting? Your mother said she was terrified, couldn't sleep the night before, threw up. But she survived. You've seen your mother's eyes light up when she tells the story."

"Yup, many times, but . . ."

"Trish, if you back out, you're gonna miss the chance to share something very special with your mom."

"Yeah, terror."

"If things go badly, I'll clip onto your horse's bridle and lead you back." I showed her the leather lead shank neatly coiled to my saddle. I mounted Carpet, an ex-racehorse fresh from the track and new to hunting. Carpet was jazzed by standing among so many horses milling around, and I had trouble keeping him calm. He was much happier walking around the horse trailers. True to his racehorse training, Carpet felt precise in turning to the left but mushy in the right turns. I'd have to remember to allow for it.

The master of foxhounds for Loudoun Hunt was Anita White, splendid in her scarlet coat. She had held the position for over twenty years and commanded considerable respect. Jane had helped Anita train and exercise her horses for most of those years. As Jane got older and had heart problems, part of her morning routine was to call and let Anita know she was okay. If Jane failed to call, Anita would check on her. Anita knew Jane's progeny had been riding in summer camps but had not met them. Hunting protocol required me to introduce them to the master at the beginning of the hunt, but in the scurry of getting ready, I had not seen Anita.

The huntsman's horn sounded, signaling he was moving the hounds to begin. We fell in behind the field master with thirty others. The first jump came immediately, a coop from the barnyard into a pasture as big as our kitchen counter. My wards drifted to the back of the file queuing for the coop to delay their public trial. Ricky knitted his brow, and Ashley had a death grip on Kiki's reins, telegraphing her fear to the little horse. Nose to tail, the line progressed over the jump.

Ricky went over without incident, his legs and posture reminiscent of his grandmother's. Sensing Ashley's anxiety, Kiki refused, and they went to the rear of the queue to try again. On the fourth try, they made it over beautifully, but seconds later, cantering on the flat, Ashley inexplicably fell. Although she was not hurt, a whip in a scarlet coat ordered her to ride with the hilltoppers for her own safety. Ashley was crestfallen at not being allowed to continue with those jumping fences.

Carpet had a hell of a jump in him and was game to try anything, for which I was grateful. Stuck in the middle of the field of riders, cantering nose to tail in single file through the woods, he didn't have much time to judge his fences, but he never balked. However, true to his Thoroughbred breeding, he hated being held back and was wearing me out keeping him in check.

"Poor Carpet with that lousy rider on him," Carpet's owner, Cindy Shreeve, rightfully yelled at me.

My son and I wound up on a narrow trail deep in the woods below Gobbler's Knob, my grandfather Rust's old farm where I had lived briefly as an infant, sold and developed into housing long ago. Anita was at the head of a line of twenty or so riders on this trail when the hounds changed direction. She needed to reverse her path and asked us all to pull off the trail so she could pass. The woods were littered with fallen trees from a recent hurricane. It was nearly impossible to find a place off the trail.

"*Please* move your horses," Anita said, losing patience. She fought her way down the line, grumbling, brushing knees with riders who could not get off the trail.

She got to Ricky and recognized his tattered hunting cap. She paused, disoriented, staring into his eyes with her mouth open, and burst into tears. Jane had worn that cap for years on their rides together. Unaware of the cause of Anita's distress, Ricky thought he had committed some unforgivable breach of hunting etiquette.

"Where's your father?" she demanded hotly, recovering from an emotional display not appropriate for a master of foxhounds.

Ricky was tongue-tied, dreading upbraiding in front of the entire field. Anita pushed by him, not waiting for an answer.

Moment's later, Ricky noticed his saddle slipping to the side. The girth was too loose. The saddle and its pad would have to be reset on Blinky's withers. Others offered to stay and help, but I was confident we could fix it. As the last horses departed, Carpet went nuts at being left behind with Blinky. He reared up and started backing uncontrollably on his hind legs into a web of knee-high deadfall timber. I hooked an arm around his neck, pulled to stay upright, pressing my chest into his mane, and kicked urgently to move him forward. Blinky jigged and wove, also searching for a way to wrestle control from Ricky to join the herd disappearing in the woods.

"Ricky, I can't get off Carpet," I said. "He'll never hold still long enough for me to get back on. You'll have to fix it on your own."

"No problem, Dad," he said, dismounting. He'd been riding only four weeks over as many years. I hoped he'd inherited his grandmother's horse sense and focus. He held Blinky's reins in his left hand and struggled with the saddle using his right hand. Blinky whirled away, and Ricky chased him. With Blinky's head tethered to Ricky's left hand, they went round and round in tight circles, drifting toward the fallen trees. I had visions of broken legs. Fighting to keep Carpet from bolting, I was powerless to help and asked myself, a dozen times, what Jane would try.

I told Ricky to lead Blinky back onto the trail and pin his right flank up against a tree so that he couldn't wheel away. Ricky had to take the saddle off and start over. By the time he remounted, the field of riders was miles away, and we had no idea where we were. We trotted uphill through dense woods, stopping periodically to catch the cry of hounds or bleats from a hunting horn for direction. At these checks, Blinky and Carpet pulled and danced sideways, impatient to rush on rather than stand and listen.

A whip for the hunt came by us, returning several lost hounds to the pack. We rode behind her, dodging through the woods at speed. I looked at Ricky. He was smoothly centered in Blinky's gallop, grinning. Near the crest of a hill, the whip pointed us toward a pasture and pushed on with her hounds to find the pack. Ricky and I jumped a coop into the pasture, where Carpet was glad to be reunited with the field of riders and the hilltoppers. I was relieved to find Trish in good spirits. Ashley broke free of the hilltoppers, joining Ricky and me over jumps for the rest of the day.

That night in the basement of Jane's house, now my house, I laundered a pile of muddy, sweat-soaked riding clothes. Upstairs, Ashley was on the phone with her girlfriends back in North Carolina. "Oh . . . my . . . gawd . . . ," she said loudly in prefacing each of the day's disasters and triumphs. I remembered Jane's saying about overcoming adversity: "Work with the hand that's dealt and draw another card."

SHOW RECORD

Shows and classes in which Fitz did not place are omitted.

Vassar, New York, 1941–1944

2nd knockdown-and-out at five feet

4th open jumpers at four feet

4th scurry

2nd bridle path hacks

1st touch and out

North Carolina, 1945

In ten shows, he won eight Jumper Championships and one Reserve Jumper Championship

Virginia, 1945

Jumper Champion, Fairfax

1946

Jumped five feet six inches at Hot Springs, Virginia, August

1st knockdown-and-out, Warrenton, Virginia, August 31–September 2

Champion jumper, Forrestville (Middleburg) (won all classes entered, cleared five feet in high jump), October

Champion jumper, Hagerstown, Maryland (six feet ten inches in skyscraper)

Champion jumper, Almas Shrine Show, Meadowbrook, Maryland (six feet six inches)

Champion jumper, McLean, Virginia, October

Madison Square Garden, November 4–9

3rd open jumpers (fifty-three horses entered), went clean in morning elimination; clean in first evening round, two front ticks in jump-off

National Capitol Show, Fort Myer, Virginia, December 6–8

Jumper champion

1st open jumpers

3rd Olympia

1st in-and-out (five jumps staggered between sixteen and twenty-four feet, three feet six inches to five feet six inches and then two jump-offs to six feet)

4th jumper stake

Missed reserve working hunter champion by one point

1st ladies' working hunter

1st working hunter stake

1947

Reserve champion, Modified Three-Day Olympic events, Maryland Hunter Show

Reserve jumper champion, Berryville, Virginia

Champion jumper, Cremona Farm Horse Show, Mechanicsville, Maryland (July)

Champion jumper, Mt. Vernon Horse Show, Grovetown (1st triple bar, five feet high, nine-foot spread)

Champion jumper, Bull Run Hunt Club, Manassas, Virginia, August 3

Champion jumper, Warrenton, Virginia, September

Reserve champion jumper, Forrestville (Middleburg), September 27

Champion jumper, McLean, Virginia, October

Madison Square Garden, 1st, knockdown-and-out (two jump-offs, five feet to five feet six inches)

Virginia Horse Show Association champion jumper, 171 points

1948

Champion jumper, Loudoun, Virginia

1st leg on Master's Bowl (Loudoun Hunt hunters)

Tied for reserve jumper champion, Warrenton, Virginia, tossed a coin and lost

    1st knockdown-and-out at five feet six inches

Champion jumper, McLean, Virginia, third time in three years, retired championship trophy

Madison Square Garden, qualified in all classes

4th Virginia Horse Show Association champion jumper points list

1949

Reserve champion jumper, PHA Show, Middleburg, Virginia

Champion Jumper, Loudoun, Virginia

    2nd leg on Master's Bowl

    1st junior hunters

Working hunter champion, Altoona, Pennsylvania

    Missed reserve champion jumper by half a point

Tied for reserve jumper champion, Berryville, Virginia, tossed a coin and lost

Tied for champion jumper, Forrestville, lost toss and awarded reserve champion Jumper

Working hunter champion, Ohio State Fair (won all his classes), August

Reserve jumper champion, McLean, Virginia

    1st handy working hunter

    1st working hunter preliminary

Bryn-Mawr, Chester County, Pennsylvania

    1st handy working hunters

    1st working hunter preliminary

    1st working hunter pairs with Brandywine

Reserve working hunter champion, Trinity, Upperville, October 7–8

Reserve working hunter champion, Madison Square Garden

8th Virginia Horse Show Association jumper points list

1950

3rd Virginia Field Hunter Championship Trials (chosen by MFH to represent Loudoun Hunt. Four judges, two picked him first, and other two said he was too thin)

Hunter champion, Middleburg Hunter Trials (criteria: best, safest, and most brilliant horse on which to ride to hounds), March 25

Reserve working hunter champion, Casanova Hunter Show (lost by one point)

Reserve working hunter champion, Foxcroft

Champion jumper, Loudoun, retired the Master's Bowl (won it three years in a row), May 13

Madison Square Garden

> 1st pen class with one and a half faults (his performance in elimination rounds was used as standard for manners and time limit)
>
> 4th Working Hunter Championship points

He was retired after Madison Square Garden at age twenty.

Fitz hunted regularly for nine seasons (1941–1950) with Rombout Hunt, New York; Moore County Hounds, North Carolina; and Middleburg and Loudoun Hunts, Virginia.

GLOSSARY

Conformation: the structure and appearance of a horse's body, as it relates to the ideal.

Coop: a type of jump typically found in the hunting field in a fence row, constructed of wood in the shape of a prism, usually 3' high (i.e., chicken coop).

Field Master: an officer of a hunt club responsible to the Master of Foxhounds for keeping the field of club members as close as possible to the hunting pack without interfering with them.

Huntsman: a person who cares for and hunts a pack of foxhounds under the direction of the Master of Foxhounds; often an employee of the hunt club.

Lightweight hunter: a horse capable of carrying up to 165 pounds to hounds. A "heavyweight" hunter is capable of carrying 200 pounds or more to hounds.

Master of Foxhounds: the chief officer of a hunt club responsible for all aspects of hunting in the field, equivalent to a general in the field of battle.

Show Hunter: a horse that exhibits that he is a safe and sure jumper over the type of natural obstacles actually met in the hunting field, that he can gallop comfortably at a uniform pace and in good control, that he is tractable and has good manners; these traits are judged by his style of jumping and his manner of going.

Show Jumper: a horse required only to clear satisfactorily the obstacles prescribed, usually painted, artificial ones, intended to represent any conceivable obstacle a horse might encounter. The manner and way of going are not considered. The judging is entirely mathematical on the basis of ticks, knockdowns, refusals, or time.

Whipper-in: an appointed or hired individual in a hunt club who assists the Huntsman and Master of Foxhounds in the hunting of the pack, equivalent to a scout in the field of battle.

BIBLIOGRAPHY

Cothran, Ben J. "Enter: His Royal Highness the Horse, Madison Square Garden Makes Ready for the 61st National Horse Show," Sunday supplement in unknown (possibly New York because of a reference to Ben commanding a regiment in New York's 77th [reserve] Division) newspaper with sketches by Paul Brown, unknown date.

Devereux, Walter B. "New York Again Hails the Horse." *National Geographic Magazine*, November 1954, 697–720.

Taylor, Henry. "Riding Lesson." In *An Afternoon of Pocket Billiards*. Salt Lake City: University of Utah Press, 1975.

INDEX

Aitkins, Alex: at Capital Area Horse
Show, 162, 164–65; at National
Horse Show, 7, 13, 144, 149, 151
Albrurae Farm, 149
alcoholism: David Rust and, 171–74;
Herman Pohl and, 24, 115–16,
160–61
Altoona horse show, 205–6
American Horse Show Association:
Conformation Hunter Champion
of the Year, 231; investigation of
amateur status, 231–39
Ashley (great-niece), 273–77
Atwell, Hunton, 203

Bacon, Robert, 10
Bailey, Thompson, 124–25, 211–12
Ballantrae Farm, 127, 149
Bartender, 135
Beauty, 263
Beck, Ethel, 18, 153, 184, 207
Belle of the Valley, 48, 50–51, 53–56
Bellwood horse show, 206
Bill Star, 155
Black Sparkle, 220–21
Black Watch, 184, 206

Blinky, 273, 276–77
Blue Ridge Hunt, 242
Bonham, Max, 126
Borah, senator, 24
Bosley, Betty (Bird), 159, 205–6
Brown, Paul, 15, 25–26, 198,
260–61
Brown, Rita Mae, ix–xi
Budd, Steven, xvii
Burke, Bobby, xv, xvi, 35–36, 106,
220–21, 266
Burke, Jackie, 159
Burkhart, Willi, 266
Burton, Jack, xvii, 35
Busch, August, 126

Calico Cat, 220
Camp Davis, 107
Camp Redwing, 20
cantering, 87–88
Canty, Steve, 170, 194
Capital Area Horse Show, 161–65
Caprilli, Federico, 33
Captain D'Arcy, 127
Carpet, 275–77
Cateer, 132, 135, 144, 147

Catholicism, Jane and, 99–100, 178, 188–89, 228, 244, 248
cavalletti, 90
Chamberlin, Harry D., 33–34, 43–44
Chamorro: at Capital Area Horse Show, 163, 165; at National Horse Show, 7, 13–14, 135, 144, 149
Charles Town, WV, 136–37, 168, 171–72
Chin, Rojah, 123, 228
Circus Rose, 205–6
clothes, 12, 17, 58, 206, 273–74; and mentoring, 221–22; at National Horse Show, 148, 151
communication, with horse, 52–53
confidence, and jumping, 114, 155, 158, 163
conformation, xiii; definition of, 283
Conformation Hunter championship, xiv, 182–84
coop, definition of, 283
Corinthian class, 17
Cothran, Mary, 261
Cotter, Maggie, 135
Count Stefan, 205–7
Craven, Honey, 147, 183–85
crow-hopping, 102
Dalling, Jim, 149–50
Devereux, Walter, xvii, 143
Devine, Walter, 250
Devon horse show, 175
Divarty's Eagle, 251
dressage, 70, 223
Duke of Orange, 179–80, 190–91
Duvall, Robert, 166

Eisenhower, Dwight D., 199

Fairfax horse show, 127, 129
falls, Jane and, 55–56, 179–80, 182, 272–73
Fayetteville horse show, 114
Fédération Equestre Internationale (FEI), 152, 238
Field Hunter Championship Trials, 212
field master, definition of, 283
Fitzgibbon, 27
Fitzrada: background of, 27–39; bad habits of, 36–37, 63–80; character of, 3, 31, 89, 106, 216; connection with Jane, 103, 109–12, 203–4, 226–27, 261; death of, 225–29; debut of, 121–38; paintings of, 25–26; rescue of, 9, 77–80; retirement of, 20–22, 215–16; ribbon display box, 186, 229; show record of, 204–5, 216, 279–82; in transit, 37–39, 80–106
flooring, at Madison Square Garden, 6, 138, 141
fly-fishing, 255–56
flying change, 53
Flying Dutchman, 195–96, 231
Fort Bragg, 72–73, 81
Fort Riley, 31
Fort Robinson Army Remount Depot, 27
forward seat riding, 33–34, 43, 239
Four Get, 177, 235
Fout, Paul, xvi, 205–6
foxes, Jane and, 16, 211
foxhunting, 90–92, 102–3, 270–72; hilltopping, 209–12, 273–77; return from, 202–4; terminology in, 283–84

Geoff (second husband), 244–48
geology, Jane and, 107–9, 254–55
Gimbel, Caral, 7, 207
Glass, Carter, 23
Glebe Plantation, 202, 263
Godfrey, Mary, 212
Golden Chance, xvi, 205–6
Graham, Barbara, 126, 219–22, 266
Graham, Gail, 196–97, 202, 219–20, 222, 266
Graham, Nancy, 219, 221–22, 266
Graham, Sam, 221
Grayrada, 231, 237
Greenberg, Hank, 7
Green Dunes Farm, 212–13, 231
Greenhalgh, George, 176–77, 180–81
Greenhalgh, Marie, 126, 176–77, 179–81, 190–91, 235
green hunter classes, xiv, 213
gymkhana, 54

Hagerstown horse show, 131–34
Haines, Marjorie, 231
Halo Miss, 222
Harrisburg horse show, 237
Haslip, Wade, 115
Hawaii, 41–61, 92–93
Hawthorne, Adele (Miller), 18, 219–22, 251–52, 270–71
hilltopping, 209–12, 274
Hoffman, Jeanne, 18, 153, 207
Holmelund, Paul, xvii–xviii
horse liniment, 19
horsemanship, x, xvii–xviii, 53, 223
horse shows, structure of, xiii–xv
hunter classes, xiii–xiv, 113
huntsman, definition of, 283

Iceland, 255
Intrepid, 135
Irish Lad, 7, 13, 127, 149, 164–65

jumper classes, xiv, 18, 58–61, 113–14, 220–21
jumpers, characteristics of, xvii, 104
jumping: changes in, xvi–xvii; confidence and, 114, 155, 158, 163; Fitzrada and, 32, 70; risks of, 132; terminology in, 283–84; training in, 54–61, 112–13

Kay, Alvin I., Dr. and Mrs., 126, 176
Keith, Ellie Wood, 182, 206–7
Kephart, Clayton, 270
Kiki, 273, 275
King, Ned, 142
knock-down-and-out class, 128–30, 164, 184
Kusner, Kathy, 238

Lawrence, Larry, 14, 130, 138
Leesburg, VA, 122–25, 170–71, 176, 219, 248–49; and National Horse Show, 8, 135–38
lightweight hunter, definition of, 283
liniment, 19
Lipscomb, Ross, 195–96
Littauer, Vladimir, 239
Liverpool, 197
Loudon Hunt, 202, 272–73; Horse Show, 195–96, 213, 220–21
Lowe, W. H., Dr. and Mrs., 127
lunge line, 28–30
Lutz, Raymond, 149

MacArthur, Douglas, 42
Madison Square Garden: 1946, 3–14,
    137–53; 1947, 181–85; 1949,
    206–7; 1950, 213–14; 1952,
    237–38
Mairs, Mary, 238
Marshall, George C., 205
Martin, Dave, 132, 144
Maryland Hunter Show, 130,
    175–76
master of foxhounds, definition of,
    283
Master's Challenge Bowl, 196, 205
Mauka Farm, 121–25, 241
McCashin, Arthur, 215
McElvoy, John, 95–98, 100–101
McLean horse show, 175
McMorrow, Anne (Pohl), 167, 191
media, 130, 136–37, 207; on female
    riders, 165; on National Horse
    Show, 8, 14; and obituary, 228
Melville, John, 104, 106
mentoring, Jane and, 220–22,
    251–52
Metacles, 251
Middleburg, 126; horse show, 175;
    Hunter Trials, 212
Middleton, Harry, 256
Miller, Bill, 216
Miller, Carol, 159
Miss Budweiser, 206
Montgomery, Andrew, 231, 233–34
Mope, sergeant, 46–47, 49–51, 54–
    56, 58–61, 64, 117
morning glories, 54
Morningstar, Anne, 164–65
Moss, Pappy and Ginny, xvi, 112,
    266–67

Mount Vernon horse show, 175
My Bill, 212–13, 231

National Horse Show: 1946, 3–14,
    139–53; 1947, 181–85; 1949,
    206–7; 1950, 213–14; 1952,
    237–38; background of, 3, 9–10;
    preparations for, 137–38
National Horse Show Association,
    137
Newman, Harry, 149
Nini (roommate), 87, 93, 101, 104,
    106

O'Connell, Joseph, 212
Octagon, 270–71
Ohio State Fair, 206
Old Fashioned, 241–42
Olympia classes, 152
Olympic equestrian events, xv, 199,
    231; Army Team and, 33–35;
    civilian contestants in, 152–53;
    female contestants in, 207
open jumper class, 58–61; judging
    criteria in, 4; National Horse
    Show, 3–4, 148–52; women and,
    18
O'Reilly, Tom, 207

Pabst Brew, 164–65
Parole, 163
Pat, 56–61
Payne, Shirley, 212, 231
pen class, 213–14
Pennsylvania National Horse Show,
    179–81
Perada, 27
Perry, Bill, 232–33

Pershing, "Black Jack," 162

Philadelphia National Horse Show, 220–22

Piping Rock horse show, 175

Play Girl, 164

The Plunge, 254, 267

Pohl, Buck (uncle), 98–100, 244

Pohl, Gus, 23

Pohl, Herman H. (father): background of, 23; career of, 21, 86, 93, 107–8, 115–17, 160–61; and Fitzrada, 66–67, 76–80, 225–26, 228–29; and Jane's pregnancy, 187–88; later life of, 241–44; and marriage, 41, 85; and Mauka, 121; writings by, 205, 220, 228–29

Pohl, Jane Andrews (mother): background of, 23–24; character of, 85–86; and death of Fitzrada, 225–26; and investigation, 233–34, 236; at Jane's events, 58, 139, 146; and Jane's pregnancy, 178; in later life, 241, 244, 250, 257; and marriage, 41–42, 85; and war, 86–87

Pohl, Jane (Rust): amateur status of, 231–39; appearance of, 21, 44; character of, 3, 42, 67, 232, 238; connection with Fitzrada, 103, 109–12, 203–4, 226–27, 261; death of, 259–67; first marriage, 167–74, 187–99, 201, 208; first meeting with Fitzrada, 63–80; first ride, 43; glasses, 6, 15, 148, 184; health issues, 18–19, 259–60; last class, 241–57; in late life, 15–26; and pregnancy, 177–79, 187–95;

second marriage, 244–48; as teacher, 248–50

Pohl, Jennet (sister): character of, 42; and family, 24, 96, 115, 244, 250, 257; marriage of, 167, 192–93, 196–97; and riding, 57, 193–96

Pohl, Kitty (aunt), 98–100

Pohl, Richard (brother): character of, 42; death of, 248, 250–51; and riding, 43; at West Point, 93–97, 107–8

poling, 4

polo, 32

ponies: Club, 223; Icelandic, 255; shows, 219

Portmaker, 176–77, 179–84

Portrush, 176

practice reins, 31

Princess Peroxide, 13, 149–50

Prompt Payment, 183

Pulliam, Matt, 136

quicksand, 109–12

racing, 32–33, 242

Rainslicker, 213

Raleigh horse show, 114

ramps: Fitzrada and, 3–4, 130–31, 140; Smith on, 157

Randolph, Jesse, 8, 137

Randolph, Theodora, 159

Rector, Tully, 134, 166

relationships, Jane and, x, 103, 167–74, 201–2, 244–48

Rhode Island, 242–43

Rice, Lester, 183

riding: awareness in, 89; family and, 42–43; and pregnancy, 178–79,

191–92; Richard and, 263–64, 269–77
riding style: Cappy's, 156; Jane's, x, 57, 113, 197–98, 239; at National Horse Show, 7; women and, 17–18
Ringmaster, 175
Rivers Country Day School, 248
Rives, lieutenant commander, 149
Rogers, Carolyn, 222, 266
Rogers, Elizabeth, 252
Rokus, Bill, 262–63, 266
Roosevelt, Franklin Delano, 41, 93
Roosevelt, Teddy, 162
Ross, 43
Royston, John, 137
rubber reins, 137
Runanplay, 212
Rust, David (first husband), 168–74, 187–99, 201, 208, 265
Rust, father-in-law, 170, 172, 202
Rust, Joanne, 248, 265
Rust, Mary, 168
Rust, mother-in-law, 201–2
Rust, Peter, 168
Rust, Richard (son), 16, 20, 241, 251, 254, 259; birth of, 194–95; and death, 261–62, 267; and Fitzrada, 20–22; and Geoff, 246–47; and riding, 263–64, 269–77
Rust, Ricky (grandson), 273–77
Ryan, Alan, 104, 106

Sampson, 273–74
Sanjo, 127
schooling, 53, 56
show hunter, definition of, 283
show jumper, definition of, 283–84

Shreeve, Cindy, 276
Shreeve, Laurie, 272
Sindy, 262–63
Sir Gilbert, xvii
sitting trot, 52
Skakel, Ethel, 184
skiing, 254, 267
skyscraper class, 131–34
Smith, Cappy: at Capital Area Horse Show, 162–63, 165; last jump, 166; at National Horse Show, 7, 13–14, 135, 144, 149, 151; and training, 126, 151–52, 155–60, 197–98, 212
Smith, master sergeant, 47–48, 53; and Fitzrada, 4, 63, 66, 68–69, 76
Snitch, 123–24, 195
Southern Pines, NC, 81, 109–12
Spillers, Harry, 167, 196–97
sportsmanship: Herman Pohl and, 42; Jane and, 135
Springsbury Farm, 176
spurs, 156
standing martingale, 92
steeplechase, 32–33
Steinkraus, William, xxi–xxii
stirrups, 51–52, 197
Stone, Whitney, 148
strip horses, xiii–xiv
Substitution, 182, 206–7
Sultan, Dan, 37, 63, 117; and Fitzrada, 64–66, 77–78
Surtees, Robert, 272
Sweetie, 123–24, 195
Sweetie Pie, 38–39

tanbark, 141
Taylor, Henry, 223

Taylor, Mary, 242
Taylor, Tom, 222–23, 241–42
Thoroughbreds, xvi–xvii
training: in Army, 28–33; Cappy
  Smith and, 151–52, 155–60,
  197–98; at Fort Bragg, 84; Jane
  and, 49–52, 222–23, 269–70;
  Jennet and, 193; in jumping, 54–
  61, 112–13; poling, 4; at Vassar,
  87–91
Trayser, Don, 255–56
Trish (great-niece), 273–77
trout fishing, 255–56
Truman, Harry S., 199
twitch, 36

United States Army Cavalry School,
  31
United States Army Equestrian
  Team, 33, 149, 199; at National
  Horse Show, 6–7, 145
United States Equestrian Team, 231,
  237
United States Jumping Team, 214–15
Upperville, 126

VanAuken, Ken, 267
Van Deusen, colonel, 50, 52, 54, 79,
  117
Van Sinderen, Adrian, 238
Vassar, 84–85, 87, 104–7
Vietnam War, Jane on, 251
Virginia Horse Show Association,
  186, 216

Wainwright, Jonathan M., 162–63
Wakefield, Lyman, 238

War Genius, 238
Warrenton Horse Show, 127–30,
  176
Washington National Horse Show,
  252–53
Weather Permitting, 104, 106
Weaver, Jane, 127
Webb, Gerald, 242
Westerly, RI, 242–43
West Point, 20, 23, 93–101, 254
whipper-in, definition of, 284
White, Anita, 251, 275–76
White, Lige, 266
White, Ridgely, 238
Whitney, Liz (Tippett), 126, 158–60,
  207
Wilkins, Delton, 11–12, 148–49
Wimert, Paul, 29
women: Brown on, xi; at Capital
  Area Horse Show, 164–65;
  cavalrymen on, 12; Chamberlin
  and, 43; and Fitzrada, 70; Herman
  Pohl on, 161; and international
  jumping, 215, 238; Jane and, 103,
  135, 207, 247–48; and jumping,
  5, 134; mentoring, 220–22,
  251–52; at National Horse Show,
  145, 147; and Olympics, 153; and
  riding, 17–18, 207; war and, 167
Working Hunter Championship,
  206–7
working hunter classes, xiv
World War II, 92–93, 107–8, 115–
  17, 169; preparation for, 80–81,
  86; and women, 167

Yandle, Rodney, 11–12, 148–49

NOTE TO THE READER

This is my mother's story. Most of it occurred before I was born. As Jane's son, I grew up perusing her scrapbooks of sports headlines. The celebrity was brief, both Jane and Fitzrada are long dead, and the newsprint is yellow and crumbling. However, aging strangers seek me out to reminisce. The beauty of the recollection is in the telling. Their faces are lit with nostalgia. A few have an axe to grind, and those tones are equally immediate.

As anywhere, there are more than two sides to every story. People and articles conflicted over the order in which things occurred as well as substance. For example, the family story was that the vet put Fitz to sleep. I was recently told that Jane killed him, minutes after her carelessness left her no other choice. Considering the source, the caveat under which Jane admitted it to him, and the guilt it implied, I believe this to be true. Where discrepancies existed, I chose the version that would make for a better story. I bridged gaps from what I knew of surrounding events and my speculation on motives.

Aspects of this story are told through scenes. The dialogue is from what might have been said. I learned of Sergeant Mope only recently from a composition Jane wrote in college. I suspect Mope is his real name, but I have no idea what he looked like, how he acted, or how much time he spent training Jane. He and other characters are synthesized from memories of horse people I have treasured. So this work is a dramatized biography. My aim was to do justice to the beauty of the story.

Many have asked me, "Why did Jane stick with it? Most adolescent girls go through a phase of being horse crazy and then go on, leaving horses behind for boys. So what drove her to spend her high school and college years trying to fix a rogue horse?"

There are several answers. Jane was an easy target for adolescent peers. She was tall for her age, had buckteeth, wore glasses, and was a German Catholic when the Nazis were attempting to conquer the world. Her younger sister was her father's favorite, and Jane never got over it. However, Pop was a West Pointer and valued athletic achievements. Horses were a refuge, and blue ribbons were a measurable identity that impressed her father. Jane was seventeen when she was asked to work with Fitz and failed. She held herself accountable for his scheduled destruction as an outlaw and, motivated by loneliness for connection with an innocent and noble creature, was determined to vindicate him.

It took five years of sweat, a few tears, and some spilled blood. By then, they trusted each other to safely jump fences that stood a foot and a half above his ears in competitions that were the domain of professional men. From Jeanne Hoffman's article for the *Sunday American,* "Girls Risk Limbs for Show Honors" (New York, November 26, 1949): "Generally considered America's greatest rider is small, youngish looking Southern belle named Jane Pohl Rust of Leesburg, Va., who looks about fourteen, is twenty-four, and for the past five years has made her reputation mainly with one mount, the temperamental Fitz-rada." Fitz was old by the time they came into their own, so his time at the top was short. Appreciation for what she and Fitz accomplished sustained her through later disgraces.

Horses hold particular fascination for us since faith in the connection is proved by riding them. Paul Holmelund, Norwegian cavalry officer and member of the Norwegian Army Horse Show Team for the 1912 Olympic Games, wrote, "The goals of horsemanship came from war and are as valid today as they were in the days of sabers. The cavalry trooper had to be educated to forge an integral unity with his horse. The trooper had to ride his mount actively, balancing with him to economize his strength over a twelve hour forced march, saving energy for an all-out burst of speed at the end, without being *discouraged* by fences and ditches. The communication between horse and rider had to be more reliable than a set of signals. It had to function without interruption and without thinking. During training for these goals, discovering the many 'latent' talents of the horse, and how to develop and take advantage of them, makes horseback riding the most rewarding of all sports" (*Ride Gently–Ride Well*, 1970).

Both man and horse are naturally playful and move in herds. The innate joys of running fast and competing to win are independently rooted in both species. It follows that horse sports, by design, emulate the intoxicating thrill of a cavalry charge.

Yet old quotes apply: "A horse is nothing but a leather bag full of trouble," and, the other that comes to mind, "The outside of a horse is good for the inside of a man." Both can be said of the same horse on the same day. Horses, I'm sure, feel the same way about us.

ABOUT THE AUTHOR

Richard R. Rust was a practicing civil engineer and amateur sportsman. As a child, he rode his tricycle under Fitz's belly and started riding ponies at age four. His mother is the subject of this book, and his father, D. N. Rust III, was an amateur steeplechase trainer and rider with two wins of the Virginia Gold Cup.

Richard was a junior member of Loudoun Hunt and the Loudoun Hunt Pony Club in the early 1960s. He played third-string polo for the University of Virginia in 1966–1967 and was hired to train ponies and play polo for a splinter team in Oilville, Virginia, to rival the Deep Run Polo Club. As a private in the army at Fort Belvoir, Virginia, and as a West Point Cadet, he played polo with retired cavalry officers, some of whom had been the best players in the country prior to World War II. He was a National Collegiate Athletic Association Nordic skier (ski jumping and cross-country) for West Point. A 1972 graduate of West Point, he served in nuclear artillery and then in construction engineering in the United States and abroad. He played polo and hunted where the opportunity arose—Menlo Park, California; Midland, while at Fort Benning, Georgia; and Arapaho, while at Fort Carson, Colorado. As an army engineer colonel constructing a health clinic in Moldova in 2000, he discovered Brezhnev's private racing stable and brood stock.

Richard exercised his cousin Snowden Clarke's horses near his hometown of Leesburg, Virginia; rode trail motorcycles and snowboards; and hunted and fished. He died in 2008.